NEW TESTAMENT

UNICIO J. VIOLI
ASSOCIATE PROFESSOR OF ENGLISH
FAIRLEIGH DICKINSON UNIVERSITY

MONARCH
PRESS

Copyright © 1964 by
SIMON & SCHUSTER

Published by
MONARCH PRESS
a Simon & Schuster division of
Gulf & Western Corporation
Simon & Schuster Building
1230 Avenue of the Americas
New York, N.Y. 10020

MONARCH PRESS and colophon are trademarks of
Simon & Schuster, registered in the U.S. Patent and
Trademark Office.

Standard Book Number: 0-671-00625-8

Library of Congress Catalog Card Number: 65-7191

Printed in the United States of America

TABLE OF CONTENTS

A DICTIONARY OF TERMS WIDELY USED IN THE
NEW TESTAMENT 5

LIFE OF JESUS: AN INTRODUCTION 10

THE SPREAD OF CHRISTIANITY 13

MANUSCRIPTS AND TEXTS OF THE NEW TESTAMENT 15

A NOTE TO THE READER 16

MATTHEW: A PREFACE 16

REVIEW AND COMMENTARY ON THE GOSPEL ACCORDING
TO MATTHEW 17

MARK: A PREFACE 64

REVIEW AND COMMENTARY ON THE GOSPEL ACCORDING
TO MARK 64

LUKE: A PREFACE 81

REVIEW AND COMMENTARY ON THE GOSPEL ACCORDING
TO LUKE 82

JOHN: A PREFACE 101

REVIEW AND COMMENTARY ON THE GOSPEL ACCORDING
TO JOHN 101

ACTS: A PREFACE 120

REVIEW AND COMMENTARY ON THE GOSPEL OF ACTS 120

THE EPISTLES: A PREFACE 137

REVIEW AND COMMENTARY ON THE EPISTLES 137

REVELATION: A PREFACE 154

REVIEW AND COMMENTARY ON REVELATION 154

QUESTIONS AND ANSWERS ON THE NEW TESTAMENT 165

BIBLIOGRAPHY 169

A HARMONY TABLE OF SYNOPTIC PARALLEL PASSAGES 170

A DICTIONARY OF TERMS WIDELY USED IN THE NEW TESTAMENT

ACTS OF THE APOSTLES: A sequel book written by Luke after he had completed his gospel. Date, between 80-90 A.D.

ADULTERY: Often means idolatry and infidelity to God as well as its usual meaning.

AGRIPPA: Herod Agrippa II, great grandson of Herod the Great; Agrippa was King of Judea when Paul, the prisoner, "almost persuaded" him to become a Christian.

APOCALYPSE: The Greek name for Revelation. A form of literature created by the Jews after the Babylonian exile. The word means *to disclose;* such works claimed to reveal the future. A complex system of metaphors, symbols, and allegory was used, understandable only to the initiate interested in predictions of the end of the world and the ushering in of the New Kingdom of God under the messiah. See the book of Revelation in the New Testament.

APOCRYPHAL GOSPELS: The N.T. contains 27 books as of today. But many gospels were not included in the official canon of the N.T. for various reasons. In many of the apocryphal gospels legend and fact are mixed; many are "heretical," but most are good reading still, even if not canonical.

APOSTLE: *One sent forth* in Greek, not merely as messenger, but carrying with him a special message. Jesus from many *disciples* chose a select twelve *apostles.*

ASIA: Used in the N.T. for what we call Asia Minor today.

ATONEMENT: A payment to cancel a debt, a reconciliation. The *atonement* of Christ on the cross for man's sins.

BAPTISM: A Greek word meaning *to immerse,* to dip. The ceremony required of all Christians as symbolic of cleansing of sin.

BEATITUDES: Latin *beati* = very happy, hence beatitudes. In Jesus' Sermon on the Mount a series of his sayings begin "Blessed are . . ." = a beatitude.

BIBLE: Greek *biblia* = little books or scrolls. Similar to the word *Scriptures* or *Writings.* The King James version of the Bible contains 66 separate Books, 39 in what is termed the Old Testament and 27 in what is called the New Testament. The King James version appeared in 1611 A.D. and included other books called the Apocrypha. The N.T. was written, most scholars believe, in Greek (Koine Greek), but some believe that the synoptics were originally written in Aramaic. The first complete translation of the Bible into English was made by Wycliffe in 1382 A.D. The first translation printed in English was that of Tyndale in 1526, the first complete English translation being Coverdale's in 1535. The King James Bible is the masterpiece of all English translations and has permeated the fabric of the English language and literature. No person can truly call himself educated or cultured unless he make himself familiar with the King James Bible. All terms which are changed herein or are obsolete in meaning today are immediately translated in parentheses.

BLASPHEME: Means *to speak injuriously against.*

BLESS: God blesses man = *praise;* man blesses God = *praise.* Man blesses man = *to speak well of.*

BLOOD: Symbol for life, the vital element in sacrifice.

BRETHREN: An old form of *brothers.*

CAESAR: In the N.T. = *Emperor.*

CANON: The standard whereby á decision is reached; specifically, the decision as to which books should or should not be included, called *canonical.* Canon controversies ranged until 397 A.D. when a *canon* list was adopted. *Canonicity* is a human matter, not a divine decision.

CATHOLIC: A Greek word = *universal.*

CEPHAS: The Aramaic word for *rock,* given by Jesus as a title to Simon; Greek = *petros,* where the name, Peter.

CHARITY: Latin = *caritas* = love (Greek: *agape*). Hence, *charity* = spiritual love, not alms-giving.

CHRISTIANS: The followers of Jesus were called Christians first in Antioch (Syria) in 42 A.D.

CHURCH: Greek: *ekklesia* — a group called or assembled for a religious purpose.

CIRCUMCISION: A ritual removal of the foreskin, before 1000 B.C. common among all inhabitants of the Palestine area except the Philistines. Associated with puberty first (Gen. 17:25), then with marriage (Ex. 4:26), it became a sign of the Covenant (Gen. 17:1-27) and a mark of membership in the community of the chosen (Ezek. 28:10).

DAVID: Hebrew: *beloved.* Born around 1090 B.C., the youngest son of Jesse of Bethlehem; he became the second King of Israel, reigned 40 years. He was divinely anointed by the prophet Samuel. He was a great hero, a generous friend, a fine organizer and statesman, and perhaps even a poet and musician.

DAY OF ATONEMENT: Most solemn Jewish ceremony, Yom Kippur, in which the sins of the people are transferred to a goat, and thus "expiated." Occurs about mid-September.

DAY OF THE LORD: A day when all wickedness will be overcome and the reign of righteousness established. The earlier Hebrews interpreted this nationally: that God would lead Israel to triumph over rival nations. Christianity took the concept over as the Day of Judgment.

DEACON: Greek: *server* or *minister.*

DESERT: Dry plains, wild areas, desolate waste places.

DEVIL: Greek: *accuser* or *opponent.* In the N.T. always means demon. Among the Greeks it originally meant the spirit of the dead, whether good or bad: but by N.T. times = all evil and illnesses were caused by *demons* or *devils,* hence, "casting out of *demons.*"

DIVINATION: Means in Scriptures clairvoyance, hypnotism, magic, mediumship, necromancy, occultism, sorcery, witchcraft.

DOCTOR: A teacher.

DRAGON: In .the N.T. symbolizes evil; more aggressive and less subtle than "serpent."

EAGLE: Often a symbol for clear-sightedness, dominion, protection; The symbol of the gospel of John is the eagle.

EASTER: Found only in Acts 12:4; Greek: *pascha* and Hebrew: *PeSaCH* = *Passover*. A lamb is sacrificed at the *Passover* meal; hence the "lamb of God" in John 1:29. The "lamb" is slain on Good Friday and resurrected on Easter Sunday. The date of our Easter = first full moon following the vernal equinox, a former ancient world-wide spring ritual festival.

ELIJAH: About the ninth century B.C. he restored to life the son of the widow of Zarephath; he triumphed over the 400 prophets of Baal; he was taken to heaven in a fiery chariot—one of the greatest of O.T. prophets. He appears with Christ on the Mount of Transfiguration.

EPICUREANS: Disciples of the Greek philosopher, who taught that happiness is the chief aim of life, and that it is foolish to fear the gods.

EUCHARIST: Greek word = *Thanksgiving*. Jesus at the Passover supper instructed his disciples to commemorate his own sacrifice — hence the *Eucharist*.

EVANGELIST: One who voices *"good tidings."*

EXORCIST: One claiming ability to cast out demons of illness.

FORTY: Twice the number of fingers and toes—the largest number primitives could reach. Symbolizes the perfect period to develop the human capacity; 40 years in the wilderness for the Israelites; 40-year reign for David and Solomon; 40 days of the flood; 40 days of Jesus' fast in the Wilderness; and 40 days between his Resurrection and Ascension; and obviously the 40 days of Lent before Easter.

GEHENNA: Literally, the Valley of Hinnom near Jerusalem; a place for burning refuse and dead bodies; hence, a symbol for *hell* and everlasting punishment.

GENTILES: Originally = *nations*: a few times in N.T. = Greeks, most often = non-Jewish.

GOSPEL: Old English *god-spel* = good message (*evangelion* in Greek).

GRACE: Latin: *gratia* = gratitude, favor, love; implies a divine gift to man, not humanly earned, but rather essentially characteristic of its source.

GRECIANS: Greek-speaking Jews only (in N.T.).

HEATHEN: Originally = *nations;* gradually, *idolators.*

HEBREW: Language of the O.T. A member of the Semitic language group such as Arabic, Aramaic (Syriac), Babylonian, Egyptian, etc. The Hebrew language was replaced by Aramaic between the fifth and first centuries B.C.

HELL: Hebrew *SHeoL* = the unseen, the grave, the pit; Greek: *Hades* = the unseen, the grave, the underground world; *Gehenna.*

HEROD: The name of the ruling family in Judea during N.T. times.

HEROD ANTIPATER: Governor of Idumea and Judea; died 43 B.C.

HEROD THE GREAT: Antipater's son; a clever, forceful, but ruthless politician; ruled until 4 B.C.

HEROD AGRIPPA I: Nephew of Antipas; ruled until 44 A.D.; he slew

James, and had Peter imprisoned (Acts 12).

HEROD AGRIPPA II: Son of Agrippa I; "almost persuaded" by Paul to become a Christian.

HEROD ANTIPAS: The tetrarch (ruler of a quarter province or kingdom) of Galilee and a son of Herod the Great, he is best known today as the slayer of John the Baptist. His cunning earned him the nickname "fox" (Luke 13:32) and enabled him to stay in power from 4 B.C. until 39 A.D.

HOLY GHOST: Greek: *pneuma* (wind); translated as *spirit*. Holy Spirit.

HOST: Army or 1. the sun, moon, and stars or 2. *army of angels*.

IDOLATRY: Worship of false gods or created things. The tendency of the unenlightened to impute to a symbol the characteristics and the powers inherent in what the symbol is intended to represent.

IMMANUEL: "God is with us."

ISAIAH: The eighth- and seventh-century prophet who reformed religious thinking in Judah. His denunciations of sin, his hope in a reformed Israel, and his prophecies of the future are well known to Jesus.

ISRAEL: Descendants of Jacob (Israel), the son of Isaac. Now the nation of Palestine. From his twelve sons sprang the twelve tribes of Israel from which all Jews are supposedly descended.

JAMES: 1. James "the son of Zebedee," one of the apostles and brother of John.
2. James, "the son of Alphaeus," one of the apostles and brother of Matthew.

3. James, "the Lord's brother," author of the Epistle of James.
4. James, father of the apostle Judas (not Iscariot).
5. James "the Little," or "the Less"; very probably the same as number 2.
6. James, the brother of Jesus and Judas and Simon; possibly number 2 or number 3.

LAMB: A symbol of gentleness, innocence, and purity; frequently the sacrificial animal.

LAW, THE BOOK OF THE: 629 B.C., while Josiah was King of Judah, a scroll was found in the Temple of Jerusalem and identified as the Law of Moses. See Chapters 12 to 28 of Deuteronomy in the O.T.

LAYING ON OF HANDS: A ceremony = transference of a divine blessing.

LORD: Hebrew *JHVH* = Lord = "The existing One." Small *lord* may mean captain, chief, master, sir, etc.

MADNESS: N.T. = senselessness.

MAGI: Members of a sacred caste of Persians who interpreted dreams and stars. They taught that each human has a spiritual "double," an angel who remains in heaven and with whom the human is to be reunited after death.

MAGICIANS: Derived from *Magi;* those able to deal with the obscure and occult, and to perform "supernatural" acts.

MARTYR: This Greek word simply means *witness*. Persecution of the *witnesses* of Jesus led to their deaths by *martyrdom.*

MEGIDDO: A famous battleground of ancient Canaan; hence, the name *Ar-maggedon* in Rev. 16:16.

MOSES: The great lawgiver and leader lived from about 1320 B.C. to 1200 B.C. He was thought at one time to have been the author of the first five books of the O.T.

MSS. = manuscripts.

MYSTERY: Greek: *mysterion* = a *secret* whose meaning is known only to selected initiates.

NAME: Names in N.T. indicate place of origin, occupation, personal qualities, impending events. It was not unusual for a man to change his name to indicate an internal change: Jacob = Israel; Saul = Paul; Simon = Cephas, Peter.

NAZARITE: O.T. name for one who has taken a vow of separation or consecration. Do not confuse with Nazareth.

NEW TESTAMENT: The name given to the last 27 books of the Christian Bible, accepted as Canonical Scripture, recording the life and teachings of Jesus the Christ and of his apostles and disciples.

NUMBERS AND THEIR SYMBOLISM: Numerical values were assigned to the Greek and Hebrew alphabets for symbolic number purposes. See Revelation 13:18.

ONE: One = divine Unity of God, and man's spiritual unity with God.

ONESIMUS: Greek: *profitable* (Onesimus = name of slave in N.T.)

PATRIARCH: The head of a family (a "family" head of the Jews).

PENTECOST: Greek: *fiftieth*, the Jewish feast celebrated on the fiftieth day (7 times 7 plus 1) after Passover. On the first Pentecost after Jesus' resurrection, the apostles received the outpouring of the Holy Spirit (Acts 2). Whitsunday in English.

PROPHET: Speaking, talking, uttering; spokesman of God.

REMISSION: Forgiveness.

RESPECTER OF PERSONS: The Greek means "one who accepts the face."

RIGHTEOUS: Begin right or correct; conforming to divine rules; right motives as well as acts.

RSV: Revised Standard Version, 1952; translation in English.

SABBATH: Hebrew: to *"cease from";* perhaps from the quarter phases of the moon every seven days. The period of cessation or rest is the Sabbath, as the Lord had commanded. By N.T. times the formalities and rituals of Sabbath had become exaggerated.

SACKCLOTH: A loin cloth of goat or camel hair worn as a sign of penitence or mourning; often a symbol of repentance.

SACRIFICE: The wrath of a deity appeased by a slaughtered animal offered to him. The supreme sacrifice = Christ as Lamb.

SAINT: A church member.

SCHISM: A division or separation in religious doctrine.

SEA: Symbol of danger and evil. See Revelation.

SECOND COMING: Before the crucifixion Jesus' disciples thought the Second Coming would be a new political order for Israel with Jesus on the throne of David. Many Christians believed in a physical Second Coming of Christ, who will be joined by the living and resurrected saints to enjoy a milennium of 1000 years of victory over Satan. Other Christians of the Pauline type believe the Second Coming is not of this world but an inner experience, as in the gospel of John.

SEVEN: Very sacred number; 7 days of creation, the Sabbath, the seven spirits of God, the seven apostles at the Resurrection breakfast, 7 churches, 7 Pleiades, etc.

SOUL: a person; a life; a spirit.

SPIRIT: God; invisible, ever-present power of God.

TALENT: 3000 shekels or 1,500 dollars (silver), or 30,000 dollars (gold).

TEN COMMANDMENTS: Exodus (24:12-18) shows Moses on Mt. Sinai receiving the laws from God. The basis for both Hebraic and Christian ethics, morality, religion.

TESTAMENT: *Covenant* in Greek.

THEOPHANY: God physically present in a human body.

TORAH: The Law. The Five Books of Moses (Pentateuch). Prophets insisted that the Torah take precedence over the rites and ceremonies of organized' worship.

TWELVE: Sacred number: 12 sons of Jacob; 12 tribes of Israel; 12 minor prophets; 12 apostles; 12 occurs several times in Revelation.

VENGEANCE: Justice = revenge.

WHEAT: A symbol for divine ideas; especially when contrasted with chaff or tares.

WIZARD: "One who knows" hidden or forbidden knowledge.

WORD: The Word of God is the divine message which God's prophets felt inspired to proclaim.

ZION: Jerusalem was built on four hills; the southwest one was called Zion or Fortress. Eventually the name was applied to the entire city, and by metaphor to the Jewish Nation, then to the Church of God, and to Heavenly Jerusalem.

LIFE OF JESUS: AN INTRODUCTION

Modern scholars place the birth of Christ around 5 B.C., toward the end of the reign of Herod the Great (d. 4 B.C.).

In northern Palestine is the hilly province of Galilee where Jesus grew up and spent most of his life and work. On the eastern borders of Galilee lies the lake of Galilee and the Jordan River (the lake being but a widening of the river), which flows south and empties into the Dead Sea. Jesus was born in the small town of Bethlehem, which is located in the southern part of Judea, and he was the oldest child in a family of at least seven children, four brothers and at least two sisters. His father was a carpenter, and one would have no doubt that Jesus adopted his father's trade, since that was the customary procedure for most male children in that day. The family itself was descended from the great King David of Israel; accordingly it was one of many eligible families from which the Messiah could come, according to Jewish thought and tradition. His father seems to have died when Jesus was still a young man, and very likely he took on himself the burden of providing for his brothers and sisters, as well as his widowed mother.

In about 26 A.D. there was great excitement in Galilee: John the Baptist (the Immerser), a strange prophet indeed, called for the Jews to repent, that the Kingdom of God was near, that baptism or immersion in the Jordan River would cleanse people of sin and prepare them for the coming Kingdom of God. At about 30 years of age Jesus was himself baptized by John, but soon after ceased following John to form his own ministry and gather his own followers or disciples.

Now the Jews did expect a Messiah, a warrior-king who would release them from enslavement to the Romans and institute a rule on earth of peace, joy, and plenty; and the Messiah himself would be seated on the throne. He would be the redeemer of Israel and the saviour of the state; he would be the Son of Man so often mentioned in the Old Testament (hereafter referred to as O.T.), the man selected by God himself to save Israel. God's anointed, chosen, and divine son would one day suddenly and unexpectedly appear amidst earthquakes, thunders, eclipses, and other terrible natural manifestations and would institute a reign of terror for the sinful and greedy, but the good, the poor, and the virtuous Jews would be saved from his wrath and win eternal life and happiness. This, or some variant of it, was the messianic hope so strongly felt by the great mass of Jews in the days of Jesus. But Jesus bewildered the Jews: yes, he spoke with authority, as if he were God's spokesman with divine rights of biblical interpretation; but he was opposed to violence or re-

bellion against the Roman rulers, which opposition seemed pusillanimous to the more revolutionary and radical groups of Jews known as Zealots. Instead, Jesus advocated an inflexible pacifism, a policy of no reprisals against injustice and cruelty by the state; he preached the returning of good for evil; he preached repentance of sins, and reformation of the inner and outer man so that he would be ready for the imminent coming of the Kingdom of God, at whose right hand Jesus Christ (Christ means messiah in Greek) would be seated.

Such policies as Jesus advocated were endorsed by the Pharisees (FARE uh seez), that religious party which reflected the views and habits of most Jews; but the Pharisees objected to Jesus' rather casual treatment of the Laws of Moses, the traditional laws, the habits, and the customs so long solemnly and punctiliously observed by Pharisaic Jews. On the other hand Jesus opposed most fiercely the party of the Sadducees (SAD you seez). [Note that this pronunciation system will be used throughout this book; all new and unfamiliar names and places will be respelled by this simple phonetic-syllabic system.] The Sadducees were the ruling, aristocratic party who held the reigns of power so long as they cooperated closely with the Roman authorities—which they most zealously did. Jesus looked upon them as opportunists and vicious exploiters of the poor and miserable of Israel. Both parties looked upon Jesus as a demagogue and dangerous revolutionary who not only associated with villains, whores, and knaves, but also collected a following who worshipped his every word. True, Jesus did not preach active rebellion, but he did attract the very poor (if awakened) to his standard of love and repentance and reform. The Sadducees were especially fearful that such messianic activity and social disturbance might foment rebellion, for messianic views are based upon a passionate nationalism. The Romans could easily have taken away the small modicum of independence and self-rule that the Jews up to then were enjoying. On the other hand, any relaxation of the Laws of Moses, any loosening of religious observance, would break up the religious unity of the Jews and allow the always omnipresent pagan religions to seep in and subvert Judaism. The pagan religion of the Greeks, for example, was widespread throughout the Empire, as was their language; no wonder then that the two major parties looked upon Jesus' popularity with the masses as downright treachery!

Now the big problem was the one of stopping the spread of Jesus' teaching and stopping Jesus himself either by murdering him, or by arresting and then murdering him. Certainly, his popularity made open arrest quite difficult since a popular rebellion in his name might be initiated and upset the political situation. Especially risky was the arrest of a person during the Passover festival, when all Jews celebrate their national liberation from Egyptian slavery. A "nationalist" like Jesus would at such a time have been extremely popular. We do know that he chose the Passover for his triumphal entry into the holiest of holy cities, Jerusalem, while riding on an ass. The city greeted him with great ovations, actually strewing palms before his entire path into Jerusalem and hailing him with great joy and exultation as their liberator-Messiah. Unfortunately, his arrest was made possible by one of his disciples, Judas, who had betrayed him to the authorities. Jesus singled out by Judas Iscariot by what is known today as the Judas-kiss; and Jesus, arrested in haste and secrecy, was brought before the hastily convened Jewish Council, the Sanhedrin

(SAN hee drin). First, Jesus was charged with practicing magic, with being a magician or wizard who practiced the black arts from devilish sources. When this charge failed, he was charged with the political crime of claiming to be the King of the Jews, the Jewish Messiah so long predicted by the prophets of the O.T., especially Isaiah, Zechariah, and the Psalm singers. Since Jesus was king in the religious sense only, the charge of treason against the Roman state could not be legally placed against him; but if the laws against treason were generously interpreted, Jesus could be arrested on a technicality. The next day he was brought before Pontius Pilate, the Roman procurator (governor) of Judea (the province in which Jerusalem lay), who unwillingly sentenced Jesus to death by crucifixion (the Roman method of capital punishment for criminals who were non-Roman citizens) on a charge of high treason. Jesus never did deny that he was the divine King of the Jews, their Messiah, although such a denial might have very well saved his life. In short, the "trial" was little more than a "frame-up," and like all "frame-ups" the legal motions were painstakingly gone through.

Jesus was buried on the third day, and our gospels tell of his disappearance from the tomb on the third day; they also tell how his disciples and others had seen, talked, felt, and dined with Jesus after his death by crucifixion, thus testifying to his having risen from the grave, alive in body and soul: In addition, these same sources testify that he appeared not as a ghost but as a man of flesh and blood. The last glimpse his disciples had of Jesus was his bodily ascension into heaven, but not until Jesus had given them a series of detailed instructions on the spreading of the good news ("gospel" in Greek). What is the good news? That

Jesus is the true Messiah so long expected by the Jews; that he died willingly on the cross as a redeeming sacrificial victim for the sins of man. With the death of Jesus, the doors of heaven and the eternal life are now possible, since Jesus the Christ had removed the burden of sin and guilt earned by man through the disobedience of their first parents, Adam and Eve. Before long, as the prophets of the O.T. had also testified, he would return with trumpet-blowing angels and vast cataclysmic omens to announce his reign on earth and the establishment of the New Kingdom of God. Jesus the Crucified initiated a new messianic movement which was known as Nazorean by the Jews and as Christian (*Christianoi* = *Christos* or Christ = Hebrew *Meshiach* or Messiah), and Messiah in Hebrew means the anointed one— anointed because the O.T. describes that process essential in the choosing of kings, an act of divine approval in the choice.

THE SPREAD OF CHRISTIANITY

The Book of Acts of the Apostles of Jesus Christ is the fifth book of the New Testament, and it tells of what happened after Jesus had risen to heaven. The original twelve followers of Christ had been reduced by the suicide of Judas Iscariot; so Matthias was elected to replace him. Filled with the force of the Holy Spirit (*Epiphany* = ee PIFF uh nee), the disciples spread the good news everywhere, but not without great difficulties. The Jerusalem church, with James, the oldest brother of Jesus, as its leader, was the original and first Christian Church, the base of the Movement, but soon branches of the Church were established everywhere, especially in Asia Minor in such cities as Antioch and Caesarea Philippi and in Greece (Athens and Corinth). The greatest of the apostles was Simon Cephas (*Cephas* = Peter = Rock), better known as Peter; but a self-appointed apostle, Saul or Paul, soon became his rival. Paul had become converted to Christianity while on the road to Damascus, obtaining there an ecstatic vision of the Lord, a vision which was to turn him into an indefatigable worker for the Cause. He preached Christ to the Gentiles (pagans) at a time when the Gentiles were seeking a religion of puritanical promise, free of corruption and salacity. Christianity, with its attractive monotheistic God, its doctrine of charity and love, its promise of the New Kingdom proved well-nigh irresistible to many pagans; so much so that the state became alarmed and tried to suppress the movement. Worse, the political situation throughout the empire was steadily deteriorating; in Palestine, for example, the Zealots (political radicals) advocated revolt against the Roman tyranny. Other persons claimed to be messiahs also ("false messiahs") and many of these, too, obtained a following, some of them even obtaining entrance into the Church. Indeed, disturbances—political, social, and economic—created a mighty impetus for a belief in a better world to come, the new Kingdom of God, a new era of hope and joy. Incredible as it may seem, many in the Movement had to be warned to keep from steadily peering into the heavens and awaiting the appearance of the heavenly deliverer momentarily. Hence, the doctrine that the Messiah would come unbeknownst and secretly, by surprise like a thief in the night, when we would least expect him!

Paul was a scholarly Pharisee, born a Roman citizen, who had become a Christian through a dramatic conversion. Since Greek was an international language, Christianity was preached and spread in that tongue. Paul would invariably visit the synagogues first to spread his message, but he also chose pagan areas in which to preach. Thus it is that he became hunted and repeatedly persecuted by both Jewish and pagan authorities. Paul even had his enemies in his own hurch, the orthodox Jewish-Chris-ns, who believed the very essence Christianity was the Mosaic Law and the Judaic heritage. They found most unpalatable Paul's rejection of circumcision and the dietary laws as prerequisites for conversion to Christianity. Faith in Christ, a normal life, baptism in the Spirit, and the eating of animal blood were the main requirements he preached. There is good evidence that the apostle Peter was at the head of the orthodox Jewish-Christians and Paul at the head of the newly converted Gentiles (non-Jews), and that both of these great men might have been rivals. There are lines in Acts that reveal a Petrine-Pauline rivalry in spite of the many attempts at covering up such evidence, attempts at healing the breach, that all was not rosy in the early Church. Paul's epistles (letters) to various individuals and churches show great skill in organizing the unorganized, in uniting the schismatic, in harmonizing the discordant, in healing the imminent breaches in the Church—in short, a genius of teaching, administrating, and preaching. His epistles follow the book of Acts in the New Testament; here is some of the greatest and most fervid writing in the New Testament.

Christians refused to worship the Roman emperor as the incarnate god; to the pagans an oath of loyalty was mere lip service to one god of hundreds available to them.

Only a fanatic would take such oaths seriously. Well then, the early Christians were fanatics—many refused to take the oath, even if non-compliance meant death! One recalls how easy it is today to take a non-Communist oath, whatever the job, and one recalls with what horror we view those "fanatics" who refuse today to take a loyalty oath to their own government. The Christians, besides, were often confused with the Zealots, who believed in the imminent overthrow of the Empire by the coming Messiah, and *actively* helped prepare his way! The Emperor Claudius ordered the expulsion of foreign Jews from Rome because of the messianic agitation. Paul himself was arrested as a fomentor of revolt, a ringleader of the Nazarenes (Acts, chapter 24, verse 5, hereafter written as Acts 24:5). Their enemies accused the Christians of perverted practices at their love-feasts (Agape), of immorality, and even cannibalism! Nevertheless, the movement spread among the lower classes especially, for it offered salvation from sin, immortality in heaven, brotherhood, and communism in life. Slaves were not barred and were free in Christ; but many of the unwanted and unwashed were attracted to Christianity (remember the Salvation Army converts in the Bowery of New York!), causing much trouble and pain to the Movement. In 64 A.D. Nero persecuted the Christians for having (so he said) set fire to Rome; later the movement was even outlawed by the Flavians, thus cleansing the Church of much riff-raff. Read the epistles of Judas and II Peter.

Paul's concept of Christ was more esoteric than the rather human figure of the synoptic (Matthew, Mark, and Luke) gospels. His Christ is a pre-existent being, the man of heaven created by God before the creation of the world, the very Pattern of the universe itself; this archetypal Son of Man and Son of God was incarnated into Jesus at his baptism by John. This mystic Jesus appealed both to Paul and the writer of the gospel of John. In the Acts this "Christ of Glory" and Spirit was the Force that inspired and led the disciples in their tribulations and trials.

After a bitter siege by the Roman armies, Jerusalem fell in 70 A.D., an important date to both Jews and Christians, and readers of the New Testament. The Antichrist had triumphed; the great and glorious Coming had not occurred; the situation was more desolate than ever before. No wonder then that many of the believers hearkened to various heresies and sundry expressions of semi-pagan doctrines. The Christian Gentiles became anti-Jewish in the sense of disowning the Judaic heritage initially, so important a part of the Christian doctrine. Heresies like the gnostics, the Docetists, the Marcionites, etc., sprang up like weeds everywhere. A reading of the epistles gives one a strong introduction to this phase of the struggle.

Towards the end of the first century a new persecution commenced, its Satan and Antichrist being the Emperor Domitian. He demanded worship as a god. In the last book of the New Testament, the Book of Revelation, better known as the Apocalypse, the author (who is called John) constructs a glorious vision of the New Jerusalem and the coming Judgment; but he also prophesies ruin and damnation for the Antichrist Rome and its emperor. After John's great work the Movement consolidated and grew stronger, constantly rejecting major heresies like gnosticism and Marcionism. By the early part of the fourth century Christianity was the state religion of the Roman Empire.

MANUSCRIPTS AND TEXTS OF THE NEW TESTAMENT

The various writings were collected together on Easter Day in A.D.367, 27 books in all, and the collection was called, for the first time, the New Testament. A process of collection and selection accompanied by much discussion and even violent quarreling had been going on for more than 200 years before certain books were selected as canonical, and others were left to join the legion of the New Testament Apocrypha (see Dictionary for definition of all unfamiliar terms). After the death of Jesus the words of the Saviour and of his deciples were maintained as oral testimony only. Soon a great need was felt for preserving those words and explaining them; hence, our gospels were all written down by the end of the first century. Naturally there has been much addition and interpolation by later editors, since such activity was not considered reprehensible. The study of such editorial additions and interpolations as well as downright forgeries is a complicated study in textual problems with which only Biblical experts can deal. Needless to say, not one original manuscript of the gospel exists. What we have are manuscript copies of the original documents:

1. Manuscript Aleph: The Codex Sinaiticus (4th Century), N.T. in full.
2. Manuscript A: The Codex Alexandrinus (5th Century), N.T. almost

complete.

3. Manuscript B: The Codex Vaticanus (4th Century), N.T. almost complete.

The two best manuscripts and the most dependable are the Codices Sinaiticus and Vaticanus, both copied from copies of further copies of the original first-century documents. When more than 200 years intervenes between a manuscript and its copy of copies, one can expect changes of various kinds. But most orthodox scholars insist that the Codices are accurate copies of second-century texts, which themselves were copies of the originals. Establishing the correct text from the different available Codices is a thorny problem. For one thing a vast and intimate knowledge of Koine Greek is required in order to translate the Greek; but in addition a good knowledge of Aramaic (the language Jesus and his contemporaries spoke) would be invaluable, along with a firm foundation in Hebrew and Latin.

The New Testament was written in Greek because that was the world language of the time, and the authors wanted a language that was understood by the many foreigners in the movement; moreover they wanted a language that surmounted political barriers, a language spoken by most of the peoples of the Roman Empire.

A NOTE TO THE READER

The quotations are taken from the King James version of the Bible (1611), because that version has entered our language most deeply and intimately. All obsolete and unfamiliar words are immediately translated in parentheses. The most complete commentary to the synoptics is that of Matthew, since that gospel is an English favorite and the most pervasively influential in our language and literature. Since the other gospels largely repeat details and incidents of the life of Jesus, the commentary on the gospels of Mark and Luke is devoted to the episodes that are not repeated in *all* three synoptics.

MATTHEW: A PREFACE

WRITER: There is common agreement that Matthew, a Galilean Jew (also called Levi), is the author of his gospel. He worked as a tax-gatherer ("publican" in KJV) for the Romans, and consequently was hated and despised by his fellow Jews.

DATE: About 80 A.D., but this date is in dispute.

THEME: How Jesus fulfils the Davidic Covenant of kingship (that the Messiah would be David's descendant) and the Abraham Covenant of promise as seen in Genesis 15:18. The commentary will explain these concepts as they arise in the gospel. Christ is the King sprung from David as the prophets had predicted. Matthew records his genealogy, his birth in Bethlehem, his ministry, and his predictions of his second coming in power and glory.

DIVISIONS: 1. The manifestation to Israel and rejection of Jesus Christ the Son of David, born King of the

Jews.
2. The sacrifice and resurrection of Jesus Christ, the Son of Abraham.
3. The risen Lord in ministry to his own.

SOURCES: The *gospel of Mark* in both the frameworg and the general order of events, although there is some rearrangement of Mark's material.
A collection of Jesus' *logia* (sayings)

that were written down.

COMMENT: Jesus is primarily a teacher in this gospel, and the world has gathered these teachings to its bosom. Jerusalem had fallen in 70 A.D., and this seemed a just punishment to Christians, for the Jewish nation had rejected its own Messiah. The six great discourses form the framework of the gospel, often called "the greatest book in the world."

DETAILED REVIEW AND COMMENTARY ON THE GOSPEL ACCORDING TO MATTHEW

CHAPTER 1

1. THE GENEALOGY OF JESUS (1:1-17): The gospel begins by listing Jesus' family descent beginning with Abraham, Isaac, Jacob, Judas (Judah), etc., through Thamar (Tamar), Phares (Perez), etc., through Rachab (Rahab), Booz (Boaz), Ruth, Obed, Jesse, David, Solomon, Bathsheba etc., until we get to "And Jacob begat Joseph the husband of Mary, of whom was born Jesus, who is called Christ." Verse 17 summarizes by saying that from Abraham to David are included fourteen generations; from David to the Babylonian captivity are included fourteen also; and from the captivity to Christ are also fourteen generations.

COMMENT: The genealogy of Jesus is interesting for the following reasons:
1. Matthew's purpose is to show that Jesus is the true Messiah (the expected king and deliverer of the Hebrews from bondage and misery), descended from Abraham, David, etc., as stated in the Jewish law.
2. The 42 mainly male ancestors are artificially divided into three groups of 14 each. In addition, the list contains inaccuracies and gaps.

3. Why the five women (Tamar, Rahab, Ruth; the wife of Urias, Bathsheba, and Mary the mother of Christ)? Because Rahab, a prostitute, helped Joshua take the city of Jericho; Tamar committed incest with her father-in-law to teach a lesson to him; Ruth, although a foreigner, was the mother of Obed, the father of Jesse, who was the father of David. Besides, the God of Israel could create the saviour of man even from women like Tamar, Rahab, and Bathsheba, who herself was an adultress who had married David; the son of David and Bathsheba was Solomon.

4. The Greek **Codex Sinaiticus** reads: "Jacob begat Joseph; Joseph, to whom the Virgin Mary was betrothed, begat Jesus who is called Christ." Many scholars believe the true reading to indicate that Jesus was Joseph's true son. Matthew's awkward change shows a wish to stress the Virgin birth doctrine.

5. Luke gives a genealogy which is much longer and less inaccurate and without the artificial "14" grouping. Luke takes the ancestry right up to God himself!

2. THE BIRTH OF JESUS (1:18-25):

When Jesus' mother Mary was engaged to Joseph she became pregnant by the Holy Spirit ("Holy Ghost" in KJV); this occurred before Joseph and she had had any sexual intercourse. Her husband Joseph, a just man (one who observes the Jewish law), was unwilling to make her a public example (expose her by bringing her to court on charges of adultery or divorce her in the presence of two witnesses), and resolved to quietly divorce her. But in a dream an angel tells him that Mary is impregnated by the Holy Spirit and that her son will be given the name Jesus "for he will save his people from their sins" (*Jesus* means "God is salvation"; Joshua and Jesus are the same in meaning). The angel adds that this happened because a prophet had foretold that a "virgin shall be with child, and shall bring forth a son, and they shall call his name Immanuel, which being interpreted is, 'God with us'." Joseph awoke from his sleep and obediently married Mary, but he did not have sexual intercourse with her until after she had given birth to a son, which he named Jesus.

COMMENT: Note the following:
1. In verse 20 Mary is called Joseph's wife, but in verse 18 they are only *engaged* to be married.
2. Several miraculous births occur in the Old Testament, but there was always a father participating; moreover, pagan mythology contains many tales of intercourse between gods and mortals.
3. A Jewish tradition was that sin would disappear on the arrival of the Messiah.
4. The prophet quoted is Isaiah (7:14), and the Greek word for virgin is not quite accurate for the Hebrew *almah* (young woman). The translation *virgin* for *young woman* is then perhaps an error.
5. Mary could not have been a perpetual virgin, for the text implies intercourse with Joseph *after* the birth of Jesus. Later we will hear of Jesus' sisters and brothers.
6. In art, the Holy Ghost is often visualized as a dove (the dove was sacred to Ishtar, Astarte, and Venus); during conception the Virgin is pictured holding a lily (symbol of purity; an odd belief common in medieval times was that eating lilies caused pregnancy without the agency of man).
7. The same Isaiah text, referred to in 4 above, is misunderstood by Matthew to mean that a *virgin* would conceive without man; the meaning is that a young girl would give birth —no divine virgin birth is intended or implied. Matthew's eagerness to push his virgin-birth thesis (this may have been in his sources) is not reflected in the other gospels.

CHAPTER 2

3. THE VISIT OF THE MAGI (2:1-12):

Chapter 2 begins by telling of Jesus' birth in Bethlehem in Judea when Herod was king. Wise men from the East come to the central and main city of Judea (Jerusalem) asking for the whereabouts of the newly-born King of the Jews. They have seen his star in the East and are come to worship the child. All the city, along with King Herod, is troubled at this news. Calling to council all the chief priests and scribes (official teachers of Jewish Law), Herod asks them where the Christ (Messiah) was to be born. The scribes and priests tell Herod that the Christ was to be born in Judea in the town of Bethlehem (about five miles south of Jerusalem); their prediction is based upon a quotation of the prophet Micah 5:2 (Micah predicts that from little Bethlehem shall come forth the ruler of Israel). Herod summons the wise men in secret and learns from them what time the star, which they had seen rise in the East, had appeared in the sky. Herod sends the wise men to Bethlehem to search diligently for this child; when they have found him they are to tell Herod the news so that, as Herod explains, "I may come and worship him also." Miraculously the same star they had seen rise in the East now guides them and finally comes to rest over the child's birthplace. They are exceedingly overjoyed, and entering the house they see the child with Mary his mother. They then fall down and worship him, after which they open their precious gifts and present the child with gold, frankincense (a tree resin used by the Jews for incense), and myrrh (another tree resin used for incense and embalming). That night they are warned in a dream not to return to deliver the news to Herod, and so they go home by another route.

COMMENT: There is no parallel or scholarly support for the magi story. In addition:

1. The Roman Senate appointed Herod king in 40 B.C. and he died in 4 B.C. Magi or wise men may mean members of the Persian priestly caste or simply astrologers and magicians. Often the word has an evil tinge to it (black magicians) when we find the word in the N.T. in other places. Matthew here probably intends astrologers from the East (Babylon?).

2. Stars have often announced the birth of great men, such as Moses and many pagan heroes.

3. Scribe (expert in Jewish religious law) was often called "rabbi" ("my great one"). The chief priests and scribes made up the Sanhedrin of Jerusalem (the civil, religious, and criminal supreme court).

4. Bethlehem of Judea was also the birthplace of the great David, whose issue would be the Messiah. Some scholars see the Bethlehem tale of birth as a legend fulfilling the O.T. prophecy of Micah. Herod's anxiety to know what time the star appeared indicates that he wants to know the age of the child.

5. "Treasures" means containers for gifts; the resins were used for worship, embalming, perfume, and medicine.

6. Herod was a deeply worried man, constantly on the watch for signs of conspiracy or revolt; nor was he a popular king, with his Roman ways and lack of religiosity. His cruelty, cunning, and hate as a politician and Roman underling are well known.

7. Psalm 72:10-15 and Isaiah 60:6 talk of kings who offer gifts to the lord; in the Psalm it is the "kings of Sheba and Seba" and in Isaiah it is "all they from Sheba shall come: they shall bring 'gold and incense'."

4. THE FLIGHT INTO EGYPT (2:13-15): Now Joseph in a dream is told by an angel to flee to Egypt with his wife and child ("the child and his mother" says the gospel) and to stay there until further notice by the angel. Joseph follows instructions and stays in Egypt until Herod's death. This fulfills the prophet's prediction, "Out of Egypt have I called my son."

COMMENT: Egypt was not far from Bethlehem (see map). An old Jewish story has it (second century A.D.) that Jesus learned his "magic" there in that land of magic and witchcraft. The quote may be from Hosea (11:1): "When Israel was a child, then I loved him, and called my son out of Egypt." The Jewish Exodus was looked upon by the Christians as a symbol of Christian redemption; the Jews saw it as a time of miracles that would be re-enacted at the coming of the Messiah. Some historicists (believers in a historical but not divine Jesus) believe the sojourn in Egypt is merely an imitation of the sojourns of Abraham and Moses; the Hosea text is misapplied since "Israel" means the Jewish people and not. the infant Christ.

5. THE SLAUGHTER OF THE CHILDREN (2:16-18):

Herod, furious at the trick played upon him by the wise men, proceeded to kill all the male children in and around Bethlehem who were two years or less in age. Two-year-olds and younger was the age he had ascertained from the wise astrologers. Here is fulfilled what the prophet Jeremiah had foretold: "A voice was heard in Ramah, wailing and loud lamentation, Rachel weeping for her children; she refused to be consoled, because they were no more."

COMMENT: Josephus, a Jewish historian at the time of Christ, does not record this story. There is no historical data to substantiate it, although Herod was indeed a ruthless killer of political and family opponents. Similar tales of infant slaughter surround Moses, Hercules, Sargon I, Cyrus the Persian, and the fabled founders of Rome, Romulus and Remus.
1. Ramah was a town several miles from Jerusalem, and the quote deals with the Jewish exile to Babylon.
2. Some historicists say this is nothing but the myth of the divine child, a kind of solar god whom an evil dragon wants to devour at birth. In Revelation (12) the myth occurs in its pristine form.

6. REMOVAL FROM EGYPT TO NAZARETH (2:19-23):

When Herod died, an angel in Joseph's dream tells him to take his family to Israel, "for they are dead which sought the young child's life." When Joseph hears that Archelaus (Are kuh LAY us) is ruler in Judea as successor to his father, he is afraid and flees (after another angel's warning) to Galilee to live in the city of Nazareth, as foretold by the prophets that "He shall be called a Nazarene."

COMMENT: Archelaus was king of Judea, Samaria, and Idumaea until the Roman Emperor reduced his rank to ethnarch, a kind of governor. He was as brutal as his father, says Josephus. In 6 A.D. Archelaus was thrown out and Palestine became a Roman province ruled by a procurator (governor) of Roman blood.
1. Matthew seems unaware that in Galilee another cruel son of Herod rules, Herod Antipas.
2. The Nazarene (or Nazorean) reference is difficult to pin down. In Judges (13:5) the barren wife of Manoah is told by the angel that she shall bear a son, "for the child shall be a Nazarite" who shall deliver Israel from the enemy Philistines. He was of course Samson. In Isaiah 11:1 it is written that "there shall come forth a rod out of the stem of Jesse, and a branch shall grow out of his roots," a possible reference to the coming Messiah's descent from David (Jesse was David's father). The words Nazarene and Nazarite all sound somewhat alike in Hebrew. In short, a kind of clever pun, something of a game rabbis were fond of playing.
3. There is no mention of the town of Nazareth in the O.T. nor in Josephus. The whole thing is another one of the evangelical legends.
4. Other scholars have identified Nazareth with the town of en-Nasira, "no doubt correctly" says *The Interpreter's Bible*.

CHAPTER 3

7. THE MINISTRY OF JOHN THE BAPTIST (3:1-12): John the Baptist has been preaching in the Judean wilderness, calling for the people to repent "for the kingdom of heaven is at hand." As the prophet Isaiah had foretold: "The voice of one crying in the wilderness: Prepare the way of the Lord, make his paths straight." John was wearing a garment of camel's hair and a leather belt around his waist; he fed on locusts and wild honey. The people from Jerusalem, all Judea, the area around the Jordan river—all came to him often to be baptized in the Jordan river and to confess their sins. Among these people were Pharisees (strict keepers of the Jewish ritual and Rome-haters; religious separatists like our Puritans) and Sadducees (SAD you seez; FARE uh seez), religious conservatives who rejected the Pharisees' stress on the oral law and belief in the resurrection. Many Sadducees were wealthy land-owners who settled in Jerusalem and cooperated in a friendly way with the Romans. At both the Pharisees and Sadducees John hurls the following: "O generation (brood) of vipers, who hath warned you to flee from the wrath to come?" He tells them to repent and do good, and not to boast of having Abraham (an ancient Jewish patriarch, "father of the Jews") as their father, for God can create children of Abraham from the very stones. The axe is ready to chop down all bad fruit trees, which will then be thrown into the fire (all sinners will come to no good end). "I indeed baptize you with water unto repentance: but he that cometh after me is mightier than I, whose shoes I am not worthy to bear (to carry): he shall baptize you with the Holy Ghost (Spirit), and with fire." This person will gather the good wheat and burn the useless chaff in "unquenchable fire."

COMMENT: The wilderness of Judea includes the Jordan valley and the mountainous area west of the Dead Sea.
1. In Mark (1:15), our earliest and most reliable gospel, it is Jesus who announces the kingdom of heaven at hand; John's message is invariably one of doom.
2. In the passage from Isaiah the Lord is God (Yahweh), not Christ, as interpreted here by Matthew. Elijah (11:14) also wore a leather belt but not a camel's hair garment. Locusts are still a delicacy among some Arabs today: locusts = grasshoppers.
3. John shows that the special protection Jews felt in being the children of Abraham could be easily gainsaid by God. The fire generally means the final day of judgment when the good will be saved and the sinful burned in hellfire.
4. John's disciples faithfully followed his doctrines long after he had died. There is good evidence to show that Jesus himself was a disciple of John in spite of the evangelical cover-ups.
5. Historicists claim that John's call was to the common people and not the Pharisees and Sadducees. John is deliberately subordinated to Jesus, evidence of Christian "doctoring" here. John's conscious imitation of the robes of Elijah shows he follows in Elijah's tracks.

8. THE BAPTISM OF JESUS (3:13-17): Then Jesus left Galilee in order to be baptized by John in the Jordan, but John desists, saying "I need to be baptized by you, and do you come to me?" Jesus replies that he wants baptism now because it is fitting for him to do all righteous things. John then consents and baptizes Jesus. Just after baptism the heavens open and Jesus sees the

Spirit of God "descending like a dove and alighting upon him"; and at the same time a voice from heaven says, "This is my beloved Son, in whom I am well pleased."

COMMENT: In Mark, Jesus happens to be in the area, but Matthew has Jesus leave Nazareth in order to be baptized. Some interesting points follow:

1. Why should a sinless Jesus need baptism, which is the cleansing of sin? This question bothered the Christians of the first century. One unofficial gospel (*According to the Nazarenes*) has Jesus say: "In what have I sinned, that I should go and be baptized by him (i.e., John)?" Theologians explain this by saying that even though Jesus needed no baptism, he "no doubt assumed that any right-minded man would associate himself with John's movement" (*I.B.*).

2. Luke says the Holy Ghost descended in bodily form in the shape of a dove. Mark says the heavens "split" open, and both Mark and Luke have God addressing Jesus—not the bystanders—directly: "Thou art·my beloved son, etc."

3. Historicists find this dialogue between John and Jesus interpolated— that John needed to be baptized by Jesus, not otherwise. The baptism story is mythical, but there is historical foundation for Jesus, as a follower of John, to be baptized by him.

4. Note that the assumption is that Jesus is now a mature man. We last had heard of him as an infant settling in Nazareth. The intervening years are often known as the "lost years" of Jesus' youth. Mythicists claim Jesus himself to be mythical, and like all divine beings he suffers "lost years" from adolescence to maturity.

CHAPTER 4

9. THE TEMPTATION (4:1-11): Then Jesus is led into the wilderness by "the Spirit," there to be tempted by the devil. Jesus fasts for forty days and nights, becoming very hungry. The devil-tempter challenges him to change stones to bread to prove Jesus is the "Son of God"; Jesus' reply is to quote, "Man shall not live by bread alone" but by the word of God. Secondly, the devil takes Christ to the holy city (Jerusalem) and sets him on a high point of the Temple, challenging Christ to throw himself to the ground. The tempter quotes words to the effect that God will send angels to catch and bear him up before striking the ground; Jesus' reply is a simple quote, "Thou. shalt not tempt the Lord thy God." Lastly, the tempter takes Jesus to a very high mountain and displays to him all the glorious kingdoms of the world saying, "All these things

will I give thee, if thou wilt fall down and worship me," but the Lord's reply is a curt "Get thee hence, Satan," for God only is to be worshipped and served. Then the devil leaves, and, behold, angels appear to serve Jesus.

COMMENT: Such temptation stories are common to founders of various religions, such as Zoroaster and Buddha. The anecdote is not historical (very likely), but it does serve as an illustration of Jesus' inner struggle with three major temptations constantly facing him: to effect miracles for immediate satisfaction, to convince with signs, and to wield political power. The word devil meant slanderer; when **Satan** is used the word means adversary or accuser. Jewish teaching says that Satan arouses evil in man, tempts him into sin, accuses man before God, and then punishes man with death. Note the following:

1. Forty is a convenient number in the Bible (the period of Moses' fasting was 40 days and nights; the Israelites wandered 40 years in the wilderness, etc.).

2. In the O.T. (*Old Testament*) Son of God can apply to angels, to the Israelite nation, and even to a king. Often it means God-related; the important fact is that the Jews did not apply the term to the Messiah (two apocalyptic books, Enoch and II Esdras, use it as a term for the Messiah). It was used early by Christians to refer to Jesus; and it denotes many things, such as saviour of man, healer of man, and with both human and divine traits—Son of God.

3. The third temptation assumes the devil possessed the entire world, but for Jesus to possess it and bring about his reforms he would have to sell his soul to the devil. The serving angels follow the promise in Psalm 91:11-14.

4. Some scholars see here two myths combined: the initiation of a man of God before launching upon his sacred mission on earth and the combat between God's agent and the Power of Darkness. The three challenges and replies are nothing but theological question and answer. Important too is the fact that Christ will not show himself to be a common magician or conjurer, not a Simon Magus (see Acts), not an impostor sent by Satan, like the Roman emperor. The mountain, etc., is mythical, like the entire anecdote, perhaps.

10. JESUS' PREACHING IN GALILEE: THE PROPHETIC SETTING

(4:12-17): At the news of John's arrest by Herod Antipas, Jesus returns to Galilee, first to Nazareth and then to Capernaum (kah PURR nay uhm), on the northwestern shore of the Sea of Galilee. Isaiah had foretold of this area that "the people who sat in darkness have seen a great light"; and from that time on Jesus begins to preach, saying "Repent: for the kingdom of heaven is at hand."

COMMENT: The point of the Isaiah quote is that even this poor, rejected land would be saved by the Messiah Jesus. Judea, the richer land and the expected area of Jesus' ministry, was spurned for Galilee. Jesus' call to repentance, "for the kingdom of heaven is at hand," requires some explanation:

1. The phrase "kingdom of heaven" means the rule of God. In the days of Noah man turned away from the kingship of God on earth, but under Abraham and Moses the Israelites accepted his rule on earth. Through Jewish disobedience the heathen gained lordship of the world and God returned to heavenly rule. The return of God's kingdom on earth is the central concept in Jesus' teaching. Man must prepare for it by repentance and moral effort, but it still remains as God's gift. Already signs of the approaching kingdom are visible in the appearance of the Messiah, and the near future (very near, indeed) would bring the full reign of God's glory on earth. *Eschatology* involves, then, a belief in an approaching God's kingdom, a visible sign of the first seeds of that kingdom, and a very exquisite sense of expectation of future glory to come. Jesus laid no national or racial conditions for sharing in such a kingdom (as the O.T. Jews had): rules for entrance are only religious and moral. Jesus is the announcer of the new kingdom, but some critics believe that he himself expected to be the bringer of the New Kingdom to man.

2. The kingdom of God and the coming of the Messiah (Son of man) are not logically connected, but the two ideas are commonly associated together in the Gospels.

11. CALLING OF THE FIRST DISCIPLES

(4:18-22): Jesus, walking by the sea of Galilee, sees the brothers Simon (nicknamed Peter) and Andrew fishing; they are fishermen. Jesus says to them, "Follow me, and I will make you fishers of men," and they immediately abandon their nets to follow him. Next, Jesus sees the brothers James and John in a boat with Zebedee (ZEB uh dee) their father. They are mending nets, and at Jesus' summons they immediately leave their boat and their father to follow Jesus.

COMMENT: Simon is Greek for the Hebrew "Simeon"; it was common for Palestinian Jews to bear Greek names; Andrew is also Greek. Fishing was an important activity around the Sea of Galilee. The nets were probably circular drawnets. Becoming "fishers of men" was a pun meaning their job will be to save men. Like the Jewish rabbis, Jesus had pupils or disciples, who learned by following their teacher's examples as well as his lectures and rules. These disciples, unlike the followers of the rabbis, are not going to learn legal niceties and ritual but only a few simple principles; their main duty is to announce the coming kingdom of God.
1. Elijah in much the same way cast his mantle over Elisha, who immediately ran after him to follow him (I Kings 19:19-21).
2. See Luke (5:1-11) for a different and highly elaborate story of Jesus' first disciples' catch. Incidentally, Peter, James, and John are the disciples closest to their master in all the Gospel.
3. Historicists find the immediate following of Christ without regard to family or living highly improbable; they feel the zealous jump to the call is the evangelical (gospel writers') addition to the basic fact that Jesus did have disciples who did follow him.

12. SUMMARY OF HIS FIRST ACTIVITY (4:23-25): Then Jesus travels throughout Galilee teaching in "their synagogues," and preaching "the gospel of the kingdom"; he heals all diseases and infirmities ("those which were possessed with devils"), and so his fame goes throughout Syria. Brought to him for healing are the sick, the demoniacs, the epileptics, and the paralytics. Great crowds follow him from Galilee, Decapolis, Judea, and the Trans-Jordan.

COMMENT: This section summarizes this part to be found in the original Gospel from which Matthew has drawn much of his material (Mark). Any competent layman could teach in the synagogue in those days. The "lunatics" means the epileptics; and the "demoniacs" are the insane. Decapolis was west of the Jordan, an area including Damascus and Gadara.

CHAPTER 5

13. THE SERMON ON THE MOUNT: INTRODUCTION (5:1-2): Jesus, seeing the great crowds who follow him everywhere, decides to climb to the top of a mountain. There he sits down with his disciples to teach them.

COMMENT: This is the introduction to what the *I.B.* calls "the most striking and characteristic feature of his (Matthew's) entire Gospel." The sermon will be rules for those who wish to inherit the new kingdom. They are *not* rabbinical legalisms so much as exhortations to moral righteousness. The Sermon on the Mount is a wholly new teaching tradition and not just another rabbinical lawbook or *Torah* (the first five books of the O.T., in which is to be found much of Jewish laws on ritual, etc.). "The sermon is made up of aphorisms, maxims, and illustrations" (*I.B.*) taken from many different speeches made at different times by Jesus.
1. The discourse is addressed to the four disciples only, but Matthew in-

tends it to apply to all Christians.

2. Later Jesus will use a mountain for his transfiguration (see 17:1) and the giving of his parting commandment (28:16). Moses received the Torah on a mountaintop also.

3. Sitting down was the classic posture of the Jewish teacher, very proper for a sermon or discourse.

4. The Sermon on the Mount is the most famous and well-known speech in the history of the western world. Ernest Renan, for this reason, calls the Gospel of Matthew the most important book in the world. Yet the entire speech can be given in twenty minutes!

14. NINE BEATITUDES, CONTRASTING FUTURE JOYS WITH PRESENT SUFFERINGS AND DUTIES (5:3-12): Jesus' sermon to his disciples is first in the form of a series of *beatitudes* (promises of the kingdom of heaven or kingdom of God):

1. "Blessed are the poor in spirit for theirs is the kingdom of heaven." How happy are the (despised, the oppressed, and the pious) poor who are "poor in spirit" (which means poor in great spiritual need; that is they are afflicted "in spirit" and "feel their spiritual need"; the last quoted phrase is that of the great theologian Goodspeed).

2. "Blessed are they that mourn: for they shall be comforted."
(Those who mourn for their own sins and the sins of Israel; moreover, they shall be comforted by God.)

3. "Blessed are the meek: for they shall inherit the earth."
(The humble minded are also the poor who will inherit the future promised land of paradise or perhaps the new age of happiness soon to come under Jesus the Messiah.)

4. "Blessed are they which do hunger and thirst after righteousness: for they shall be filled."
(Those who thirst for religious (moral) justice and right will be given

spiritual satisfaction by God.)

5. "Blessed are the merciful: for they shall obtain mercy."
(The merciful are those who show love and kindness to the unfortunate.)

6. "Blessed are the pure in heart: for they shall see God."
(The pure in heart are those who are right with God, of clean heart and mind. Seeing God means they will see him in the new paradise to come.)

7. "Blessed are the peacemakers, for they shall be called the children of God."
(In the O.T. peace is absence of war and strife; inner and outer well-being through trust and love of God. "Sons of God" means the Hebrews whom God chose as his "sons".)

8. "Blessed are they which are persecuted for righteousness' sake: for theirs is the kingdom of heaven."
(They who are persecuted on Jesus' account for having believed in his word and person as Messiah.)

9. "Rejoice, and be exceeding glad: for great is your reward in heaven: for so persecuted they the prophets. which were before you."
(God's reward is immeasurable, "for it consists of salvation in the age to come; it is a gift of God's grace, not for services rendered but for doing what is prescribed for a follower of Jesus.)

COMMENT: The sermon was never delivered in this way, since it is a collection of different sayings at different times. This sermon, often known as "The Discourse," originally was *eschatological* (ess KAT o logical): belief that the Kingdom of God is imminent and the end of the present age is at hand. Christ is to appear then and deliver a Final Judgment in which the good will be saved for Paradise and the sinful condemned to hell. Note: Some critics believe the original source was an appeal to the poor and hungry of the land, who were appealed to in a direct revolutionary sense, but that Matthew changed these "poor *in spirit*," to "those who hunger *for righteousness*," adding such non-revolutionary sentiments as the gentle, the merciful, the pure in heart, and the peacemakers. These additions made the gospel less subversive and revolutionary to the suspicious and ever-wary Roman rulers.

The Sermon on the Mount is only one-fourth as long in Luke (6:20-49). The Beatitudes (the list of rewards in heaven and blessings, in a form taken from the Psalms) form the very heart of the Christian ethic.

15. THE RELATION OF THE DISCIPLES TO THE WORLD (5:13-16):

Jesus now defines the nature of the listening disciples, whom he calls "the salt of the earth"; "but if the salt have lost his savor (its taste), wherewith shall it be salted?" The disciples are the "light of the world"; one does not put a lighted candle under a bushel, but lets it shine before men so that they may see your good deeds, and by so doing they will glorify God on earth.

COMMENT: The disciples will keep the world from going bad, as does salt. Pure salt never spoils; the meaning must be that the disciples will no more lose their character than salt will its taste.

1. The rabbis often called God, Israel, and the Torah (Jewish ritual law) "the light of the world."

2. To be useful light must be like salt, applied in a practical way.

16. THE NEW LAW IS THE COMPLETION OF THE OLD, NOT ITS DESTRUCTION (5:17-20):

Jesus then adds a reassurance to the disciples: "Think not that I am come to destroy the law, or the prophets: I am not come to destroy, but to fulfill." Not a dot shall pass away from the law as laid down in the O.T. until Christ's mission on earth is ful-

filled. Jesus warns that those who break the law will suffer in heaven, but those who practice and teach it will be glorified in heaven. In fact, their righteousness shall be more strict and pure than / that of the "scribes and Pharisees." Six examples of what Jesus meant / by this injunction follow:

16. CONTRASTS BETWEEN THE OLD INTERPRETATION OF THE LAW AND THE NEW (5:21-48)

a) MURDER AND ANGER: The Law says "Thou shalt not kill" but Jesus says that even anger (which leads to murder) without reason ("cause") may bring about a loss of heaven; moreover those who say "Raca!" (wretch or fool) shall burn in hell. Be reconciled; make friends with your adversary quickly before going to court to avoid going to jail and paying the last penny of the fine.

b) ADULTERY AND LUST: The Law (Sixth Commandment) forbids adultery, "But I say unto you, That whosoever looketh on a woman to lust (sexually desire) her hath committed adultery with her already in his heart." Pluck out your right eye if it causes you to sin (by stimulating you visually) and throw it away; better that than the whole body go to hell. The same goes for the right hand.

c) DIVORCE: The O.T. allows divorce, but Jesus forbids it entirely unless the wife has committed adultery.

d) OATHS: The O.T. forbids false swearing of oaths, but Jesus forbids swearing by heaven, by earth, by Jerusalem, and by your head, "for you cannot make one hair white or black." Anything more than "Yes" or "No" is evil (oaths are solemn invocation of God or heaven, etc., to make your promise more binding).

e. RETALIATION: The O.T. says "An eye for an eye, and a tooth for a tooth," but Christ urges the disciple not to resist evil persons by self-defense, but if slapped on the right cheek, to turn the left cheek to be slapped; and if one sues in court for your coat, give him your cloak as well.

f) **HATRED AND LOVE:** The O.T. tells you to love your neighbor and hate your enemy, but Christ says love your enemies, bless your cursers, return good for hate, and pray for those who hurt and despise you. The God of the Israelites makes the sun rise on both the good and evil people and rains on both the just and unjust. It is not enough just to love those who return your love anyway Even tax collectors can do that. "Be ye therefore perfect, even as your Father which is in heaven is perfect."

COMMENT: By the time Matthew was writing (late first century A.D.) many Jews believed in a hell (*Gehenna* in Greek) of fire to torment sinners. This could happen after the final judgment or just before it. The ideal of a fiery hell arose from the valley of Hinnom near Jerusalem, a garbage dump and a former place of human sacrifice — this plus Isaiah's (31:9; 66:24) quoting the Lord "whose fire is in Zion and his furnace in Jerusalem," and as for sinners "their worm shall not die, neither shall their fire be quenched; and they shall be an abhorring unto all flesh."
1. By *adultery* (see 'b' above) Christ means illicit sexual intercourse with any woman. The rabbis were less inflexibly demanding perfection than Jesus since they gave little account to evil intentions if not succumbed to. However, evil desires were just as forbidden by the Law as by the Gospel!

2. The certificate of *divorce* (see 'c') was a writ of the divorcing husband given to his wife, which was legal and valid in every respect. The grounds of unchastity is the Gospel writer's addition to his source and the original tradition. Originally, Jesus allowed for no exceptions, but the early Christian church had to allow for them; hence the interpolation (editorial addition).
3. With *oaths* (see 'd') Jesus means to prohibit idle and useless swearing to affirm one's honesty. Swearing by God (or his equivalent) was binding, but Jesus equates it with trivial oaths by the head, by Jerusalem, etc. The good disciples need no such reenforcement of their honesty.
5. In *retaliation* (see 'e') the coat is a long-sleeved undergarment, and the cloak was worn over the coat; it (the cloak) was also used by the poor as a night blanket.
5. In *hatred and love* (see 'f') Jesus misquotes, since the O.T. never says the Jews should hate his enemy, although except for the Books of Ruth and Jonah and in a few other places, the O.T. generally displays a virulent hatred of the enemies of the Jews. Love here means the love of God for "man and of man for God and the benevolent loving kindness which seeks the material and spiritual good of others (*I.B.*)." Even as today, tax collectors were hated and despised, classified with sinners.
6. Verse 48: "Perfect" meant in New Testament times that "you must be honest with him (Yahweh or God), upright and sincere, having wholeness and integrity, not double-dealing" (F. C. Grant in *The Earliest Gospel*, 1943).

CHAPTER 6

17. CONTRASTS BETWEEN THE OLD PRACTICE AND THE NEW (6:1-18)
a) **AGAINST OSTENTATION:** Do not (says Jesus) show how religious you are in public, for you will not be rewarded in heaven.
b) **ALMSGIVING:** When giving to

charity do not go blowing your own horn as do the hypocrites in the synagogues (Jewish place of worship) and in the streets so that men will praise them for their high devotion. When giving alms (charity) "let not thy left hand know what thy right hand doeth"; give anonymously and secretly and God will reward you secretly.

c) **PRAYER:** Don't pray like the hypocrites who stand and pray in the synagogues and streets to make an impression. They will get what they deserve. Pray in private, in secret, and you shall be rewarded in the same way. Do not pile on meaningless phrases in your prayers like the Gentiles, but pray then like this:

Our Father which art in Heaven,
Hallowed be thy name (glorify thy name).
Thy kingdom come (reign of God).
Thy will be done in earth, as it is in heaven.
Give us this day our daily (necessary? faithful? for the morrow?) bread.
And forgive us our debts (sins), as we forgive our debtors (sinners forgiven by us).
And lead us not into temptation (trial, persecution, or perhaps God will remove things that cause sin in us), but deliver us from evil (often "the evil one").
For thine is the kingdom, and the power, and the glory, for ever. Amen ("Amen" is the *doxology*, that is, the prayer in praise of God, ending; it means "so be it".

COMMENT: The "hypocrites" are very likely the Pharisees, who try to please men rather than God. The great Lord's Prayer shows a need for us to pardon other sinners if we ourselves wish to be pardoned. Luke gives the same prayer in a shorter form and in a different context. It is almost entirely Jewish in its sentiments, and portions of it can be traced easily in the O.T.

d) **FASTING:** Fasting (a kind of "starvation" period, in which one seeks forgiveness and atonement through hunger)among hypocrites is too obvious by a show of unwashed ("disfigured") faces in public. Jesus urges the disciples to anoint (pour oil on) their faces which are to be washed; that the fasting is to be done in private for God's sake. Thus you will earn your reward, says Jesus.

e) **THE RIGHT USE OF PROPERTY** (6:19-29): Do not build up property and riches in life, where they will be subject to moths and rust ("worm") and thievery, "For where your treasure is, there will your heart be also." So, if your eye (man's moral spirit) is sound, then will your whole body be sound morally and religiously. But if your eye is evil (i.e., a selfish person), then shall your whole body be so. "No man can serve two masters: for either he will hate the one, and love the other" or he will be true to one and despise the other. "You cannot serve God and mammon" (*mammon* = property-lover, materialist, not always meant to be used in the evil sense). Therefore, do not fret over eating, drinking, the care of your body, or clothing. Is not life (with God) worth more than food, and your body worth more than mere clothing? Look at the birds: they do no labor and yet God feeds them. Are you not more precious to God than they? "And which of you by being anxious can add one cubit to his span of life?" (*cubit:* the length of your arm from elbow to fingertip). As for anxiety about clothing, "Consider the lilies of the field, how they grow; they neither toil nor spin; even Solomon (fabulously wealthy Hebrew King of the O.T.) cannot compare with them in dress. God then will clothe man even more splendidly, "O ye of little faith." The Gentiles (non-Jews) seek food, clothing, etc., but you (the disciples) are to seek first the kingdom of God "and all these things (prope ty, food, etc.) shall be added unto ou" (shall be yours as well). There- ore, forget about tomorrow and let your present troubles be enough for you now ("Sufficient unto the day is the evil thereof").

COMMENT: Verse 21 has modern equivalents: a man's mind is where his money is. Verse 23 on selfishness can be better understood if it is translated this way: your actions are guided by the selfish spirit; then how much more selfish must your entire character be. Worry over material security in life may be of more concern than spiritual salvation to many of us. Jesus tells us to replace that

concern by faith in God's providing for us if we show trust and faith in him. The meaning is eschatological since Jesus felt his own death and resurrection were near and the kingdom of God very, very near. The lilies of the field (28-29) is a term for all kinds of wild flowers in the Bible. In 32-33 one must be aware that the Gentiles prayed to Jupiter (for example) to give them material benefits. Jesus "quite frankly bids his disciples pray for daily bread" (*I.B.*). Origen, an early church father, found an alleged saying of Jesus telling man to seek the great things and the little will be obtained, and "seek the heavenly things and the earthly things will be added to you."

CHAPTER 7

18. THE CENSORIOUS SPIRIT (7: 1-6): "Judge not, that ye be not judged." Do not, says Jesus continuing his sermon, judge others, for God will as surely judge you with the same measure of justice that you dealt out. Why look for the speck ("mote") in your brother's eye when you cannot see the log in your own? You hypocrite, first remove the log in your own eye, and then you will be able to remove the speck from your brother's eye. ("First cast out the beam out of thine own eye; and then shalt thou see clearly to cast out the mote out of thy brother's eye.") Do not give holy things to dogs, "neither cast ye your pearls before swine, lest they trample them under their feet" and turn to attack you.

COMMENT: 7:1 is found in the *Mishnah* (Jewish law digest) and in Luke (6:37). It means that you are not to be so severely self-righteous, not that one must never make a judgment on a moral issue. See Shakespeare's *Measure for Measure*,

where the treatment of O.T. justice is contrasted with Christian mercy; for that is how Shakespeare saw the issue. 3-5 tell us to improve ourselves first before attempting to improve others. The pearls-swine verse (6) is out of place here, but it can mean that religious teaching is useless before the unappreciative. Incidentally, dogs and pigs are abhorrent to the Jew.

a) **CONFIDENCE IN PRAYER** (7: 7-12): "Ask, and it shall be given you; seek, and ye shall find," says Christ. All who ask of God will recieve what he asks. If your son asks for bread would you give him a stone? Then how much more your Father in heaven will give to those who ask: "Therefore all things whatsoever ye would that men should do to you, do ye even so to them: for this is the law and the prophets." *Translated*: Act the same towards others as you would have them act towards you.

COMMENT: The emphasis is on *ask*

— the religious person must find prayer essential. This does not say that all wishes shall be granted you. Verse 12 is known as the Golden Rule, a central concept among Christians. In Judaism it was put in a negative form by Hillel, a rabbi contemporary of Jesus: "What is hateful to you, do not do to your neighbor; this the whole Torah, all else is interpretation." Jesus put it in *positive* form. Righteousness is in doing good, *not* avoidance of sin.

19. WARNINGS (7:13-29): "Enter ye in at the strait gate: for wide is the gate, and broad is the way, that leadeth to destruction." Enter the narrow gate where the path is hard and few will venture it—but that is the way to heaven. The road to hell is broad and easy to entrance. [Two ways there are: to life and to death (life is "eternal life").]

a) **FALSE PROPHETS:** Beware also, Jesus says, of false prophets dressed in sheep's wool who inwardly are ravenous as wolves. You will recognize them by their actions ("fruits"). A good tree bears only good fruit, and a bad one evil fruits. All trees not bearing good fruit are to be cut down and burned. "Wherefore by their fruits ye shall know them."

b) **LIP SERVICE:** Those only shall enter heaven who do the will of God. Of course many will have only spoken of and not *done* the will of

God. To those Jesus will say, "I never knew you: depart from me, ye that work iniquity" (do evil). Those who hear and perform the words of Christ will be like the man who built his house on a rock: rain, floods, winds did not make it fall because it was built on a rock. Those who only hear but do not *do* Christ's teachings will be like the fool who built his house on sand; it fell before the storms. And now Jesus ends his sermon, leaving the crowds astonished at his doctrine, for "he taught them as one having authority, and not as the scribes."

COMMENT: V.22 "In that day" is a phrase for the messianic age or the world to come. The disciples who act "in thy (Jesus') name are able to cast out devils (illness was thought to be caused by certain devils within the body; they were "cast out" by the use of Jesus' name and certain sayings). The parable (anecdote-with-moral) of the houses on stone and sand was known to the Jews. The astonishment of the people must have been at certain radical departures from Jewish law. In addition, unlike other rabbis, he failed to document his teachings with the citation of chapter and verse. He even referred to himself as "Lord" and judge. The lack of documentation and citation showed he needed no higher authority than himself, the Lord: "For he taught them as one having authority, and not as the scribes."

CHAPTER 8

20. THE HEALING OF A LEPER (8:1-4): Finally Jesus descends from the mountain and great crowds follow him. Behold, a leper kneels before him, asking to be cured. Stretching out his hand Jesus cures him by saying, "Be clean." Jesus enjoins him to say nothing to anyone but to go to the priest and offer a

gift (in the purification ceremony one offered up two birds in the temple at Jerusalem). "Unto them" could be proof to the critics of Jesus or to the people.

COMMENT: 1. The story of the leper is from Mark (1:40-44). Leprosy was a common enough disease in Palestine then. It was regarded as a punishment for sins. Curing it was as difficult as raising the dead. The disease could be a loose term for ringworm, psoriasis, leucoderma, and vitiligo. Actual leprosy was unknown in Palestine.

2. Stretching out the hand and touching the ill one were the usual gestures of healing. To cleanse a leper on the spot is a supernatural act.

3. The injunction to remain silent comes from Mark, who "probably thought that Christ's messiahship must remain secret" (*I.B.*). If the words are Jesus', then he said so because he did not want too much publicity about his miracle powers; too many curious people would cry for more displays, which was not Christ's purpose.

21. THE HEALING OF A CENTURION'S SERVANT (8:5-13):
When Jesus enters Capernaum, a *centurion* (an officer in the Roman army) begs him to cure his paralyzed servant ("sick of the palsy"). Jesus offers to go home with him, only to be told by the officer "I am not worthy that thou shouldest come under my roof." Jesus is only to say the curative words and his servant will be healed. The man's great faith in Jesus makes Him marvel, saying there is no such faith in any Jew as there is in this Roman. Jesus predicts that many people will come from the east and west to sit with Abraham, Isaac, and Jacob (the three great Jewish patriarchs) in heaven. But the sons of the kingdom of heaven (the Jews) "shall be cast into outer darkness: there shall be weeping and gnashing of teeth." To the centurion he says, "Go thy way: and as thou hast believed, so be it done unto thee," and at that very moment the servant is cured.

COMMENT: Matthew emphasizes how a Gentile showed faith in Jesus

and was praised for it. A centurion was a non-commissioned officer in charge of a hundred soldiers in the police force of Herod Antipas. Often Lord can mean simply "sir" as in v. 6; and "servant" can mean *boy*. The paralysis might have been hysteria.

1. Vss. (verses) 11-12 indicate an old idea, to be found in Isaiah 45:6, 49:12, and elsewhere, that many Gentiles will be accepted as well as the natural heirs to the kingdom of heaven (the Jews).

2. This tolerance for Gentiles is in harmony with his other teachings, as in the great Sermon on the Mount.

22. THE HEALING OF PETER'S MOTHER-IN-LAW AND OTHERS (8:14-17):
Jesus went into Peter's house, where he cured Peter's mother who was sick of a fever. In the evening of the same day many who came to him were cured ("casting out their demons"). This was foretold by Isaiah 53:4: "He took our infirmities, and bare our sicknesses." (The quotation has Isaiah referring to the servant of God who "took our infirmities" by getting ill himself. Matthew twists it to refer to Jesus' healing power.)

23. INTERLUDE: TEACHING ABOUT DISCIPLESHIP (8:18-22):
Seeing great crowds all around him, Jesus decides to cross the lake of Galilee. When a scribe offers to follow Jesus everywhere, Jesus says that unlike the birds and foxes, the Son of man "hath not where to lay his head." One disciple asks permission to bury his dead father, but Jesus says to him, "Follow me; and let the dead bury their dead."

COMMENT: Taking by the hand and raising up the invalid is a classic gesture of healing in many ancient stories. Verse 20 is inappropriate since Jesus has a home in Capernaum. In Luke 9:57 the scribe is merely a man.

Son of man can also mean a human being, as it does here; or it can mean "the celestial figure who comes on the clouds at the end of the age to establish the final order" of the Kingdom of God. Referring to himself as the Messiah who would return in *apocalyptic* (end-of-world judgment-day) glory would be unusual, for this was not the prevalent idea in Jesus' day (i.e., that the *Son of man* and the *Messiah* were one and the same). Burying one's father was a sacred Jewish duty, a very sacred one indeed, and for Jesus to put the claims of the coming kingdom of God over family duty was a daring requirement. Those who do not follow Jesus are spiritually dead anyway: let them bury their own dead.

24. POWER OVER NATURAL FORCES (8:23-27): Jesus gets into the boat with his disciples to cross the sea of Galilee. A great storm arises but the sleeping Jesus does not awake; they finally succeed in arousing Jesus, telling him they are about to die. "Why are ye fearful, O ye of little faith," says Jesus, who then gives a scolding to the winds and the sea, and immediately all is calm on Galilee. Naturally, the disciples are thunderstruck.

25. POWER OVER DEMONS (8:28-34): Reaching the other side of the lake, Jesus and his disciples are met by two demoniacs (men possessed by demons), "exceeding fierce, so that no man might pass by that way." They want to know what the Son of God has to do with them; has he come to torment them "before the time?" The demons beg Jesus to send them away into a herd of passing pigs. Christ says, "Go"; so the demons came out of the two men and enter into the bodies of the swine, and behold, the whole herd jumps over a steep bank and into the sea where they perish. The pig-keepers fled to the city of Gadara (ten miles southeast of the western shore of the lake) and tell all that has happened. The Gadarenes all come out to meet Jesus and beg him to leave their neighborhood.

COMMENT: Jews, of course, did not keep pigs, so such a story is impossible about Jews. The point of the anecdote is that demons recognize Jesus as the Son of God even when humans like the Gadarenes, who had rejected him, do not. A fabulous story, but one showing dramatically men being delivered from evil.
1. The storm-delivery and power-over-the-storm story is meant to show how Jesus could deliver his people from either literal or symbolic storms, although sudden storms are not uncommon on Galilee.
2. Note that the disciples themselves have not recognized Jesus as divine yet.
3. Mark (from whom Matthew takes most of his material) wrote Gergesenes (the town of Gerge was on the eastern shore); Mark has only one man possessed by demons; Matthew has added one more for good measure. Demons are the angels of the devil who bring mankind all his woes; some of their favorite dwelling places are tombs and water.

CHAPTER 9

26. POWER TO FORGIVE SINS, NOW AVAILABLE TO MEN (9:1-8): Jesus and his disciples return to Capernaum across the lake where they meet a paralytic brought to them by the townsmen. Seeing their belief in him, Jesus forgives the paralytic his sins, thus shocking the scribes who know only God could forgive sins (not even the Messiah

THE NEW TESTAMENT

33

had this right). The scribes call it *blasphemy* (really means cursing God in his own name; perhaps used loosely in this instance). Jesus informs them that the Son of man had authority on earth to forgive sins. He then tells the paralytic to rise, take up his bed (a light cot or rug) and go home, which the paralytic does. The awed crowds praise God for giving authority to forgive to man.

COMMENT: Sickness was a product of sinning; so due repentance could make healing possible. The paralytic was duly repentant. *Son of man* means the Messiah in Mark and perhaps Matthew; here the power to forgive sins passes from God to man.

27. CALLING OF A TAX COLLECTOR (9:9): Soon after, Jesus sees a man named Matthew working as a tollhouse keeper. Jesus says to him, "Follow me. And he rose and followed him."

28. JESUS ASSOCIATES WITH SINNERS (9:10-13): While reclining at his home in Capernaum, many tax collectors and sinners (both "light" and "heavy" sinners) enter to sit with Jesus and the disciples. The Pharisees are shocked, asking why Jesus sits with such riff-raff. Jesus says that well people do not need a physician, but sick ones do. What Jesus desires is mercy and not sacrifices: "For I am not come to call the righteous, but sinners to repentance."

29. HIS DISCIPLES DO NOT FAST (9:14-15): The disciples of John the Baptist come up to Jesus asking why his disciples do not fast, to which Jesus replies: wedding guests mourn only when the bridegroom is taken from them: "and then they will fast." Similarly, unshrunk cloth is not sewn to an old garment since a big tear would result; nor do "men put new wine into old bottles," else the bottles (leather ones in those days)

would break. New wine in new bottles saves both.

COMMENT: Vss. 10-13 is a "paradigm" or controversy story: its point is in v. 12. The statement in v. 13 about mercy and not sacrifice is from Hosea 6:6, taken quite out of context. Fasting in private was voluntary; Jesus and the disciples violated this part of the code.
1. Wedding guests ("children of the bedchamber") and even rabbis could break ritual laws, a Jewish custom. The Jews often told about the days of the Messiah being like a wedding. The bridegroom is of course Jesus, the sons, disciples.
2. The cloth and wine comparisons mean that the coming new kingdom of God will burst "the framework" of the past order (*I.B.*); or it may mean that Jesus' teachings cannot be contained in the old Jewish law.

30. POWER OVER CHRONIC ILLNESS AND DEATH (9:18-26): Just then an official approaches Jesus, bows low and begs Jesus to revive his daughter who has just died. While on his way to cure her, a woman with a chronic 12-year hemorrhage touches the edge of his cloak, thinking the touch would cure her illness. Christ, telling her to cheer up, cures her because of her faith in him. On arriving at the official's house he asks the noisy flute players and crowd inside to leave, telling them that the girl is only asleep. Their reply is scornful laughter. Nevertheless, he forces the crowd to go outside, and proceeds to revive the girl by taking her hand; the dead girl comes to life and gets up. This miracle becomes widely known. Next, while walking, he cures two blind men because they too had faith. The cure is effected by laying his hand on their eyes. He warns them not to tell about the miracle, but the cure is soon widely known. Later a dumb man "possessed by a devil" is exorcised and the devil leaves him, allowing the dumb man to talk again. The crowd is amazed; nothing like it has ever been seen in Israel, but the Pharisees claim he has power over devils because he is in league with the devil himself.

COMMENT: The woman with the "blood issue" is not named, "but a woman of Magdala (on the Sea of Galilee) whose name was Mary became later his very devoted follower (Goodspeed, *A Life of Jesus*, 1950). The "official" may have been a synagogue official.

1. The hem of the cloak was usually fringed and had sacred associations. The blood-woman came up from behind Jesus, because in menses women are supposedly unclean.

2. Funerals usually carried a musical accompaniment of two flutes and one wailing woman. To say one is "asleep" is a gentle way of saying he is dead—a euphemism. The crowd is put outside because unbelievers must not be present at divine miracles.

3. Note the blind men call him the Son of David, one of the regular names for the Jewish Messiah, who the Jews believed could work miracles. The injunction to secrecy (taken from Mark 1:43-44) meant that Jesus did not want to be merely known publicly as a miracle-worker, magician, or quack.

31. JESUS IS TOUCHED BY THE PEOPLE'S NEED (9:35-38): Jesus travels about, curing the ill and preaching the good news (*gospel*) of the kingdom. Feeling pity for the crowds, who are miserable and not guided, he says to his disciples that there is a great crop but only a few pickers, so they must pray to the Lord to send men to reap this harvest.

COMMENT: Matthew regarded the twelve disciples as heads of the church, although Jesus did not plan an organized church; he simply sent out his disciples to preach the coming Kingdom of God and be sure the good news reached the poor. Here the lost crowds are in need of a good shepherd like Christ to usher the poor into the rich harvest of the age to come. Verse 38 seems to be a plea for more men to spread the message, an increase in his ministry (disciples). This will become a thorny point in the church later.

32. JESUS SENDS OUT THE TWELVE WITH DIVINE POWER (10:1-15): Jesus now gives his twelve disciples authority to expel evil spirits and to cure the ill. Their names are Simon, called Peter, with his brother Andrew; James and his brother John, sons of Zebedee; Philip and Bartholomew, Thomas, and Matthew, the tax collector; James, the son of Alphaeus, and Thaddaeus; Simon the patriot ("the Canaanite"), and Judas Iscariot (Iss CARE ee yuht), who later turns traitor.

Jesus' instructions to them are to avoid the non-Jews and to concentrate on "the lost sheep of the house of Israel." They are to preach that the kingdom of heaven is at hand (arrived), work cures, "raise the dead," and cast out devils. Take no money, no knapsack ("scrip"), no change of clothes, sandals or staff ("staves"), "for the workman is worthy of his meat" (worth his keep). Wherever they go, they are to stay in respected homes, blessing them upon entering, if they deserve the blessing; if not, bless them not. And if you are rejected, "shake off the dust of your feet" from that place, which will suffer a worse fate than did Sodom and Gomorrah (wicked O.T. cities destroyed by God).

COMMENT: For the first time we learn how many and who the disciples are. Mark and Luke give the same lists. Here only is the term "apostles" used, a term meaning in the N.T. not only the twelve disciples but others like Paul and Barnabas Gal. 1:1; Acts 14:14). It means those commissioned to proclaim salvation through Christ. This is a late first-century view, unusual for Matthew, who prefers the term *disciples*, followers of a *rabbi* (Jewish religious teacher). This apostolic conception is not in Mark, the earliest Gospel. Simon is usually the first in rank among the disciples, his last name being Peter (his Aramaic, the language of the Jews at the time of Christ, nickname, meaning *rock*). In 9:9 Matthew was called Levi. Simon was not a Canaanite, but very likely a revolutionary agitator (Zealot) against Rome. Iscariot is of tremendous interest: his name could mean "man of Kerioth" (a village) or "the false."

1. The "lost sheep" are the poor who are careless of Jewish ritual laws. The Pharisees treated them with contempt.

2. Jews in pagan territory "shook the dust" from their feet to clear them of uncleanliness.

33. HE WARNS THEM OF TROUBLES THAT LIE AHEAD

(10:16-11:1): "Behold, I send you forth as sheep in the midst of wolves: be ye therefore wise as serpents, and harmless as doves." Watch out for men, for they will take you to court and whip you in the synagogues (the synagogue attendant did the scourging). When you are taken before rulers under arrest, let the Lord speak through you. Brothers are going to betray brothers, fathers will betray their children, children their parents. You will be hated everywhere, but he who endures will be saved in the end. Flee the town if persecuted; before covering all of Israel the Son of man (the Judger at the Final Judgment) will have arrived. Disciples and servants are not superior to their masters; what is good for the master is also good enough for the servant. The master

of the household (i.e., Jesus) may even be called the "Prince of Evil" and his disciples given similar labels, but never let them frighten you: the secret things I tell you shall all be revealed publicly. Do not fear those who can kill your body: they cannot kill your soul; but do fear those who can kill both soul and body. Two sparrows may sell for a penny ("farthing"), yet your Father determines even its fall to the ground. The very hairs on your head are numbered, so do not fear, "ye are of more value than many sparrows." Whoever confesses me (publicly acknowledges me) publicly, him will I confess also before my Father which is in heaven. But the man who denies (disowns) me publicly, I will do the same before God. "Think not that I am come to send peace on earth: I came not to send peace, but a sword." I have come to create family strife, and he who loves his family more than me is not worthy of me; and he who refuses to take up his cross and follow me also is not worthy of me. "He that findeth his life (he who risks his life for God will go to the new Kingdom of heaven) shall lose it (in martyrdom): and he that loseth his life for my sake shall find it." Jesus goes on to bless those who will receive his disciples with hospitality. When Jesus finishes his instructions to his disciples, he goes on to teach and preach in the towns in which they lived.

COMMENT: These instructions are meant for the Christian church, not only for the disciples, since the dangers recited apply to anyone spreading the message.

1. Vss. 21-22 suggest the persecutions of the Christians under Nero. They felt they were hated by all people while they suffered for Jesus' sake. (Nero, a vicious Roman emperor, 54-68 A.D.)

2. Beelzebub (chief of the devils, Satan) also sounds like "lord of the

house"—a pun (24-25).

3. V. 26 assumes that Jesus' teaching was not widely known until after the Crucifixion.

4. V. 28: The only one who can destroy both soul and body in hell (*Gehenna*) is God.

5. V. 29: The fall of the sparrow really means the death of a sparrow.

6. V. 30: Jesus exaggerates to show how much personal interest God takes in us.

7. Vss. 32-33: In Luke (12:8-9) it is the Son of man who shares in the divine judgment.

8. Vss. 34-36: (see Luke 12:51-53); God's truth is more important than family harmony or social order. Only the kingdom of God is important!

9. V. 38: Condemned men were forced to carry their own crosses before crucifixion (only the main shaft; the crossbeam was nailed on later). This form of execution was dealt out to anti-Roman revolutionaries and criminals.

10. V. 42: A cup of cold water symbolizes a minor service, the need for practical loving kindness.

CHAPTER 11

34. JOHN INQUIRES ABOUT CHRIST: CHRIST SPEAKS ABOUT JOHN (11:2-19): John the Baptist, in prison (put there by Herod Antipas), sends a message: "Art thou he that should come, or do we look for another" (i.e., redeemer). Jesus' reply to John's disciples is to tell about the miracles and the good news: happy is the man who looks on Jesus with friendly eyes. Then Jesus says to the crowds about John that they had gone to see a poor man and prophet who prepared the way for another as cited in the Scriptures (John was more than a prophet: a preparer of the way for Christ; the announcer of Christ, so to speak). Jesus says there is no one greater than the Baptist, and yet a humble member of the kingdom is greater than he (meaning that Jesus is greater than John). John himself is a kind of Elijah (O.T. prophet who prepared a prophetic movement) who must appear to man before the kingdom arrives. "He that hath ears to hear, let him hear." People today are like children, for although John came in strict austerity, people called him crazy. Then came the Son of man enjoying life ("eating and drinking") and people call him a drunkard and glutton, a crony of the tax collectors and sinners. "But wisdom is justified of her children (by her deeds)."

COMMENT: Note the following:

1. V. 11: This is an important verse, indicating that the kingdom of heaven *is* already present by Christ's very appearance!

2. Vss. 12-13: Means that from John's time "until now, Zealots or revolutionaries have sought to seize God's kingdom," but they are only ravaging it. There are other theories.

3. V. 14: In Malachi 4:5, Elijah is to return just before the day of the Lord; then he would announce the Messiah. Matthew calls John the new Elijah more than once.

4. V. 19: The Son of man "felt no embarrassment in the wholehearted enjoyment of life" (*I.B.*).

35. JESUS DENOUNCES APATHY —AND THANKS GOD THAT SIMPLE MEN UNDERSTAND HIS MESSAGE (11:20-30): Jesus then denounces the towns unchanged in heart in spite of his miracles—especially Capernaum, which he says will go to its death. Sodom (destroyed by God in O.T.) will be better off on the day of judgment than Capernaum (where Jesus had spent so much time in cures and teaching). He thanks his Father for hiding "these things" (his teachings) from the "wise and prudent" (the scribes, experts in Jewish ritual law), while the same things are revealed to babes (the unlearned, who readily accept his teachings). All has been put in Jesus' hands by his Father, and no one knows the Son— except the Father and *vice versa*. "Come unto me, all ye that labor and are heavy laden, and I will give you rest." They are heavy laden from labor to follow the now stultified Jewish rituals (stultified for many of the poor at least.) He tells the people his yoke is light upon them and to learn from him, "for I am meek and lowly of heart: and ye shall find rest unto your souls" (the yoke was Jesus' interpretation of the law in the O.T., which would give them a new birth of spiritual freedom).

CHAPTER 12

36. JESUS REBUKES THE SABBATARIANS (12:1-14): On the Sabbath (day of rest from labor) Jesus' disciples felt hungry and ate some ears of wheat from a wheatfield. The Pharisees tell Jesus they are breaking the Sabbath by eating during the spring harvest (one of the thirty-nine classes of work not lawful on the Sabbath). Jesus replied that King David (O.T. hero-king of the Jews from whose descent would come the Jewish Messiah) had entered and eaten the showbread (holy bread) from the synagogue, thus violating the Sabbath. The priests in the temple, too, are guilty, "But I say unto you, That in this place is one greater than the temple (i.e., Jesus' authority)" Again going into the synagogue he met a man with a shriveled hand. In spite of another rebuke he cured him. His justification for again violating the Sabbath is the example of a sheep falling into a ditch: would not the owner save him in spite of the Sabbath? "How much then is a man better than a sheep?" Hence, it is lawful to do good on the Sabbath. He then cures the man's hand.

COMMENT: A "paradigm" is a brief conversation in the Gospel ending in a pithy saying, like an example in a sermon; it can also be called a "controversy story": there are several in the Gospels. It is learned from a long previous oral tradition and gives an excellent insight into the way Jesus taught; not sermons in theory but in concrete situations.
V.7: "I will have mercy, and not sacrifice" means mercy is more important than sacrifice in the temple.
V.8: An unlikely statement, even from Jesus, since God himself instituted the Sabbath in the O.T.
Vss.9-13: The rabbis allowed healing on the Sabbath if a life were in danger. The man with the withered arm (hysteria?) was not in danger of his life. The sheep example is not analogous.

37. JESUS RETIRES TO CONTINUE HIS WORK (12:15-23): Jesus knew the Pharisees were plotting, and so he left the place while great crowds still follow him, "and he healed them all," charging them not to tell. As foretold by Isaiah: God has chosen his servant with whom he is "well pleased". God will fill him with his Spirit "and he shall show justice to the Gentiles," who will trust in his name.

COMMENT: It is evident that some Pharisees (not all) wanted to get rid of Jesus by reporting his activities to the ruler, Herod Antipas.
15-16: Matthew often repeats himself; sections known as doublets.
18-21: Quoted before by Matthew; the servant is the Messiah, "the suffering servant" in whom the early Christians

delighted. Jesus keeps his Messiahship a secret through his humility and modesty, but although the Jews will reject him, the Gentiles will not.

Then Jesus cures a blind and dumb man at which the whole crowd excitedly wonders whether he really is the Son of David. (The Messiah as Son of David could work miracles.)

38. THE PHARISEES DRAW AN EVIL CONCLUSION, AND JESUS REBUKES THEM (12:24-37): Again Jesus is called the prince of devils (Beelzebub) by the Pharisees. He replies that "Every kingdom divided against itself" is ruined, and "every house divided against itself shall not stand." How can Satan's · kingdom continue divided against itself? And if Jesus expels devils through Beelzebub's power, how do your children (sons = devil-expellers of the Pharisees) do the same? But if Jesus does expel by the Spirit of God, why then the kingdom of God has come unawares amongst you (if God's spirit is driving out devils, this is a sign that in some sense God's kingdom has already come: *I.B.*). You can only enter the house of a strong man by first tying him up: "He that is not with me is against me"; the unforgivable sin is blasphemy (non-belief) against the Holy Spirit (of God). "The tree is known by his fruit," and good fruit is best. "O generation of vipers (brood of serpents), like the fruit tree, a good man produces good; the bad, evil. The judgment day will judge you for every careless word uttered: "by thy words shalt thou be condemned."

COMMENT: The correct spelling is Beelzebul, not Beelzebub. The Jews charged Jesus with being a magician via the devil. 25-28: Civil war in hell would bring its ruin, etc.

29: The house is Beelzebul's and the enterer is God acting through Jesus. 30: Mark (9:40) contradicts this statement. He who does not help to save

souls is against Jesus.

31: If this is true (blasphemy against the Holy Spirit) then God's mercy is limited, and all sorts of doubts can arise.

Note: The fruit tree metaphor was already used in 7:16-20.

39. JESUS REFUSES A SIGN (12:38-42) Then some scribes and Pharisees ask for a sign (that his teaching is true), and he tells them that as Jonah was in the whale for three days and nights, so will the Son of Man be. The men of Ninevah repented when Jonah preached (O.T.), and a better preacher is with you now. In the last judgment the queen of Sheba ("queen of the south": Arabia) and the Ninevites (converted by Noah, that is non-Jews) will be witnesses against Israel. The queen came from the ends of the earth to hear the wise Solomon whereas you have a wiser one than Solomon with you now!

COMMENT: This passage seems to contradict the previous one, where the casting out of demons is a sign the kingdom is here!

39-40: This *typology* (O.T. people who prefigure Christ) is common. Jonah converted the Ninevites without a sign, yet a sign is wanted from Jesus. Even the resurrection will not convince some people.

41-42: The Ninevites and Sheba are more receptive to God's presence than the Jewish Pharisees.

Note: Matthew wrote his Gospel in Syria fifty years after Christ died, when Jews and Christians were opposed. Hence, the attitude towards Pharisaism: Jewish isolationists, anti-integrationist, dogmatists of religion —the very opposite of Christians. Pharisaism so refined the ritual laws that the poor and ignorant were unable to observe them!

40. THE DANGER OF SPIRITUAL EMPTINESS (12:43-46): An evil

spirit once fled will return with seven others to a cleaned and empty house, "and the last state of that man is worse than the first." (The last state is worse because the man has had a moral relapse.)

41. JESUS AND HIS RELATIONS (12:46-50): Jesus' mothers and brothers are announced. "Who is my mother, and who are my brothers," he said, and pointed to his disciples. calling them his mother and brothers. All those who do the will of his Father are mothers, brothers, and sisters to Jesus.

COMMENT: Small attention is paid by Jesus to his family. His mother is not important in the Gospels; she is not even mentioned as being at her son's crucifixion by the synoptists (Matthew, Mark, Luke)! His brothers are all younger than he and later were active in affairs of the church. In Mark 3:21, the earliest and most authentic Gospel, his mother and brothers think Jesus is out of his mind! The final point is that only spiritual ties are all-supreme.

CHAPTER 13

42. JESUS TELLS THE PARABLE OF THE SEED (13:1-23): Jesus tells the crowd the parable of the man who sowed seed in various bad patches of ground; but on good soil it produced a rich crop: "Who hath ears to hear, let him hear." Then the disciples ask why he spoke to the crowd in parables. His reply is that with their eyes they do not see and with their ears they do not hear—the living proof of Isaiah's prophecy (6:9-10) that the Jews could not understand him, their hearts dull, their ears closed. But you, my disciples, both see, hear, and understand me. You are indeed fortunate. Jesus explains the parable: the seed on the bad soil represents different men who hear the message (seed) of Jesus but cannot respond to it because of life's woes and illusions. But the seed sown on good soil is the man who gets the message; his life shows a fine crop, many times more than that which was sown.

COMMENT: "The parable is an application of fiction to moral instruction" (Goodspeed). Jesus did not invent the device; they were popular with the rabbis also. They were vivid and concrete with few or no abstractions; and they had the attraction of the puzzle or riddle to be solved for its deeper meaning.

14. Isaiah used bitter words for his listeners, who gave deaf ears to his prophecies.

18. *Allegory* (images representing various ideas) was a Greek method for reading and interpreting sacred texts. Teachers of the later Christian church were fond of them.

21-22: Persecution of Christians on account of the Word (Christianity); worldly care and delight in riches also made some people bad soil for the Word. These two factors help us to date some gospels: after 70 A.D., the date of Jerusalem's fall.

43. GOOD AND EVIL GROW SIDE BY SIDE IN THIS PRESENT WORLD (13:24-30): In another parable he compares the kingdom of Heaven to a man who sowed good seed in his field, but his enemy while he slept sowed weeds among the wheat. The weeds are allowed to grow with the wheat (they could not be pulled without harming the wheat); but at harvest time the weeds are collected first and burned and the wheat is stored in the barn.

COMMENT: "Tares" are weeds; "fruit" are the wheat kernels (ripe), and the housholder is the farmer.

25. The enemy is redundant to the meaning. The actual weed is the poisonous bearded darnel, which looks like wheat.

Note: "It is to be noted that the parable of the tares refers to the recruiting of members by the Christian communities, intimating that the elimination of the unworthy should be postponed to the final judgment" (Loisy).

44. THE KINGDOM'S POWER OF GROWTH, AND WIDESPREAD INFLUENCE (13:31-35): The kingdom of heaven is like a tiny mustard seed. The smallest of seeds grows to be the biggest of plants, big enough for birds to nest in. Heaven is also like yeast which raises dough. And so Jesus keeps telling his message in parables—to fulfill the prophecy "I will open my mouth in parables; I will utter things which have been kept secret from the foundation (ever since the beginning) of the world" (Psalm 78:2).

COMMENT: Matthew's parable of the mustard seed occurs also in Luke 13:18-19 and Mark 4:30-32.
31. Mustard was raised for its seed and leaves; it can grow to ten feet high, but birds do not nest in its branches.
33. Leaven (yeast); three measures = a bushel. The idea is that the message will swell amongst men like the dough.

45. JESUS AGAIN EXPLAINS A PARABLE TO HIS DISCIPLES (13:36-43): The meaning of the parable of the tares, says Jesus to his disciples, when he is indoors alone with them, is that the sower is Jesus, the field = the world, the good seed = sons of the kingdom, weeds = sons of the devil, and the harvest = the end of the world, the reapers = angels. At the judgment the weeds (defiers of the laws of the kingdom) will be thrown into a furnace and the good will shine in God's kingdom.

Men with ears should use them!

COMMENT: For Matthew the missionary field is the world. Some parables compare it to a garden also.
38. *Sons of the evil one* evidently implies that some people are inherently evil!
41. *The kingdom of the Son of Man* = the church. The angels will accompany Jesus on judgment day.
42. "There shall be wailing and gnashing of teeth" is a vivid figure for the sinners burning in the furnace of Gehenna (hell) in Jesus' time.

46. MORE PICTURES OF THE KINGDOM OF HEAVEN (13:44-53): The kingdom of Heaven is compared by Jesus to a man finding a buried treasure, or to a big net thrown into the sea to catch fish (the good fish are kept, the bad thrown away). At judgment the angels will do the same, "where there shall be wailing and gnashing of teeth." Jesus finishes by telling his disciples how everyone who knows the Law and is a disciple of the kingdom of heaven is like the householder "which bringeth forth out of his treasure things new (Jesus' new law) and old" (riches of the O.T.).

47. JESUS IS NOT APPRECIATED IN HIS NATIVE TOWN (13:53-58): Jesus goes to Nazareth and teaches in their own synagogues. The people wonder about his wisdom and powers. After all, he is only a carpenter's son, with Mary his mother and James, Joseph, Simon, and Judas, his brothers; are not all his sisters living here? They take offense at him: "A prophet is not without honor, save (except) in his own country, and in his own house."

COMMENT: The church is fond of showing Jesus as a despised and rejected man in his own time. Any competent person could teach in the synagogues. "His own country" seems to be Nazareth or thereabouts. 55. What about the virgin birth? Note that his brothers and sisters are mentioned specifically here.

CHAPTER 14

48. HEROD'S GUILTY CONSCIENCE (14:1-12): Jesus' fame comes to the ears of Herod Antipas, the tetrarch (ruler of one-fourth of a province, in this case Galilee and Peraea, from 4 B.C. to 39 A.D.), who calls him "John the Baptist, he is risen from the dead," doer of mighty works. But Herod had already arrested John at the insistence of his sister-in-law Herodias. John had opposed as sinful the marriage of Herod and Herodias (the ex-wife of his brother, or rather half-brother named Philip). From jail (see 4:12) John was still looked on as an O.T. prophet, and hence safe from Herod, who wanted him murdered. On Herod's birthday the daughter of Herodias danced so well that the pleased Herod swore an oath to grant her anything she wanted. The girl (probably Salome, suh LOH mee) daughter of Herodias (hair OH dee us), asked for John's head at the prompting of her mother; the king, aghast at her request, still kept to his sworn oath. John was beheaded in prison and the head brought to the feasting guests on a charger (flat dish) according to Herodias' daughter's wish, who then handed it to her mother. Later, John's disciples took the body and buried it, and then gave the news to Jesus. Jesus, at this news, went away by boat to a deserted place, all alone.

COMMENT: Great artists are fond of the scene, as are poets and dramatists. The dance of a strip-teasing lush Salome in veils is another invention. Do not confuse Salome and John's head on a charger with Judith (O.T. heroine) who holds the giant Holofernes' head *by the hair*. The Herods were careless about incestuous relationships; the marriage of a brother to his *living* brother's (Philip) ex-wife was strictly forbidden by religious law. Hence, John's wrath and the peoples' sympathy with John. Salome later married her own uncle! The Dead Sea Scrolls condemn marriage with a niece. Note that John was beheaded, and without a trial, both of which actions were illegal in Jewish law but common enough in Roman.

49. JESUS FEEDS A TIRED AND HUNGRY CROWD (14:13-21): A vast crowd follows Jesus in his lonely retreat, where he cures many of their sick. Evening comes and the disciples complain they have only five loaves and two fishes with which to feed the crowd. Jesus tells the crowd to sit on the grass, blesses and breaks the loaves, which were handed to the multitude: "And they did all eat, and were filled"—still leaving twelve baskets full of food! The crowd numbered 5,000, apart from the women and children.

COMMENT: This too is a famous episode. Unlike Mark (1:14), Matthew has Jesus leave because of John's arrest, showing that he took warning from John's fate. The grass and the hour, 6:30 P.M., could make this the Passover (O.T. religious holiday about the same time as Easter). The blessing and breaking of the bread suggests the Lord's supper and shows Matthew's organized church bias. This is the only miracle recorded in *all four* gospels. Some believe it happened as is, and some find it symbolic: the preaching of the Gospel (the bread of life) to the twelve tribes of Israel—note the twelve baskets; note the seven loaves, which when combined with a parallel miracle with five loaves = 12, the mystic number (see Dictionary of terms).

50. JESUS AGAIN SHOWS HIS POWER OVER THE FORCES OF NATURE (14:22-36):

Jesus leaves to pray alone while his disciples had left for the other shore and are now returning in the boat. Jesus walks right on the water toward the terrified disciples who think he is a ghost, but Jesus calms them down. Peter, in attempting to walk on the water toward Jesus, becomes frightened at the fury of the wind and begins to sink, crying "Lord, save me!" Jesus catches him up saying, "O thou of little faith, wherefore didst thou doubt?" They entered the ship as the wind dies down, while the disciples in the boat come and worship Jesus, saying, "Of a truth thou art the Son of God." Then they land at Gennesaret (fertile plain on northwest side of the Sea of Galilee). When he is recognized, the sick touch the edge of his cloak and are cured.

COMMENT: This episode teaches that the early Church (often known as a ship) when beset by storm and danger requires the staunch faith of the membership to stay above the water. Note how impulsive Peter is and how courageous. Jesus' "It is I; be not afraid" (27) really translates "I am"—words used by God for himself in the O.T. when revealing himself to Moses (Exodus 3:14). Here Jesus "reveals" himself as the person of God.

51. THE DANGERS OF TRADITION (15:1-9):

Then scribes and Pharisees from Jerusalem ask why the disciples break the ancient traditions (customs added to the Law by the lawyers) and eat their food without first washing their hands. But Jesus counters by asking why they break God's Law by adding their traditions: God says to honor one's parents, and if slandered the penalty is death; but the religious scribes and Pharisees reject their parents entirely when dedicated to God, thus denying God's meaning. "Ye hypocrites, well did Esaias prophesy of you": these people pay me only lip service, putting the doctrines of man over mine (Isaiah 29:13)

52. SUPERFICIAL AND TRUE CLEANLINESS (15:10-20):

Then he tells the crowd that it is what comes out—not in—a man's mouth that makes him unclean. Later his disciples tell him the Pharisees are insulted by his words. Jesus says that all plants not planted by his Father will be uprooted: "Let them alone: they be blind leaders of the blind. And if the blind lead the blind, both shall fall into the ditch." Peter asks the meaning of the parable, whereupon Jesus asks if Peter was also without the sense to grasp things like this: things entering into the mouth pass out the body, but the things coming out of the mouth come from one's heart and mind. Evil arises in the mind, like murder, adultery, fornications (lust), theft, perjury (false witness), and blasphemy. Eating without first washing the hands then does not make a man unclean.

COMMENT: Jesus is showing that he finds the Jewish law too strict; the Gentile Christians agree and, like Jesus, find the lawyer's traditional restrictions in conflict with God-given law; and that the spirit of the law was more important oftener than the letter. These lawyer's traditions were passed on from rabbi to student orally. The Sadducees rejected the tradition also, like ritual hand-washing.
3-6: Jesus scolds the Pharisees for evading looking after their parents by way of the tradition instead of the law.
15: Mark has the *disciples* question Jesus, but Matthew favors Peter always.
Note: Remember Jesus is attacking

the rabbinic tradition, not the Law of Moses. The blind leading the blind may refer to the downfall of Pharisaic Judaism.

53. A GENTILE'S FAITH IN JESUS (15:21-28): A Canaanite (ancient Palestinians, kin to the Hebrews) woman keeps piteously pleading with Jesus to cure her daughter. "I am not sent but unto the lost sheep of the house of Israel (i.e., the Jews)," he told her, but she kneels ("worshipped him") at his feet; said Jesus, "It is not meet (proper) to take the children's bread (i.e., message to the Jews), and to cast it to dogs (the non-Jews)." Her reply: "Truth, Lord: yet the dogs eat of the crumbs which fall from their masters' table." For her faith Jesus cures her daughter.

54. JESUS HEALS AND FEEDS VAST CROWDS OF PEOPLE (15:29-39): This episode, except for the change in numbers, is very much like that recounted in section 49 (14:13-21). There are seven loaves and a few fishes and the remnants fill seven baskets. Jesus then dismisses the crowds and sails to Magadan (perhaps Magdala on the west shore of Galilee).

55. JESUS AGAIN REFUSES TO GIVE A SIGN (16:1-4): To test him, both the Phariseess and Sadducees ask for a sign from Heaven, but Jesus said they can read weather signs but cannot interpret the signs of the times. A wicked age deserves no sign at all but that given by the prophet Jonah; and he turns on his heel and leaves them.

COMMENT: The loaves and bread miracle may be a "doublet" of the former one. Some translations omit the weather reference since the most important manuscripts omit that passage. The signs Jesus refers to are the signs of the coming day of judgment. The sign of Jonah (4) in the O.T. is

simply a call to repentance to the Ninevites.

56. HE IS MISUNDERSTOOD BY THE DISCIPLES (16:5-12): When the disciples forget to bring bread, Jesus tells them to be on guard against the "yeast" of the Pharisees, which the disciples understand not. After a reminder about the meaning of the loaves and fishes, he tells them he is not really talking about bread —simply to beware of the yeast of the Pharisees. They now understand he means the teaching of the Pharisees and Sadducees.

57. PETER'S BOLD AFFIRMATION (16:13-20): When Jesus enters the Caesarea-Phillippi district, he asks his disciples who the people say the Son of Man is; they say John the Baptist or Elijah or Jeremiah or one of the prophets. He next asks who the disciples think he is, and Simon Peter answers, "Thou art the Christ, the Son of the living God," and Christ calls him blessed and says he got the news from his Father: "And I say also unto thee, That thou art Peter, and upon this rock (*Petros* = rock in Greek) I will build my church; and the gates of hell shall not prevail against it." Jesus added that he will also give him the keys to heaven as well as heavenly power on earth.

COMMENT: This section is the climax of the gospel story: Peter's confession. From now on Jesus will not conceal his future suffering and death-to-come. This is also the end of his public ministry in the Galilean provinces. Note the two natures of Christ: the Son of Man (fleshly) and the Son of God (divine), foreshadowed here. We shall see later that this is an extremely sensitive doctrine over which much blood has been shed. Mark (8:27-30), from whom Matthew takes this incident, lacks Matthew's additions: giving Jesus words that can only issue from the immortal Messiah or Christ. Some say that a pro-Peter faction in the Church inserted this section to counter the pro-Paul faction whose claim is laid down in the epistles (letters written by Church missionaries).

1. Vs. 14: Herod thought that John was the Messiah. Elijah was expected to return before Judgment Day (cf. Malachi 4:5); note that Jesus has accepted the title of prophet (cf. 13:57) = a brave spokesman of God.

2. Vss. 17-19 are only in Matthew: see comment above.

3. Vs. 18: In Aramaic the word for rock is Kepha or Cephas; in Greek, Petros. This is a pun on the word Peter and rock. Peter's nature is unsteady and impetuous and Jesus means to make him more steady. The Roman Catholic church uses this text (tradition says Peter was the first Bishop of Rome) to indicate its authority from Christ himself. In 18:18 the privileges assigned to Peter are given to all the apostles. Peter did preach the first Christian sermon (Acts 2). Christ, says Paul, is the only foundation of the Church (I Corinthians 3:11). The word "church" meant gathering or congregation, not necessarily the organized church.

4. Vs. 19: The keys mean rule and authority, as in Isaiah 22:22. The keyholder is the steward of the house of God. Peter's decisions on earth will be ratified in Heaven by God. Peter is the acknowledged spokesman and head of the apostles in the gospels. Paul later challenges his authority (Galatians 2:11).

5. Again in vs. 20 Jesus enjoins his disciples to secrecy that he is the Christ (Messiah), but just why is not too clear.

58. JESUS SPEAKS ABOUT HIS PASSION, AND THE COST OF FOLLOWING HIM (16:21-28): From now on Jesus explains to his disciples how he must go to Jerusalem and be

persecuted and killed and then on the third day live again. When Peter remonstrates with him, Jesus says, "Get thee behind me, Satan: thou art an offense (hindrance) unto me, for you see all from man's eyes and not God's." Then said Jesus to the disciples, "If any man will come after me, let him deny (give up all right to) himself, and take up his cross and follow me. For whosoever will save his life shall lose it: and whosoever will lose his life for my sake shall find it." What good is the whole world at the price of the soul? The Son of man will "come in the glory of his Father with his angels," and then "he shall reward every man according to his works." Some of you will not know death until the Son of Man comes as king.

COMMENT: Jesus' rebuke of Peter is only in Matthew. Peter's protests against what Jesus foretells and the almost savage reprimand seem to contradict his former high praise of him. From a foundation stone Peter has turned into a stumbling-block (hindrance, offense) which trips people. Taking up the cross implies great public suffering and persecution for one's ideas. The second coming of Christ (parousia) is predicted as taking place in the lifetime of his disciples, but in 24:36 and Mark 13:32 the time of the parousia is unknown.

59. THREE DISCIPLES GLIMPSE THE GLORY OF CHRIST (17:1-13): Jesus chooses Peter, James, and his brother John to go with him high on a hillside, and here his whole appearance changes with shining face and clothes white as light; and Moses and Elijah are seen talking to Jesus. Peter offers to put up three "shelters" for them but is interrupted by a voice from a bright cloud: "This is my beloved Son, in whom I am well pleased." The frightened disciples fall on their faces, but Jesus makes them

arise, assuring them that there is nothing to fear.

COMMENT: Peter, James, and John are the inner circle of the twelve. The hill may be Mount Hermon near Caesarea-Phillippi. Moses is the Law and Elijah is the prophet; both were taken into heaven; Jesus will soon be with them. God's words divinely confirm Peter's own words that Jesus was the Messiah. Again Jesus tells them to keep what they saw secret until "the Son of Man be risen again from the dead." Jesus tells how the prophet Elijah had reappeared to reform the world in the shape of John the Baptist.

60. JESUS HEALS AN EPILEPTIC BOY (17:14-23): Among the crowds again a man rushes up to Jesus begging him to cure his lunatic son who is always falling either into fire or water. Jesus cures him by reprimanding his evil spirit, which then flees the boy. Jesus tells his disciples that they were unable to cure the epileptic because they had so little faith. In Galilee Jesus perdicts his death and resurrection, which distresses his followers.

61. JESUS PAYS THE TEMPLE TAX—IN AN UNUSUAL WAY! (17:24-27): In Capernaum the Temple tax collectors come to collect from Jesus, who tells Peter to go fishing, and from the first fish that bites he will find in its mouth the money to pay the tax.

COMMENT: Jesus' command to his disciples to keep silent may mean that he was not believed by most people to be the Messiah until his resurrection, as given in Mark; but it may mean he wants it kept secret until his triumphal entry into Jerusalem. soon to come. Mark describes the boy's convulsions when the devil left him, but the more refined Matthew leaves those details out. The second pro-

phecy of the Passion (suffering and crucifixion of Christ) shows the disciples mourning, but in Mark they are consistently dense and generally obtuse even in Christ's last days. The money-fish story is an old story, and there is more than a hint of refusal to pay the tax, which contradicts his later statement about the tax to Caesar (22:15-22). The Temple tax was paid by every male Jew over 19 for temple upkeep. The fish story is probably legend and contains a meaning probably lost.

62. JESUS COMMENDS THE SIMPLICITY OF CHILDREN (18:1-7): In answer to a question from his disciples as to who is really greatest in heaven, Jesus sets a little child in their midst and says, "Except ye be converted, and become as little children, ye shall not enter into the kingdom of heaven"; he who can humble himself like the little child will be greatest in heaven, and he who receives children in my name receives me, but he who causes a child to sin is better off dead. The world is full of pitfalls ("offenses"), which is in the nature of things; yet woe to the man responsible for them.

63. THE RIGHT WAY MAY MEAN COSTLY SACRIFICE (18:8-15): Rather than hinder your faith, tear off your limb or pluck out your eye if they lead you astray. Do not despise children, for they have angel guardians in heaven. A man with a hundred sheep will leave them all to search for a lost one; just so will your Father in Heaven be concerned if a single one "of these little ones" should perish or be lost.

COMMENT: Jesus does not put his arms around the child as in Mark (9:36), nor does he in Luke. Did Matthew and Luke erase his purely human characteristics? As children humbly revere their parents, so must adults God. The pagan world often exposed babies to die, but the rabbis taught kindness towards them.

1. Vs. 8 is a typical exaggeration, an oriental characteristic in Matthew. The Church was looked upon as a body with limbs; unworthy members are to be cut off or excommunicated.

2. Vs. 10: After the Jewish exile in Babylon (6th century), a belief in angels arose, taken from Persian sources. All men have guardian angels, often identified with stars.

3. Vs. 11: Omitted in the best manuscripts: "For the Son of Man came to save the lost." The lost sheep (12-14) are of course the disciples, or lapsed members from the fold of the Church.

64. RECONCILIATION MUST ALWAYS BE ATTEMPTED (18:15-17):

If your brother wrongs (sins against) you, tell him, and if he listens, all is well; if not, produce witnesses of his wrong, and if he still denies wronging you, accuse him in church; and if he is still denying "let him be unto you as a heathen man (a Gentile, a non-Jew) and a publican (tax collector)."

65. THE CONNECTION BETWEEN EARTHLY CONDUCT AND SPIRITUAL REALITY (18:18-20):

Whatever is forbidden on earth is forbidden in heaven; and whatever is permitted on earth is permitted in heaven. Two disciples in agreement on earth will have their request granted in Heaven. Wherever two people come together in my name "there am I in the midst of them."

66. THE NECESSITY FOR FORGIVENESS (18:21-35):

In answer to Peter's question on brother-forgiveness, Jesus replies that one must forgive him seventy times seven times. Heaven is like a king who forgave a penitent debtor-servant and canceled the debt. The same forgiven servant was unrelenting later to a fellow servant who owed him a debt and had the debtor put in prison. His master hearing of this berated him for not showing pity as he had done and had the servant jailed until the debt was repaid: "So also my heavenly Father will do to every one of you, if you do not forgive your brother from your heart."

COMMENT: Brother in Jewish usage means fellow-member of the synagogue. The law required two witnesses (Deuteronomy 19:15). If the Church congregation cannot obtain redress, the offender is no longer a true brother but a pagan or outcast.

1. Vs. 18: The authority granted to *Peter-Rock* is granted to all the disciples.

2. Vss. 21-2: This has to do with one church member wronging another in Matthew's time. The offender must apologize and make reparation. Jesus is reversing the old law of revenge (Genesis 4:24).

3. The parable's point: only a forgiving spirit can receive forgiveness.

67. THE DIVINE PRINCIPLE OF MARRIAGE (19:1-12):

Then came a test question from the Pharisees: "Is it lawful for a man to put away his wife (divorce her) for any grounds whatsoever?" Jesus replies that God made man and woman one flesh: "What therefore God hath joined together, let no man put asunder" (separate), but the Pharisees quote Moses, who allowed divorce by writ. Jesus replies that Moses allowed divorce because love was not known among men. Only the unfaithful wife can be divorced; otherwise her husband is an adulterer if he marries another. The Pharisees then say if that is the case, marriage is not worth it. Jesus said not everyone can live up to his rules of marriage: some are born eunuchs (castrated, impotent), some are made into eunuchs by others, and some are made eunuchs by self-mutilation in order to enter the kingdom of heaven. Those who can accept what I have said, accept it.

COMMENT: Two schools of Jewish thought (Hillel and Shammai) are reflected on divorce. Rabbi Hillel was the more liberal on grounds for divorce, whereas Rabbi Shammai's position was more like that of Jesus. Jesus even forbids remarriage after divorce! Some read celibacy instead of the eunuch state (castrated), a kind of enforced abstention from marriage and sex.

68. JESUS WELCOMES CHILDREN (19:13-15): Then Jesus puts his hands on and prays for some little children, done at the request of their parents. To his frowning disciples he says that children must never be stopped from coming to him: "Suffer little children, and forbid them not, to come unto me; for of such is the kingdom of heaven."

69. JESUS SHOWS THAT KEEPING THE COMMANDMENTS IS NOT ENOUGH (19:16-26): A young man is told that to earn eternal life he must keep the commandments of Moses: not to murder, commit adultery, steal, perjure, to honor his parents, and to love his neighbor as himself. The man says he had kept all the laws: was there anything missing in his life? Jesus tells him to sell his goods and give the money to the poor—and then to follow Jesus (his riches in heaven). This last the crestfallen man could not do. Says Jesus to his disciples: "It is easier for a camel to go through the eye of a needle, than for a rich man to enter the kingdom of God." They, amazed, asked who then could be saved? And the reply: "With men this is impossible; but with God all things are possible."

COMMENT: V. 15: Again Matthew omits a personal touch from Jesus, a touch contained in Mark (see 18:2).

1. Vs. 17 is a *crux* (problem): "Why callest thou me good?" But in Mark 10:18 and Luke 18:19 Jesus says only God can be called good. Matthew does not want to imply that Jesus is lacking.

2. Vs. 24: a camel is a camel, the largest beast of burden in Palestine. It may or may not be a ship's cable or gate as some translators suggest. The import is clear: the rich will never get there! Yet some rich men, like Joseph of Arimathaea (27:57) and Zacchaeus in Luke 19:19, do get there! The rich were often mistrusted both in the Jewish and early Christian traditions. In the O.T., pious men are, however, often rewarded with material wealth. The rabbis taught that riches were a blessing, and poverty punishment for sin and a testing of one's faith; this is why the disciples are so bewildered by Jesus' words on wealth.

70. JESUS DECLARES THAT SACRIFICE FOR THE KINGDOM WILL BE PAID (19:27-29): Peter complains and Jesus says to the disciples that they shall be seated on twelve thrones, judging the twelve tribes of Israel (all Jews are supposedly descended from the twelve sons of Jacob) when the Son of Man is king. And all those abandoning family and property will be rich in eternal life.

"But many that are first shall be last; and the last shall be first," Jesus adds.

COMMENT: The disciples had even abandoned their nets to follow him. The "regeneration" means the new world, a changed earth, a new world order after it is once destroyed by God's wrath (apocalyptic visions like this were common. Cf. Revelation 21:1). In the Jewish version only God can sit on that throne, and as for the judges, there will be no sinners to judge—only sinecure duties.

1. Vs. 30: Does this mean the bot-

tom order of disciples will be first in order in the age to come; or does it mean there will be class divisions even then?

2. Incidentally, Mark omits the mention of thrones for the disciples—again his hostility shows.

71. BUT GOD'S GENEROSITY MAY APPEAR UNFAIR (20:1-16): Jesus compares the kingdom of heaven to a farmer hiring laborers for his vineyard. At different times of the day they are hired at the same wage for the day's work. At paytime all, both the early and late-hired workers, are paid the same wage, and at the laborers' protest at the unfairness the farmer told them he could do whatever he wanted with his own money: did they not agree to work for a penny (worth much more then) a day? "So," says Jesus, "the last shall be first, and the first last: for many be called, but few chosen."

COMMENT: The vineyard is a symboy of Israel. See Ruskin's essay "Unto This Last" on equal pay for all workers. Vs. 15: "jealous" = "evil eye" = grudging envy.

72. JESUS' FINAL JOURNEY TO JERUSALEM (20:17-28): Jesus again predicts his passion and resurrection to his disciples. Here the mother of the disciples James and John, sons of Zebedee, comes and requests

thrones on each side of Jesus for her sons in the new kingdom. Jesus says such a grant is only in his Father's hands. The other ten are highly indignant at James and John, but Jesus calms them by saying the disciples who serve the rest will be great and first among them—just as the Son of Man has come to serve others, and to give his life for the freeing of others.

COMMENT: This is Jesus' third prediction of the Passion. The sons of Zebedee make the request in Mark, but Matthew the "apostle-sparer" brings in the mother. Luke, with good sense, omits the story altogether. The king's chief ministers also sat on his right and left.

1. Vs. 22: The cup metaphor indicates suffering. Only by sharing Christ's suffering can the disciples be glorified.

2. Vs. 23: James was the first to suffer martyrdom in Jerusalem under Herod Agrippa, 44 A.D. (Acts 12:2). John was either martyred or died naturally after writing his gospel.

73. HE RESTORES SIGHT TO TWO BLIND MEN (20:29-34): Two piteous blind men addressing him as Son of David beg for mercy and Jesus, touching their eyes, cures them —and they follow him. (This scene is a doublet of Mark; Matthew likes doubling things, since the blind man is alone in the original gospel.)

CHAPTER 21

74. JESUS' FINAL ENTRY INTO JERUSALEM (21:1-17): As they approach Jerusalem, Jesus sends two disciples into a nearby village for an ass and a colt. They are to untie them and bring them to Christ as foretold by the prophet and fulfilled now by Christ: "Tell ye the daughter of Sion (Zion), Behold, thy King cometh unto thee, meek, and sitting

upon an ass, and a colt the foal of an ass." They did as he said, found the ass and colt, put their cloaks on the animals, and Jesus takes his seat. Then, many in the crowd spread their cloaks on the road while others spread branches from the trees in his path. Before and after they shouted "God save the Son of David (Hosanna): Blessed is he that cometh in the name of the Lord; Hosanna (God save) in the highest (him from on high)!" A shock runs through the whole city, which wonders who he is; and the crowd replies, "This is Jesus the prophet of Nazareth of Galilee." Then Jesus enters the temple of God and drives out all the buyers and sellers there, overturning the table of the money-changers and the benches of the dovesellers, crying; "It is written, My house shall be called the house of prayer; but ye have made it a den of thieves." There he cures the blind and lame. When the high priests and scribes sees this and hear the children shouting for God to save the Son of David, they grow angry and ask Jesus if he hears what the children are yelling. "Yes," replies Jesus, "have ye never read, 'Out of the mouth of babes and sucklings (infants) thou has perfected praise (brought perfect praise)?'." Then he turns on his heel and leaves for Bethany (about two miles south of Jerusalem), where he spends the night.

COMMENT: This event is a holy day, celebrated as the festival of Palm Sunday (the trees were palm trees from which the branches were torn to strew his path).

1. Vs. 1: Bethphage was near Bethany about two miles southeast of Jerusalem; there, too, is Mount Olivet. The entry takes place on Sunday.

2. Matthew read the prophecy quoted from Zechariah 9:9 as meaning two animals, an ass and a colt, when actually just an ass is meant, as in Luke and Mark. The king of course is the Messiah; the crowds are those who came to Jerusalem to celebrate the Passover (feast of freedom from Egyptian bondage), and among them would be Galileans and other followers who do all the shouting. They see in Jesus the Messiah son of David who fulfills the Messianic prophecy.

3. Vss. 12-13: Mark stages the temple cleansing on Monday and John stages it at the beginning of the ministry of Jesus. (Cf. Malachi 3:1, "the Lord, whom ye seek, shall suddenly come to his temple.") In the outer court of the temple, the court of the Gentiles, sacrificial animals were for sale (birds, wine, animals, salt, etc.), which kept the Gentiles from worshipping in that place. Speculation for profit was the vogue. The money-changers changed Greek and Roman money into temple money in order to buy the sacrificial animals and other things.

4. Vs. 13: The quote is from Isaiah 56:7, but unlike Mark, Matthew and Luke omit "for all nations" even though the scene is among Gentiles. Vs. 14: Shouting was forbidden in the temple area. Vs. 16: from Psalm 8:2. Jesus sleeps outside the overcrowded, festival-minded city. In addition, his life was now literally in danger.

75. HIS STRANGE WORDS TO THE FIG TREE (21:18-22): In the morning Jesus feels hungry but finds no figs on a fig tree. He curses it and at once the fig tree withers away before the thunderstruck disciples. Jesus explains: faith in the heart can do more than this: even a hill will throw itself into the sea at your bidding. "And all things, whatsoever ye shall ask in prayer, believing, ye shall receive."

COMMENT: The point is that the Jewish religion is fair without and false within, which is also the point of the temple cleansing episode. The Jewish religion has been perverted by the priests and scribes and will wither before the true Messiah. Luke found the episode too crude to record it, and the curse is very peculiar: the lesson about faith has nothing to do with the curse!

76. JESUS MEETS A QUESTION

WITH A COUNTER-QUESTION (21:23-32): When asked for the source of his authority to teach in the temple, Jesus counters with a question on the source of John the Baptist's authority. The priests and scribes are in a quandary at this: if John's authority came from heaven, they hadn't recognized it, and if from humans, the people would attack them, for the people felt that John was a true prophet: so they answer they do not know. Jesus tells them of a man with two sons, one of whom promised to work in the vineyard but did not, and the other who refused his father's request to work but nevertheless did. The priests and scribes admitted the second had done his father's bidding. Then, Jesus tells them that the tax collectors and harlots (prostitutes) will reach the kingdom before them. "And even when you saw it, you did not afterward repent and believe him."

77. JESUS TELLS A POINTED STORY (21:33-46): Jesus tells them another story: a landowner left his vineyard to servants and farm workers, who then proceeded to drive off the owner's representatives, including his own son, whom they killed to obtain the ownership of the vineyard. Now, says Jesus, what will the owner do when he returns? They reply that he will kill the wicked workers and farm out the vineyard to good tenants. Jesus quotes the Bible: the stone rejected by the builders was made the headstone; it came from the Lord and is marvelous (Psalm 118:22-23; this refers to Israel, the despised nation, destined by God to be supreme; Jesus sees the passage as predicting the Messiah, despised by the priests and exalted by God). So, says Jesus, the kingdom of God will be taken from you and given to a nation that yields the right fruit. The priests and scribes saw what he meant and wanted to arrest him, but were afraid of the people who saw him as a prophet.

COMMENT: The point of the parable is that the leaders of the Jews have failed in God's eyes and will be rejected; others who denied God at first (said No!) but have repented and accepted God will reach the new kingdom.
1. Vs. 32: In 11:11 Jesus places John outside the new kingdom of Jesus, but otherwise the point is clear.
2. Vss. 33-46: The landowner is God, the vineyard Israel, the wicked vinegrowers the Jewish religious leaders, the servants are the prophets, and the son is Jesus and his death the crucifixion. Walls were built to protect fields from wild beasts; the watchtower had a flat roof and storerooms; the vinegrowers were tenant-farmers. Since Jerusalem was destroyed in 70 A.D. by the Romans, the readers of Matthew would see fate and truth working out in the prophecies of the Psalm.

CHAPTER 22

78. THE KINGDOM IS NOT TO BE LIGHTLY DISREGARDED (22: 1-14): Jesus tells them another parable in which the kingdom is like a king who made a wedding party for his son. The guests ignored the repeated invitations sent via the king's servants — finally, the guests even killed the servants. The king sent his troops to kill the murderers and burn down their city. Then he sent his servants to invite all on the streets, bad and good alike, to the feast. One person came improperly dressed and the king told the ushers to throw him out all tied up: "for many are called, but few are chosen."

79. A CLEVER TRAP — AND A PENETRATING ANSWER (22:15-22): To trap Jesus in a political gambit, the Pharisees ask him: Is it right to pay taxes to Caesar or not? But Jesus catches on, takes a coin from them, and asks whose face was on it; when they say Caesar's (Roman ruler) name and inscription are on it, Jesus tells them, "Render therefore unto Caesar the things which are Caesar's; and unto God the things that are God's."

COMMENT: Those invited to the wedding feast are the righteous Jews who maltreat the messengers; so the invitation goes to sinners, Gentiles, tax-gatherers, etc. The king sets fire to Jerusalem and kills the Jews, which dates Matthew *after* the destruction of Jerusalem by the Romans in 70 A.D. The improperly dressed man = a spiritually unprepared and unworthy person at the coming of the King-Jesus. The tied-up castout is thrown into hell. The chosen or the elect are the believer-Jews in Christ.

1. Vs. 16: Herod's party are the followers of Herod who support paying taxes to the Romans, while the Pharisees loathed the tax. If Jesus attacked the tax, he would be in civil trouble; if he accepted it, he would be unpopular with the people. Vs. 17 indicates a headtax upon all males over 14, and all females over 12. The silver coin carried a portrait of Caesar and an inscription of his name and titles—the emperor Tiberias Caesar or perhaps the former emperor Augustus Caesar was on it.

2. Vs. 21: Separation of church and state in a way; he recognizes the claims of political control so long as religious affairs were not interfered with. Naturally, the religious must have priority in Jesus' eyes. This answer of Jesus is very important.

80. JESUS EXPOSES THE IGNOR-ANCE OF THE SADDUCEES (22:23-33): On the same day some Sadducees (those who deny the resurrection of the body) ask Jesus: Moses says a man should marry his brother's widow if her husband left no children. Suppose seven brothers died one after the other, and lastly the woman herself died. Now in this "resurrection," whose wife "will she be of these seven men—for she belonged to all of them?" Jesus tells them that in heaven there is no marriage since men live like angels in heaven. And as for the resurrection —God is God of the living, not the dead. They are left astounded at his answer.

81. THE GREATEST COMMANDMENTS IN THE LAW (22:34-40): Now the Pharisees' turn comes and they ask him what the Law's greatest commandment is. Jesus replies, "Thou shalt love the Lord thy God with all thy heart, and with all thy soul, and with all thy mind," and the second most important is "Thou shalt love thy neighbor as thyself"— on these two rest the Law and the Prophets.

COMMENT: The Sadducees (wealthy aristocratic Jews who accepted the Law of Moses but not the traditional added law followed by the Pharisees) know the Law requires marriage of the brother with the dead brother's wife, but the question was really a test to trap Jesus. Vs. 30: shows that after death and resurrection, the body in heaven is spiritual, not flesh and blood. Vs. 32 quotes from Exodus 3:6.

1. Vs. 37 quotes from Deuteronomy 6:5; vs. 39 from Leviticus 19:18. These two form the base of the Christian ethical code, Jesus being the first to combine the two.

82. JESUS PUTS AN UNANSWERABLE QUESTION (22:41-46): Jesus asks the Pharisees whose son Christ (the Messiah) is, and they reply, "The Son of David." Jesus asks, then how can David address his son as Lord— hence the Messiah cannot be the Son of David. No one could answer this, and from that day they asked no further questions!

CHAPTER 23

83. HE PUBLICLY WARNS THE PEOPLE AGAINST THEIR RELIGIOUS LEADERS (23:1-37): Jesus tells the crowds to follow what the scribes and Pharisees say but not what they do. They are hypocrites out to impress by increasing the size of their phylacteries (religious amulets) and the length of their robe fringes ("borders of their garments") to display their piety. They love the best seats in the synagogues, love to be called "Rabbi" ("my great one" or "my Lord"), but your master is Christ. Call no man your father except your Father in heaven; the greatest is your servant, the humblest will be exalted. Woe to the scribes and Pharisees who have made the Law so difficult that heaven is unattainable among men; who devour widows' houses; who make enthusiastic converts ("proselytes") over zealous children of hell; who prefer gold to piety, who pay tithes (taxes) on petty things but omit weightier matters of the law; who leave undone matters of judgment, mercy, and faith: "Ye blind guides (i.e., of the Jews) which strain at a gnat, and swallow a camel (who harp on petty things and commit gross sins)," who are clean outside but dirty inside, who are like "whited sepulchres" (whitewashed tombs), fair without and rotten bones within, righteous without, within hypocritical; "ye serpents, ye generation of vipers (snakes)"; you crucify my men and persecute them from city to city, and may all the crimes against the good be on your heads from the murder of Abel (Cain by his brother at the beginning of time) to Zacharias (O.T. hero). "O Jerusalem (i.e., the Jews), you kill the prophets and stone them, and how often I would have made converts of you (i.e., gathered the chickens) but ye would not! Behold your house (city of Jerusalem) is left desolate, and I say to you that you will not see me again until I return in glory."

COMMENT: Vs. 5: religious charms made "broad" are showy. The enlarged borders are the tassels on the shawls, signs of piety. Vs. 6: *Alas* is a better translation for *woe* here. Vs. 16: *Oaths* are meant, not vows. Vs. 23: *Anise* and *cummin* are aromatic plants; all Jews were required by law to pay one-tenth of their produce (the tithe) to the Temple. Jesus is saying that minute points of the law should be followed but not in order to violate big points. Vs. 27: tombs were whitewashed to guard against accidentally touching them; this would be "unclean" and defiling; whitewashing them made them also lovely to look at, hiding the corruption within. Vs. 29: veneration of tombs and monuments was common. Vs. 32: means that you should live up to the standards set up by your fathers. Vs. 34 and after refers to the later persecution of Christians *after* the crucifixion. Vs. 35: Abel is the first martyr and Zechariah the last one in the Hebrew Bible: Matthew confused him with the prophet. Vs. 37: the hen-chicks' image is considered very lovely. Vs. 38: Jesus is saying he is the representative of God and that the Jews can no longer be saved in the coming judgment; the home of course is Jerusalem. Vs. 39: From Psalm 118:26, which predicts the *parousia*, the return of the Messiah.

CHAPTER 24

84. JESUS FORTELLS THE DE-STRUCTION OF JERUSALEM (24:1-14): Jesus shows his disciples the Temple of Jerusalem and foretells its destruction, stone by stone. On the slope of the Mount of Olives (hill just east of Jerusalem), the disciples ask him when he will come again to deliver judgment. He warns them of an impostor in his name, "and ye shall hear of wars and rumors of wars" but that will not be the end; war between nations, famines, plagues, earthquakes will be signs of the coming end. You (the disciples) will be afflicted (persecuted), hated, and killed "for my name's sake." Betrayal, hatred, false prophets, the waning of human love are all signs, "but he that shall endure unto the end, the same shall be saved." This good news of the kingdom will spread all over—then the end will come.

COMMENT: Jesus met his disciples privately because at that time disclosure of the apocalypse (the end of the world) was commonly done in private among the Jews. The "coming" means the final arrival or advent of Christ at the judgment. Simon Magus was one of these false prophets (Acts 8:9-11); false Messiahs are mentioned in Josephus (historian at time of Christ). There will be universal war, persecution, apostasy (desertion of Christ), false prophets (false Christian teachers within the Church).
1. Vs. 12: love (*agape* in Greek) means Christian love and good will among Christians—which will grow cold.
2. Vs. 14: "this gospel of the kingdom" = the good news that the kingdom of the Messiah is near; to reach "all nations" of the then known world—within the realm of possibility at the time the Gospels were written.

85. JESUS PROPHESIES A FUTURE OF SUFFERING (24:15-28): Jesus continues to tell of the time when they shall see the desolating sacrilege ("abomination of desolation") foretold by the prophet Daniel standing in the Temple ("holy place"); then is the time to flee to the hills or to stay wherever you are —on housetops (flat in those days), in the fields. Alas for the pregnant women, the tiny babies! No such time of misery has or ever will be known again. Beware of false Christs, false prophets who will appear to mislead you. The Son of Man will appear as instantly as lightning, for wherever there is a corpse there will be vultures.

86. AT THE END OF TIME THE SON OF MAN WILL RETURN (24:29-44): Immediately after the misery of the last days, the sky will be disturbed, the sign of the Son of Man will appear, and all the world will weep as they see Him coming on the clouds in power and great splendor. He will send out his angels with a loud call of the trumpet and his chosen will be gathered. Like the fig tree in bloom, so too you will know by all these signs that he is near, at your very door! "This generation shall not pass, till all these things be fulfilled." Only my Father—not I nor the angels—knows when that day shall come. Like the days of Noah when man was full of sin and Noah was preserved by the ark, so in the same way shall be the coming of the Son of Man. Of two left in the field, one will be taken; of two women caught grinding wheat, one shall be taken and the other one left. "Watch therefore; for ye know not what hour your Lord doth come." Know this: a householder on watch cannot be robbed: so "be ye also ready," for the Son of Man will come unexpectedly.

COMMENT: Vs. 15: "the abomination of desolation" is from Daniel 11:31, which refers to a pagan god set upon the altar of the Temple. Vss. 17-18: Many will not have time to save property. Vs. 21: Matthew refers to the days of anti-Christ (an opponent of Christ, the Devil, the enemy of God's people who would come just before the coming of the Son of Man). Vss. 26-8: the coming will be sudden and unexpected and all will know of it. Disturbance of sun, moon, planets, etc., were common signs of the Jewish apocalyptic descriptions of the end of the world, when Christ will appear with a host of angels in shining radiant light. The Judgment will be sounded by a trumpet call (Isaiah 27:13) and the dead will rise from their graves; both good and evil men will be judged by God and Christ at his right hand. The chosen will be saved for the eternal life in Paradise, the sinful will burn in hell. Be prepared! = the warning of Jesus, the End of the World is very near! Vs. 36: Jesus himself does not know the exact time of the End — only God. This "proves" Jesus somewhat inferior to God. Noah, unlike the sinful of his day, was prepared. The lesson is obvious = the Flood is like the End.

87. VIGILANCE IS ESSENTIAL (24:45-51) (25:1-13): Think of the story of the good and bad servants. The good one serves well in the absence of his master and is rewarded upon his master's return, but the bad one is caught up by the unexpected return of his master and is consigned to hell, where "there shall be weeping and gnashing of teeth." (The master is of course the Messiah returning at Judgment and the servants are the good and bad Christians.) Think too of the story of the ten bridesmaids ("virgins") who went to meet the bridegroom: five were wise and five were foolish. The wise were thoughtful enough to keep their lamps filled with oil, but the foolish procrastinated and came with empty lamps. At midnight the groom came; the maids with oil in their lamps were ready for him. But the others were not. The five foolish ones were forced to go out to purchase oil, but meanwhile the groom came and the prepared maids were able to attend the marriage party—the late-arriving foolish ones found the door barred to them: "Watch therefore; for ye know neither the day nor the hour wherein the Son of man cometh."

COMMENT: The parable of the faithful and wise servant tells the disciples that more than watchfulness is required: the trusty servant = the good disciple, the bad servant = the Jewish religious leaders or the bad Christians (depending on the date one accepts for Matthew). The reward for good service is more responsibility in the Age-to-Come. The story of the ten girls is an *eschatological parable* (anecdote concerning the end of the world). The good-and-bad-Christians allegory is obvious. The girls are really bridesmaids who must meet the groom and his friends in order to escort the couple being married back to the groom's home where the feast will take place. The girls = good and bad Christians. The moral: keep reserves of faith ("oil") within you: Be Prepared! The Groom = Christ in the second coming.

CHAPTER 25

88. LIFE IS HARD FOR THE FAINTHEARTED (25:14-30): The kingdom of heaven is like the man who before going far away gave each of three servants five, two, and one talent (one talent = $1000). The five-and two-talent servants invested them wisely and increased their wealth, but the third still had only one talent when the master returned (the third had hid his money for the entire time); the first two were rewarded by the master, and the third is berated, is cast out for being wicked and lazy, and his money given to the first servant: "For unto every one that hath shall be given, and he shall have abundance; but from him that hath not shall be taken away even that which he hath." (An eschatological parable as in no. 87.)

89. THE FINAL JUDGMENT (25:31-46): Jesus said that when the son of Man does come in splendor with angels to sit on his glorious throne, all will come before him to be judged and the sheep will be separated from the goats (sheep = good Christians; goats = bad Christians, etc.). The sheep will be on his right and the goats on his left. To the sheep he said, "I was ahungered and ye gave me meat (food): I was thirsty, and ye gave me drink: I was a stranger, and ye took me in." When the good ones asked how this was possible, he answers that by doing good to their brother Christians they did good to Christ. To the goats on his left he gave his curse into hell-fire with the devil, for they had done the reverse of the good sheep; everlasting fire to them, and eternal life to the sheep.

COMMENT: This picture of the Last Judgment forms a fit climax to the preceding five discourses. It differs from most Jewish apocalypses in that the Judge is Christ (not God). Vs. 32 refers to or implies that all men will rise from their graves to be judged by Christ. Vss. 35-6 can mean that service to Christ's disciples is service to Jesus himself; it is the nature of this service that will be judged—its loving kindness and compassion. Note how Christ identifies himself with his people.

CHAPTER 26

90. JESUS ANNOUNCES HIS COMING DEATH (26:1-2): After Jesus had finished all his discourses and teaching he said: "Ye know that after (in) two days is the feast of the passover, and the Son of man is betrayed to be (will be) crucified?"

COMMENT: In Matthew the Jewish feast of the Passover (celebration of Jews for freedom from Egyptian slavery) falls from 6 p.m. Thursday until 6 p.m. Friday, the day of the crucifixion (so also Mark and Luke). The time now is Wednesday. The Passover lambs were sacrificed in the temple in the late afternoon on the 14th day of the Jewish month called Nisan (first month of the Hebrew year) and the Passover supper eaten the same evening; the 15th of Nisan began at midnight, the actual Passover day. Of the Passover, more later.

91. AN EVIL PLOT — AND AN ACT OF LOVE (26:3-13): Now the chief priests and elders of the people assembled with Caiaphas, the High Priest, to plot to trick and kill

Jesus—but not during the festival— a riot might result. Back in Bethany we find Jesus in the house of Simon the leper; a woman comes and pours a bottle of expensive perfume on his head, to the indignation of the disciples at the waste of money that might better have been given to the poor. But Jesus says she did a beautiful thing to him, "For ye have the poor always with you; but me ye have not always" — she did it for Jesus' burial and she shall not be forgotten.

COMMENT: The Sanhedrin (temple priests and Sadducean aristocrats) form a church court. These priests are the ones who had instigated Jesus' arrest. The perfume is in a marble-like ("alabaster") bottle used for precious ointment in marriages and burials. In Luke and John the feet are anointed. Messiah means "anointed one," which translated into New Testament Greek means "the Christ." Jesus, unlike the disciples, is aware that he is being anointed *before* his death, not after, as was customary.

92. THE BETRAYAL IS ARRANGED (26:14-16):

Then a disciple called Judas Iscariot approaches the chief priests: "What will ye give me, and I will deliver him unto you?" he asked. They settle with him for thirty silver coins, and from then on he sought for a way to betray Jesus.

COMMENT: Iscariot = "man of Kerioth," a certain village, or it may mean "the false" in Aramaic, the language spoken by the Jews in Jesus' time. If the latter is correct, then "who betrayed him" is redundant in a sense. What he told them was the place where Jesus could be found. Why did he betray Jesus? An intimate disciple certainly would not have done so for money merely. 1. Was he a revolutionary who wanted Jesus to take over Israel as king in a revolt against the Romans? 2. Did he hope to save Jesus from death through assassination by placing him under arrest? 3. Was it greed for money (as in John's gospel)? But his remorse and suicide later makes this theory unconvincing. 4. Did he fear Jesus was taking the wrong path, one that might lead to bloody insurrection? 5. Did he betray Jesus to force Jesus to display his Messianic power and truth? In Genesis 37:26ff. Judah (= *Judas* in Greek) proposed the sale of his brother Joseph to the Ishmaelites for "twenty shekels of silver"; Zechariah 11:12 provides the origin probably for the sale of the Lord for thirty pieces of silver. Historicists find this incident legendary; that Judas is a symbol for Israel, the villain of the gospels; that he could not have been one of the twelve since Jesus did not institute that college (see also Matthew 29:28); in short, a handy traitor provided by legend to elaborate the drama of the crucifixion.

93. THE LAST SUPPER (26:17-35):

Now on the first day of unleavened bread (bread made without yeast) the disciples ask Jesus where they are to eat their Passover meal. He tells them to go into the city of Jerusalem to a certain man and tell him that the Master says, "My time is at hand (near); I will keep the passover at thy house with my disciples." The disciples did so; when evening came, they all sit down and eat, and Jesus says, "Verily I say unto you, that one of you shall betray me." Each becomes sad and asks him, "Lord, is it I?" And Jesus says the one who dips his hand along with his own into the dish (the sauce dish into which the herbs of bitter taste were dipped — if this were the Passover supper), "the same shall betray me . . . but woe unto that man by whom the Son of man is betrayed! it had been good for that man if he had not been born." Then Judas, who actually did betray him, says, "Master, is it I?" and Jesus replies, "Thou hast said" (= "As you say"). Then Jesus takes a loaf, blesses it, breaks it into pieces and gives it to the disciples telling them to eat it, for, it is his body; telling them to drink the wine, for it is his blood, "my blood of the new testament (agreement, contract), which is shed for many for the remission (forgiveness) of sins." He goes on to tell them that he would drink no more wine until the advent of his Father's kingdom. Then they sing a hymn and go out to the Mount of Olives where he tells them that tonight they will lose faith in him as foretold in the scriptures: "I will smite the shepherd, and the sheep of the flock shall be scattered abroad" (Zechariah 13:7). "But after I am risen again, I will go before you into Galilee," continues Jesus. Peter says that even though the others desert Jesus, he never would; the rest say the same.

COMMENT: The day is probably Thursday, Nisan 14th (Jewish calendar) when the Passover lambs were killed and then eaten in the evening. Jesus is aware of the plot to destroy him: "My time is at hand." The first day of the unleavened bread would be Nisan 15th, the day *after* the Passover—an obvious mistake; the sense is the day *before* the Passover, which could be eaten only in Jerusalem. Matthew like Mark calls the Last Supper the Passover meal. In the Gospel of John (18:28) the Passover is eaten on the evening *after* the crucifixion, but that gospel is more "theological," less "historical."

1. The Passover meal was eaten at night from a reclining position, which is the position of the disciples and Jesus.

2. Vss. 24-5: Judas is humanly responsible for his act and will be judged so. Note that Jesus goes to his death foreknowing every detail of the plot. The bread is compared to his body and the wine to his blood: in the O.T. the blood is separated from the body in sacrifices. Hence, Jesus considers himself a sacrifice to God by which a new testament (covenant, contract, bond) will be formed between God and man: the sacrifice of God's son in exchange for the forgiveness of man's sins = the New Testament. The disciples (and through them all the world) by eating the bread (body) and drinking the wine (blood) will be the beneficiaries of the sacrifice. In addition, the future will bring in the new kingdom with its messianic banquet, when they all will feast together again. The new covenant recalls that made by God with the Jews after the exodus from Egypt (Exodus 24:8).

3. Vss. 28f.: the forgiveness of sins' idea was added by Matthew, probably taken from Jeremiah 31:34. Jesus tells his disciples he will be arrested and they will desert him when he quotes Zechariah on the smitten shepherd and the scattered flock. The hymns they sang are Psalms 114-118, the Passover Psalms. Historicists insist that this supper was only a memorial prelude before the imminent kingdom when they would again dine in joy, but that mystical elements were later interpolated to transfer the meaning to Christ as sacrificial paschal lamb to redeem mankind from sin.

94. THE PRAYER IN GETHSEMANE (26:36-46): Then they go to a place called Gethsemane and Jesus goes apart to pray alone, taking with him only Peter, James, and John. Jesus becomes deeply sorrowful, telling the two to remain there and watch with him. Going off a little farther he prays: "O my Father, if it be possible, let this cup pass from me: nevertheless, not as I will, but as thou wilt." Returning to the three, he finds them asleep and scolds them: "Watch and pray, that ye enter not into temptation: the spirit indeed is willing, but the flesh is weak." A second time in prayer and again he finds them asleep. At the third time he tells them to continue sleeping: "Behold, the hour is at hand, and the Son of man is betrayed into the hands of sinners." He tells them to rise, for the man betraying him was here at hand.

COMMENT: Gethsemane means "olive press"—very likely an olive orchard. The triple disobedience of the three principal disciples indicates their fate is separated from that of Jesus': hence the separation and flight of the disciples at the critical moment. Jesus accepts the will of God although in deep affliction: "Thy will be done." Adam had disobeyed God's will and had brought misery upon us all; Jesus by complete obedience to God's will wipes out our inherited sin from Adam's transgression. Christ's spirit conquered the *flesh*—theirs did not. The bitter cup of destiny he drank and accepted—crucifixion. The same three disciples were at the transfiguration, 17:1, where they saw his glory.

95. THE BETRAYAL (26:47-56): At this, Judas the disciple enters with an armed crowd sent by the elders and chief priests. Judas gives the sign to the arresters by going up to Jesus, saying "Hail, Master" and kissing him. "Friend," says Jesus, "wherefore art thou come?" They seized him, but not before one of the disciples cuts off the ear of a servant of the high priest. To this disciple Jesus gives a reprimand: "Put up again thy sword into his place: for all they that take the sword shall perish with the sword"; if he had so desired, Jesus adds, he could pray to his Father who would immediately send twelve legions (anywhere from 3000 to 6000 men in a Roman legion) of angels to help him. But to fulfill the Scriptures (Bible) he submits, merely asking the crowds why they had come with swords and staves (staffs) to seize him when before they had left him

alone when he had taught in the temple. Again the Scriptures must be fulfilled. "Then all the disciples forsook him and fled."

COMMENT: The kiss, a sign of love, is here a sign of betrayal. John in 18:10 makes Simon Peter the one who strikes off the ear. Vss. 52-4 were added by Matthew and are not found in Mark: 1. Evil is not to be resisted. 2. To call for help would be to disobey God's purposes. Note that Jesus has been arrested as a common robber, and note too that the disciples flee as Jesus had predicted in vs. 31. Matthew omits the young man who runs away naked from the scene (Mark 14:51f.). The flight of all twelve seems incredible and is contradicted by Peter's presence later on. Some scholars insist that they might have stayed in Jerusalem and followed or heard what follows.

96. JESUS BEFORE THE HIGH PRIEST (26:57-68): He is led before Caiaphas (high priest head of the Sanhedrin: KYE yuh fahs) and diverse scribes and elders. But Peter follows to see the end. The church court can find no perjurors ("false witnesses") until two are finally found (two were required by the Law) to testify that they had heard Jesus saying that he was able to both destroy and rebuild the temple in three days—to which charge Jesus remains silent. The High Priest then asks him to swear by the living God that he was the Christ, the Son of God—to which Jesus said, "Thou hast said" ("You have said so"), and added that hereafter would be seen the "Son of man sitting on the right hand of power, and coming in the clouds of heaven"; at this the High Priest tears his clothes, calling Jesus blasphemous, and asking the court for a decision—which was: "guilty of death." Then they spit in his face, strike him and slap him, saying "Prophesy unto us, thou Christ, Who is he that smote thee?"

COMMENT: The silence of Jesus comes from Isaiah ("like a sheep that before its shearers is dumb, so he opened not his mouth" 53:7). Jesus under oath admits he is the Christ and will return in glorious judgment. Mark omits the name of the High Priest. Note Peter seems yet not to believe in the resurrection.

1. Vs. 59: Matthew adds *false* to Mark's "sought testimony."

2. Vss. 61f.: The destruction of the temple charge is inserted to delight the Christian reader who knows the body and soul of Christ is meant. Note that this evidence is not used to determine guilt.

3. Vs. 64: Power is an indirect way of saying God, a word not to be uttered or written by Jews, a taboo word of great magic and power. The Son of man coming on clouds is from Daniel 17:7.

4. Vss. 65-8: The rabbis made it a rule to tear one's robes if they heard blasphemy. The spitting and slapping fulfills Isaiah 50:6.

97. PETER DISOWNS HIS MASTER (26:69-75): Peter in the courtyard is asked by a maid if he had not been with Jesus before. Peter denies it. A second time he denies it. On the third time he begins to curse and swear—"I know not the man"—and right then the cock crows. Peter recalls Jesus' words that he would deny Jesus three times before the cock would crow, and he wept bitterly. In the morning the priests and elders met in council to decide on how to get Jesus executed. They tie his hands and give him over to the governor of the province, Pilate. (Jesus had said in 10:33 that he would deny before God those who denied him before men: a contradiction unless even the words of Jesus cannot limit God's mercy and grace.)

CHAPTER 27

98. THE REMORSE OF JUDAS (27:1-10): Jesus is delivered before Pontius Pilate, and Judas, seeing the verdict, repents and returns the thirty pieces of silver to the chief priest and elders, saying he has sinned and betrayed innocent blood; the priests and elders scoff, saying they had nothing to do with it, that it was his affair. Judas flings the coins on the floor of the Temple, goes outside, and hangs himself. The Sanhedrin, finding it blood money unfit for the Temple treasury, uses it to buy the potter's field where foreigners were buried—hence its name, "the field of blood," to this very day. As Jeremiah foretold: "And they took the thirty pieces of silver, the price of him that was valued, whom they of the children of Israel did value (price); And gave them for the potter's field, as the Lord appointed me."

COMMENT: Luke in Acts 1:18 has Judas buying the field and dying there after falling headlong in a hole and bursting his guts. Judas may have thrown the money into the Temple treasury instead of on the floor.

1. Vs. 9f: From Zechariah, 11:12f.—not Jeremiah!

The burial place is called *Aceldama* (cemetery), implying its use as a cemetery for suicides and executed criminals—in short, the place where Jesus himself might have been buried after crucifixion!

99. JESUS BEFORE PILATE (27:11-32): Pilate asks Jesus if he be the king of the Jews, to which the answer is, "Yes, I am." But he keeps silent in the face of the accusations of the priests, to the Governor's amazement. The custom at festival time was to release any prisoner whom the people chose; so a notorious prisoner named Barabbas is put next to Jesus and the people are given their choice—Barabbas or Jesus called Christ (Messiah). Pilate knows that Jesus had been handed to him in sheer malice. Even while sitting on his bench, his wife sends a message telling him to have nothing today with that good ("just") man because she had gone through agonies dreaming about Jesus last night. But the chief priests and elders persuade the mob to choose Barabbas and to have Jesus executed: in short, when given their choice between the two by the Governor, they cry out in one voice: "Barabbas!" "Then what am I to do with Jesus called Christ?" asked Pilate. They all say again, "Let him be crucified!" When Pilate wants to know what evil crime he has committed, they cry out all the louder: "Let him be crucified!" Pilate then gives up, realizing a riot might result, and so literally washes his hands of guilt in the affair, saying, "I am innocent of the blood of this just person: see ye to it." Then all the people answer, "His blood be on us, and on our children!" Barabbas is then freed and Jesus is flogged and made ready for crucifixion. The Roman guards then strip him, put on him a scarlet cloak, place a mock crown of thorn twigs on his head, and a mock king's sceptre (a stick) in his hand. Then the guards spit at him, and beat him with his own stick. The fun over, they re-dress him in his own clothes and lead him off to be crucified. On the way a man called Simon, of Cyrene (sigh REE nee, in North Africa), is compelled to carry Jesus' cross.

COMMENT: The Sanhedrin must have explained to Pilate that Christ meant *King* of the Jews (a term for the Christ used by Gentiles). Pilate knows that the Sanhedrin is envious of Jesus, that their charges are unjust, that his wife is "on his back," so

to speak. The whole aim of Matthew is to make the Sanhedrin and the Jews responsible for the crucifixion of Christ, and not the Romans, who actually carried out the sentence (crucifixion was a *Roman* method of punishment for criminals). Actually, the truth might be that the Romans feared the influence of Jesus upon the common people; that they might foment a revolution and overthrow Roman rule. Political agitators like Jesus (if he was one) would have been unmercifully tortured and crucified. Matthew omitted Mark's designation of Jesus Barabbas (his full name) as a murderer in the late insurrection. Incidentally, there is no evidence of such a custom as release of prisoners on festivals. Matthew, more than Mark, is eager to shift the blame for the crime from Roman shoulders. The washing of hands to indicate innocence of a deed is a Jewish custom—not a Roman one, and Pilate would not have done so.

1. Vs. 25: "all the people" = the entire Jewish nation asks to be eternally damned forever with the blood of Christ on their heads. Matthew's addition of this detail has caused incalculable harm—the blot of anti-Semitism.

2. Vss. 26-31: The Roman custom is to scourge prisoners before executing them. The mock worship and mock kneeling before the "King" might be a reflection of certain pagan festival practices. A spiky crown and rod of rule are common Roman emperor attributes.

100. THE CRUCIFIXION (27:33-56): They reach a place called Golgotha (GAUL go thah), which means Skull Hill, and there offer him a drink of wine ("vinegar") mixed with a bitter drug, which Jesus refuses after tasting it. After nailing him to the cross, they (the Roman soldiers) draw lots for his clothes, after which they sit down to keep guard over him. Over his

head they put a placard with "This is Jesus the King of the Jews" written on it. Now two bandits ("thieves") are crucified along Jesus' right and left. Passers-by revile him, mockingly telling him to rebuild in three days the temple he had destroyed; to save himself, to come down from the cross if he truly is the Son of God. In addition, the chief priests elders and scribes mock him, saying that he who had saved others cannot save himself. If he truly were the King of Israel (the Jews), why doesn't he come down from the cross; then he would be believed. Let God deliver him, since he said he was his son. Even the two bandits mock him. Then about midday ("the sixth hour") to three o'clock ("the ninth hour") there is darkness over all the countryside. At about three o'clock Jesus cries with a loud voice, saying, "Eli, Eli, lama sabachani? that is to say, My God, my God, why hast thou forsaken me?" Some think he is calling for the prophet Elijah ("Elias"); and one soaks a sponge in vinegar and reaches it up to Jesus on the end of a long stick. But the rest say. "Let us see whether Elias (Elijah) will come to save him." Jesus cries out again with a loud voice and dies ("gave up the ghost"). And behold the veil (sanctuary curtain) in the Temple is torn in two, the earth shakes, rocks split, and graves open and a number of holy men's bodies who were asleep in death rise again, leaving their graves after the resurrection of Jesus and entering the holy city, appearing before many people. When the Roman guard-centurion (captain) and his soldiers see this reaction in nature they are frightened, saying "Truly this was the Son of God." Many women had watched the scene from a distance; they had followed Jesus from Galilee to help him, and among them are Mary of Magdala, Mary the mother of James and Joseph, and the mother of Zebedee's sons (James and John).

COMMENT: The parable of the vineyard (21:33-41) tells of the tenants (Jews, high priests, etc.) of a vineyard (Israel) who refuse to pay the landlord (God); the tenants even kill the landlord's son and heir (Jesus). The landlord will kill the tenant-murderers and rent out the vineyard to other tenants who will pay. "And they took him and cast him out of the vineyard, and killed him" describes pretty well what was done to Jesus. The *Simon of Cyrene* who bears the cross by compulsion has the same first name as Peter to whom Jesus had said that any man who would come after him, let him deny himself and take up his cross and follow him. Jesus, weakened by the flogging, would carry the crossbeam part only, the usual practice. *The wine mingled with gall* (in Mark it is mixed with myrrh in order to act as an anesthetic, a pain-killer) is tasted and refused by Jesus because its purpose may have been to increase his torture, or on the other hand to relieve his pain. Jesus would have spurned it in both cases, according to Matthew. *Golgotha* (Skull Hill) was so-called because the hill was skull-shaped, although in art the scene is marked by the presence of bones and skulls lying around. The historical evidence for such a place is lacking; in all probability Jesus' body was cast into some unclean place used for executions of criminals. The *soldiers casting lots* for his garments is correct since the executioners customarily obtained the criminal's clothing. Matthew adds that the *soldiers sat down and kept watch* over Jesus to forestall rumors that his body was removed from the cross before he was dead, or that another body had been substituted for that of Jesus. Jesus was *fastened to the cross* in this way: the hands were nailed to the crossbeam on the ground and separated from the upright beam, which was already fixed in its hole. Then the crossbeam was nailed to the upright beam with the weight of the body eased by a peg nailed under the crotch, between the legs. Lastly the feet were nailed—but not always. Then guards were placed to insure the death of the victim, which was further tested by breaking his legs. Often the victim was merely tied to the crossbeam. *This is Jesus, the King of the Jews* was placed on a placard on the beam; it was the Roman custom publicly to display the charge against the criminal. The charge in Jesus' case was that he claimed to be the Messiah or King. In John the charge is written in three languages for the benefit of foreigners at the festival. It was a warning to all Jews that the Romans would tolerate no kings! Luke elaborates on the *two bandits,* making one good and repentant and the other evil and cruel. The *wagging of heads* is a scornful gesture and a sign of gloating. Vs. 41 is implausible since members of the Sanhedrin would have kept clear of such an unclean place on this holy day. *Darkness over all the land* is explained by Luke as an eclipse, an impossibility (except for miracles) during the paschal full moon. "*Eli, Eli,* etc." is from Psalm 22, a prayer of complaint to God but ending on a note of victory (vss. 23-31). It could mean a loss of faith in God (a few scholars), but many think it a prayer for times of adversity, which actually builds up encouragement from suffering: so used by pious Jews. *Elijah* (O.T. legend had it that he did not die but rose to heaven) was the bystanders' error for Jesus' "Eli, Eli." The *sponge on the stick* is reached up to Jesus to torture him still more. Yet it might have been the *posca,* a drink of mercy with the Romans. Jesus *yielded up the ghost* in Matthew, but in Mark (the source) it is *breathed his last;* Matthew wants to stress the voluntary act for the mortality of Mark's phrase. The *cry in a loud voice* would have been impossible after such long torture and exposure in an ordinary human. *The veil of the temple* is the curtain before the Holy of Holies; the rending = the end of the Jewish approach to God and a sign of the Christian approach. It could also mean divine judgment on the Jews for their crime and blindness. The *saints rising from their graves* means that resurrection will now be available to all who adopt Christ. Note the care Matthew takes in stating they rose from their graves *after his resurrection,* Christ being the first to offer life after death. This looks like an editorial insertion to make sure of Christ's primary ascension (cf. I Corinthians 15:20). The centurion's words are the mouthpiece for Christians who confess their faith in Jesus, but in the mouth of a pagan the words mean Jesus is a hero or demi-god; perhaps Matthew intends irony here (?). To show how much of the crucifixion is based upon O.T. sources we document:

Vs. 34: "They offered him wine to drink, mingled with gall"

Psalm 69:21: "they gave me gall (poison) for food"

Vs. 35: "they divided his garments among them by casting lots"

Psalm 22:18: "they divide my garments among them, and for my raiment they cast lots"

Vs. 38: the two bandits

Isaiah 53:12: "he . . . was numbered with the transgressors"

Vs. 43: "He trusted in God; let him deliver him now . . ."

Psalm 22:8: "He committed his cause to the Lord; let him rescue him"

Vs. 39: "reviled him, wagging their heads"

Psalm 22:7: "All who see me mock at me, they make mouths at me, they wag their heads"

Vs. 46: "Eli, Eli, lama sabacthani" = "My God, my God, why hast thou forsaken me?"

Psalm 22:1: "My God, my God, why hast thou forsaken me?"

Vs. 48: "sponge and filled it with vinegar"

Psalm 69:21: "and for my thirst they gave me vinegar to drink"

101. JESUS IS BURIED AND THE TOMB IS GUARDED (27:57-66): In the evening the wealthy Joseph of the town of Arimathea, who was a disciple of Jesus, goes to Pilate and obtains his consent to take the body of Jesus. Joseph wraps the body in a shroud and lays it in his own new tomb hewn from rock. A great stone is rolled before the door of the tomb by Joseph and he leaves. Opposite the tomb sits Mary Magdalene "and the other Mary." Next day (after the Sabbath, the first day of Unleavened Bread) the chief priests and Pharisees ask Pilate to set a watch on the tomb lest the disciples steal his body from the sepulchre and say that he had risen from the grave. Pilate consents, and the stone is sealed and a watch is set on the tomb.

CHAPTER 28

102. THE FIRST LORD'S DAY: JESUS RISES (28:1-15): Just before dawn on Sunday morning Mary Magdalene and the "other Mary" come to see the sepulchre, and behold! a great quake of the earth and an angel comes and rolls back the stone and sits upon it. His appearance ("countenance") was like lightning and his clothes were white as snow. The keepers (guards) tremble and become like dead men. The angel tells the two women to fear not, that Jesus has risen, as Jesus had predicted; and he invites them into the tomb to see. Then he tells them to quickly tell his disciples that he has risen from the dead and that Jesus will be going before them in Galilee—and there they should see him. The two women, filled with fear and great joy, do as they are bidden. On their way Jesus meets them and says, "Be not afraid" and repeats the angel's message. The guards tell the chief priest what has happened, and, calling the elders they take counsel, but not before rewarding the guards and bribing them to say that his disciples had stolen the body away at night. The guards accept the bribe and spread the tale.

COMMENT: Mark (16:1) had the women coming to anoint the body in the tomb—something the guards would have prevented. The earthquake and the angel are peculiar to Matthew. In Mark the women disobey the angel and flee in fear and astonishment. In Matthew the great joy of the women resembles the joy of the Magi—the gospel ends where it began. Mark does not have Jesus reappear after death; Matthew has two appearances: one here and one in Galilee in the next paragraph.

103. JESUS GIVES HIS FINAL COMMISSION (28:16-20): The eleven (no Judas) went to Galilee, where they see Jesus on the appointed hillside. They worship him, though some were still doubtful. To the disciples he says: "Go ye therefore, and teach all nations, baptizing them in the name of the Father, and of the Son, and of the Holy Ghost: Teaching them to observe all things whatsoever I have commanded you: and, lo, I am with you always, even unto the end of the world. Amen."

COMMENT: This passage prepares for the life and work of the Church: the disciples (founders of the Church) are to spread Christ's teachings and messages to all nations (Jews and Gentiles everywhere). Christ will be with the Church until the day of final judgment. Christianity actually began in Jerusalem (i.e., the early Church); there is no historical basis for its commencement in Galilee. The hillside was unmentioned by Jesus in his directions to the two women. Why Matthew inserts doubt by some of the disciples is puzzling, and no answer is attempted here. Vss. 18, 19 contrast with Jesus' narrower aims to convert Israel in 15:24 and 10:6. The baptism in trinity is the first time Jesus explicitly commands baptism. Vs. 20 sounds like a similar command given by God to Moses: Jesus the second Moses, giving the New Testament of teachings to the new Israelites—the entire world!

MARK: A PREFACE

WRITER: It is believed that Mark was Peter's interpreter while Peter was imprisoned in Rome, and while with Peter he took down Peter's recollections of the life, words, and actions of Jesus. Peter's language was Aramaic, and Mark was forced to set his words down in Greek, the universal tongue. Many of the curious things in Mark are the result of this odd origin of the gospel of Mark.

DATE: Around the year 70 A.D.
SOURCES: Peter the apostle of Jesus provides the main facts, but in addition Mark drew on an *oral gospel* long used by Christians from earliest times. This oral gospel was a memorized account of the acts and teachings of Jesus (cf. Paul's letter to the Corinthians). Mark wrote his gospel to supplement the oral tradition, not to replace it.

THEMES: Mark's is the earliest and first of a long series of Christian gospels. His is the model for all successive gospels, especially the canonical ones of Matthew, Luke, and in some respects John. Certainly the synoptic Luke and Matthew borrow anywhere from half to three-quarters of their material directly from Mark. If the reader consults the Harmony Table, he will discover parallel passages in Luke and Matthew that correspond amazingly with the originals in Mark. In Mark, Jesus is less a teacher than a doer, "a man of action, of amazing power" (Goodspeed tr., p. 78). It is almost a primitive document, filled with demons, devils, and miracles. The style is simple, direct, and concrete—no learning, no embellishment—often naive and innocent, but here Jesus comes to more life than in the more learned and sophisticated Matthew and Luke. There is real drama beneath the unpretentious words, real intensity beneath the rugged vividness of its language!

DETAILED REVIEW AND COMMENTARY ON THE GOSPEL ACCORDING TO MARK

CHAPTER 1

1. PROLOGUE: (1:1-8): This is the beginning of the gospel of Jesus Christ, the Son of God. God's messenger, John the Baptist, as prophesied in Isaiah, is sent to prepare the way for Jesus Christ. John is "the voice of one crying in the wilderness" who began to baptize men, a rite which marks a complete change of heart and God's forgiveness of the sins of the baptized ones. And John preached to the Jews telling of One who is coming after him who is stronger than he, "the latchet (laces) of whose shoes I am not worthy to stoop down and unloose."

2. THE ARRIVAL OF JESUS (1: 9-13):

Jesus came from Nazareth (his home town) in Galilee and was baptized by John in the Jordan River. During his baptism the heavens were "rent asunder" and God's voice came: "Thou art my beloved Son, in thee I am well pleased." Then the Spirit drove Jesus into the wilderness for forty days where Satan tempted him. His only companions were wild animals, and only angels were there to care for him.

3. JESUS BEGINS TO PREACH THE GOSPEL, AND TO CALL MEN TO FOLLOW HIM: (1:14-20):

After John's arrest (by Herod), Jesus went to Galilee preaching the gospel of God, "the time is fulfilled, and the kingdom of God is at hand." He calls upon the Galileans to repent and believe in the gospel. Passing by the Lake of Galilee he attracted the brothers Simon Peter and Andrew as followers. Later on James and John, the sons of Zebedee, "left their father Zebedee in the boat with the hired servants, and went after him."

COMMENT: The quote from Isaiah (40:3) is also partly a quote from Malachi (3:1). John is the forerunner and subordinate to Christ. Some critics say that the two originally represented rival sects and that the inferiority of John to Jesus is a result of later interpolations and additions. The problem of baptism, the change from sin to virtue in repentance, seems superfluous in the case of Jesus, who obviously needed no baptism. John here is the herald of the Messiah (the saviour of the Jews, the bringer of peace, justice, and plenty to the Jews, a descendant of the house of King David). At this time the Jews were seeking for a God-sent Messiah to deliver them from Roman misery and oppression, and in fact there are records of "false" Messiahs at the time of Jesus. Notice that God speaks directly to Jesus and not to the entire multitude, as in Matthew and Luke. Perhaps the "messianic secret" begins here: Jesus is not recognized as the Messiah of God by the Jews and for a time not even by his disciples. In Mark we shall note a persistent desire on Jesus' part to keep his messiahship secret. Just as the angels had fed Elijah in the O.T. (I Kings 19), so do they aid Jesus in the desert. The victory of Jesus over Satan means that Jesus has undone Adam's original sin and the possibility of paradise available again to man is now open. The father Zebedee, left with the hired servants, may mean the sons have abandoned their father to evil hirelings (*misthotos* in Greek means servant in a bad sense), or it may mean a contrast between hireling servants and true servants of Christ.

4. JESUS BEGINS HEALING THE SICK (1:21-39):

At Capernaum on the Sabbath a man in the grip of the evil spirit appeared in the synagogue and shouted to Jesus, "What have we to do with thee, thou Jesus of Nazareth? art thou come to destroy us? I know who thou art, the Holy One of God." Jesus cut him short ("rebuked" him) and ordered the evil spirit to leave the man's body. At this, the spirit convulsing the man screamed and left him. The people were astounded at the man who could order evil spirits around—a man with authority (a teacher of the scriptures who has God's ear, so to speak). Jesus then cures Simon's wife of the fever and many others who were sick or possessed by evil spirits ("possessed with devils"), "and he suffered not the devils to speak, because they knew him."

5. Very early on the next morning, while it was still dark, Jesus went apart to pray. Simon and the companions found him after a search saying, "Everyone is looking for you." Jesus replied that they will go then elsewhere - to preach in the neighboring towns. But he continued to makes cures in all Galilee.

6. JESUS CURES LEPROSY (1:40-45): Moved with compassion, Jesus "stretched forth his hand and touched" a leper and cured him ("made him clean"). Jesus enjoined the man to keep the cure secret, but the man broadcast the news so that it became impossible to show his face in the towns. But even in the lonely places the people came from all quarters.

COMMENT: Jesus' supernatural powers are confessed to by the very demons themselves! The gospel of John finds these demoniac cures uncomfortable and omits them all, but the synoptic gospels (Matthew, Mark, and Luke, because they have parallel scenes showing close collaboration in the story of Jesus) make quite a point of demoniac cures. Jesus' constant injunction to silence is editorially inspired to account for the fact that he was not recognized as the Messiah until his resurrection. The editors indicate in this way that he was the recognized Messiah, but the recognizers of the fact had kept it secret—the messianic secret (see Loisy, p. 93).

CHAPTER 2

7. FAITH AT CAPERNAUM (2:1-12): When a group bringing a paralytic could not get near Jesus because of the great crowd, they removed the rooftiles and let down the paralytic's bed through the opening. Jesus said to the paralytic ("palsy") that his sins were forgiven and to rise. The scribes called this blasphemy since only God can forgive sins. To demonstrate he had such power Jesus said to the patient, "Arise, take up thy bed, and go unto thy house." The man did so and all were amazed.

8. JESUS NOW CALLS "A SINNER" TO FOLLOW HIM (2:13-17): Jesus recruits Matthew (called Levi in Mark, but Matthew in the gospel of that name), the tax collector. Later when Jesus was seen dining with publicans (tax collectors), the scribes (authorities on Jewish law) criticized this violation, but Jesus answered: "They that are whole have no need of a physician, but they that are sick: I came not to call the righteous, but sinners."

9. THE QUESTION OF FASTING: (2:18-22): When criticized over his disciples' not fasting as often as the law required (i.e., Jewish religious law), Jesus tells the story of the wedding guests who do not fast in the groom's presence; he also illustrates with similes on patching old cloth with new, and putting new (fresh) wine into old wineskins (winebottles made of leather).

10. JESUS REBUKES THE SABBATARIANS (2:23-28): The Pharisees (the popular form of Judaism, strict followers of the law of Moses) criticize Jesus for allowing his disciples to violate the Sabbath by picking wheat ("corn"). Jesus tells of King David who ate the holy bread in violation of the law: "The sabbath was made for man, and not man for the sabbath: so that the Son of man is lord even of the sabbath."

COMMENT: Jesus' conflict with the Pharisees and the scribes indicates a time somewhat later than the days of Jesus, since the friction with Jewish legalism by a separated body of Jewish Christians indicates a later era. In Mark the Son of Man is not the Judaic version but the Christ of mystery who redeems man from sin; but some say that he is a mixture of the Jewish Son of Man (a man who will be sent by God to save the Jews) and the Christian redeemer. The dining with publicans and sinners means that Jesus is out to save what the Jews considered unworthy—especially the non-Jews (Gentiles). This of course is the mission of Christianity to this day. The fasting on the day of his death (crucifixion) by his disciples indicates new fasting periods out-dating the "obsolete" Jewish laws of fasting. The attitude of Jewish legalism being obsolete indicates a period somewhat later than the so-called apostolic era (50 A.D.-90 A.D.). The ears of corn episode points to the Christ of mystery who can dispense his disciples from the sabbath observance—a power obtainable only in God.

10. (3:1-6): Jesus effects the cure of the man with the shriveled hand on the holy Sabbath because it was right to do good on the Sabbath regardless of legalisms. Here the Pharisees discuss with Herod's party how they can dispose of Jesus.

CHAPTER 3

11. JESUS' ENORMOUS POPU-LARITY (3:7-12): Great multitudes come to Jesus to be cured and to hear him, some wanting to touch him and thus be cured. The evil spirits on seeing Jesus would fall down before him saying, "Thou art the son of God." He instructs them not to tell about his powers.

12. JESUS CHOOSES THE TWELVE APOSTLES (3:13-19): Jesus on the mountain appoints his twelve disciples to follow him, to spread his word, "and to have authority to cast out devils." There were Peter (Simon), James, John, and these three he called the Boanerges, meaning "Sons of thunder'; then came Andrew, Philip, Bartholomew, Matthew, Thomas, James, the son of Alphaeus, Thaddeus, Simon the Canaanite, and "Judas Iscariot, which also betrayed him."

13. JESUS EXPOSES AN ABSURD ACCUSATION (3:20-30): Such large crowds gathered that it became impossible to eat a meal. When his friends (really relatives) heard of this, they set out to take charge of him ("to lay hold on him"), for people were saying that he was mad ("beside himself"). To the charge of the scribes that his power came from the chief devil Beelzebub, Jesus said that a divided kingdom cannot stand, nor a divided house, nor a divided Satan. One can rob a strong man only by binding him first. All sins are forgivable except blasphemy (cursing) against the Holy Spirit. All this Jesus said in answer to the charge he was in league with the devil.

14. THE NEW RELATIONSHIPS IN THE KINGDOM (3:31-35): Jesus is told that his mother and brothers are outside looking for him, but Jesus looking at those about him said, "Behold, my mother and my brethren!" For who does the will of God, that is the brother, sister, and mother of Jesus.

COMMENT: The choice of the Twelve was not actually made during Christ's lifetime; very likely, they were the leaders of the first believing group in Jerusalem some time after the crucifixion. The attempt of Jesus' family to bring him back home (Joseph, Mary, etc.) heaps no honor upon them for not recognizing the Christ. The incident may be symbolic of the new family of Gentiles Jesus has found outside his old family (Judaism). The blasphemy-against-the-Spirit as being unforgivable seems a late addition to refer to the Spirit as that which replaces Christ in the guidance of the Church (Loisy).

CHAPTER 4

15. THE STORY OF THE SOWER (4:1-20): At the lakeside Jesus taught in parables (little sermons, allegory stories). He told of the sower who threw his seeds in various bad places, but only on good soil did the seed thrive. When he was alone with his close followers and the twelve, he was asked about the parables. He told them that only those "in on the secret meaning" of the parables would know the truth. The sower is the spreader of the message, but various receptions are given the seed-message until it strikes good soil—and a crop increased by as much as a hundred times is the result.

16. TRUTH IS MEANT TO BE USED (4:21-25): He added that a lamp is not made to be hidden under a bushel: "If any man hath ears to hear, let him hear." He enjoins them to be careful in listening, for whatever justice you deal out, the same shall be dealt you. The man that has the truth, shall be given more; he without the truth has nothing, and even that will not remain.

17. JESUS GIVES PICTURES OF THE KINGDOM'S GROWTH (4: 26-34): Jesus tells of the kingdom of God (the imminent rule of God when man shall be in bliss again and regain his lost paradise) being like a rich harvest from a small seed, like a mustard seed which becomes a giant plant. He told all things in parables and then explained their meaning to his disciples.

18. JESUS SHOWS HIMSELF MASTER OF NATURAL FORCES (4: 35-41): On a trip across the Lake of Galilee there arose a great storm while Jesus lay asleep "on the cushion"; the disciples said, "Master carest thou not that we perish?" Jesus told the wind and sea to be still, and it was so. The disciples marvelled at this miracle, this power over nature, and wondered who Jesus really was.

COMMENT: Isaiah (6:9-10) indicates the blindness of the Jews to the meaning of parables, but the followers of Jesus shall not be made blind to their meanings. They alone shall obtain the mystery of the Kingdom of God. Actually, parables were common among the rabbis and their meanings were relatively easy to obtain. Certainly the parables of Jesus are beautifully simple and clear as to their allegorical significances. What is difficult is to ascertain just *exactly* what Jesus had in mind in many of his unexpounded parables. In v. 10 the people about Jesus request an explanation—and not the disciples. Was it actually the disciples who were a bit blind too? Elsewhere, too, we shall see more instances of disciple blindness to the message of Jesus.

CHAPTER 5

19. JESUS MEETS A VIOLENT LUNATIC (5:1-20): They reached the other side of the lake at Gadara (on the east shore). A man from the tombs, where he was living, rushed to meet Jesus. He was in the grip of a demon and could not be restrained by chains or fetters, for he would break them to pieces. All night and day he could be heard crying and cutting himself with stones. "What have I to do with thee, Jesus, thou Son of the Most High God? I adjure thee by God, torment me not." Jesus told the demons to come out of the tortured man, and when asked their name, the answer was, "My name is Legion; for we are many." Jesus sent them into a herd of 2,000 swine, who then jumped into the lake and all perished. The cured man was told to go home and broadcast in Decapolis "how great things Jesus had done for him: and all men did marvel."

20. FAITH IS FOLLOWED BY HEALING (5:21-43): Coming back to the west shore a certain Jairus, a synagogue president, begged him to cure his little daughter "at the point of death." In the crowd was a woman with a twelve-year hemorrhage ("issue of blood") who had spent all her money on doctors who had made her worse, not better. She touched Jesus' cloak, and realizing a drainage of power, he asked who had touched his clothes. His disciples inquire how could he ask such a question in such a jostling crowd. The scared woman, now cured of her "issue," confessed. Her faith had healed her, Jesus said. He called for Peter, James, and John (the brother of James) to follow him into the president's house, where there was a great hubbub and wailing. He scolded them for their wailing: "The child is not dead, but sleepeth. And they laughed him to scorn." He turned them out of the

house, and taking the father, mother, and his disciples where the child was, he said, *"Talitha cumi"* ("Damsel, I say unto thee, Arise."). The 12-year-old girl got up and walked immediately. He charged all to secrecy, and ordered that something should be given the girl to eat.

COMMENT: The four miracles: 1: The stilling of the sea storm, 2. the cure of the madman of Gadara, 3. the cure of Jairus' daughter, and 4. the cure of the hemorrhage. They are all wonderfully and beautifully told. The slight mockery of the disciples at the "silly" question of Jesus as to who had touched him in the crowd, and the order to give the newly-living child something to eat are only a few of the delicious touches. Mark is ever so much the better storyteller—simple, often naive, and filled with living detail that makes for great art.

21. THE "PROPHET WITHOUT HONOR" (6:1-6): Jesus came to Nazareth with his disciples and preached in the synagogues, but his reception was not good since they knew him as the son of a carpenter and Mary with brothers named James, Joses, Judas, and Simon, as well as some sisters. The townsmen were deeply "offended" with him. "A prophet is not without honour, save in his own country, and among his own kin, and in his own house," said Jesus. He could do there no great works because of their unbelief in him, and at this he was astonished.

22. THE TWELVE ARE SENT OUT TO PREACH THE GOSPEL (6:7-13): Here Jesus gives his disciples power over evil spirits: how to travel with nothing except a staff; how to shake the dust of the hostile host from their feet and leave. So they went out and preached a new life and healed many sick ones.

23. HEROD'S GUILTY CONSCIENCE (6:14-29):

John the Baptist had become well known; some even thought him to be the new-risen prophet Elijah of the O.T. Herodias wanted him killed for his opposition to her marriage with her brother-in-law Herod. Herod, fearing John for his righteousness and holiness, protected him. He used to listen to him, was disturbed, but nevertheless enjoyed listening to John. At Herod's birthday party with many high-placed people, the daughter of Herodias danced and the king was so pleased he promised her anything, even half his kingdom. At her mother's instigation she asked for John's head on a "charger" (wooden plate) and obtained it from the unwilling king. She presented the head on a "charger" to her mother. When John's disciples heard of this, they took up John's corpse and laid it in a tomb.

24. THE APOSTLES RETURN: THE HUGE CROWDS MAKE REST IMPOSSIBLE (6:30-38):

The apostles returned to Jesus and they left for a private place to rest, but the crowds followed. Jesus took pity on them and taught many things. They eventually got hungry, so Jesus told them to sit down in ranks of hundreds and fifties.

25. JESUS MIRACULOUSLY FEEDS FIVE THOUSAND PEOPLE (6:39-44):

Taking a mere five loaves of bread and two fishes Jesus was able to feed the five thousand in the crowd amply, even leaving twelve basketfuls of bread and twelve of fishes.

26. JESUS' MASTERY OVER NATURAL LAW (6:45-56):

Jesus went alone to pray while the disciples sailed for the other side to Bethsaida, but the wind stalled their rowing and the disciples were distressed. Jesus came to them walking on the surface of the lake and calmed their looks of fright at the thought he might be an apparition. He entered the boat and to their astonishment the wind stopped blowing, "for they understood not concerning the loaves, but their heart was hardened." They did not see who Jesus really was. When the boat reached Gennesaret, the people brought the sick on their very beds to him, and wherever he went they laid their sick in the marketplaces for him to cure. Many were cured by the touch of his garment hem, "and as many as touched him were made whole."

COMMENT: The failure of Jesus' teachings in his own home town reminds us of his earlier failure in Capernaum. Here the meaning is that Christian thought fell on no fertile soil among the Jews. The family touch points strongly to a historical incident. The instruction to the disciples to go out and preach prefigures their missions to the Gentiles. The story of John the Baptist's death is probably legendary, and its placement between the mission of the Twelve and their return is most unfortunately purposeless. Its sole aim seems to be a final disposal of the rival John the Baptist's following so that Christ's mission is left clear. The miracle of the loaves and fishes is purely symbolic and represents the holy Christian communion meal in which the body and blood of Christ represents spiritual nourishment. The walking on water miracle shows Jesus' power again over natural forces. The Gennesaret cures, etc., form a transition to the next section.

CHAPTER 7

27. JESUS EXPOSES THE DANGER OF MAN-MADE TRADITIONS (7:1-23): From Jerusalem came scribes and Pharisees who saw that some of the disciples ate without first washing their hands, which was against the tradition of the law laid down by the elders (custom). Jesus denounced them for following man-made traditions and not those of God, for they violate God's laws as to the treatment of parents. To the crowds he said that what enters a man's mouth cannot defile him: that which leaves, "which proceed out of the man" are the things that can defile the man. In the house with his disciples he explained the parable: anything entering a man from the outside cannot make him "common" or unclean because it doesn't reach his heart but passes out of the body, so that all food is clean enough. Whatever comes out of a man comes from his heart and mind, like veiled thoughts, lust, theft, murder, adultery, greed, wickedness, deceit, sensuality, envy, slander, arrogance, and folly. These make him unclean.

28. THE FAITH OF A GENTILE IS REWARDED (7:24-30): A Greek woman, "a Syrophoenician by race" (i.e., a Gentile), came to him and begged him to cure her daughter, but Christ refused saying he must take care of his children (the Jews) first rather than feed the dogs (non-Jews). When she replied that even the dogs eat the children's crumbs under the table, he said, "Go thy way, the devil is gone out of thy daughter," and at her home she found this so.

29. JESUS RESTORES SPEECH AND HEARING (7:31-37): A deaf man who could not speak intelligibly was brought to him. Taking him aside, Jesus put his fingers in the man's ears, "and he spat and touched his tongue" (put saliva on it) and said *"open"* in Aramaic (*Ephphatha*), and the man was cured of his deafness and speech defects. Again he charged the people not to tell, but they broadcast the news all the more.

COMMENT: The instruction on man-made traditions is given in rather crude terms in this one case, for example: the food enters the "belly, and goeth out into the draught (i.e., privy), purging (eliminating) all meats (foods)." The passage shows a breaking away from Jewish food traditions and scruples about food and a basis for newer Christian attitudes. The cure of the daughter of the Greek woman signifies that Christianity will spread without missionaries to non-Jewish lands, which actually happened. Nations unvisited by Jesus will nevertheless receive his blessing and spiritual cure—just as the girl was cured from a distance without the necessity of a visit by Jesus. The deaf-mute was cured in pagan territory (Decapolis) for an obviously similar symbolic reason. The cure of the blind man in Bethsaida (8:22-26) is a similar cure. One gets a vivid picture of the methods of magic-healing (exorcism) in the deaf-mute cure. The itinerary of Jesus is well-nigh impossible to follow and seems to follow no logical scheme whatsoever.

CHAPTER 8

30. HE AGAIN FEEDS THE PEOPLE MIRACULOUSLY (8:1-10): With seven loaves of bread and a few fishes Jesus again fills the hunger of a crowd of four thousand, with this time seven baskets full of food left over.

31. JESUS REFUSES TO GIVE A SIGN (8:11-21): Going into the boat again they forget to take bread. Jesus said to them (the disciples) to keep their eyes open and be on guard against the Pharisees' yeast and the yeast of Herod! The disciples got excited and Jesus called them dense, unable to understand and grasp what he had said, like people with unseeing eyes and un-hearing ears. He reminded them of the twelve and then seven baskets of food left over at the two fish-bread miracles: "And do ye not yet understand?"

32. JESUS RESTORES SIGHT AND PETER'S INSPIRED ANSWER (8:22-31): At Bethsaida he took a blind man apart and spat on his eyes and put his hands on him and cured him. He sent him away to his home, enjoining him not to enter the village. On the way to the village of Caesarea Philippi (Gentiles ruled by Rome) he asked his disciples about the rumors of his identity. They told him that some say he is John the Baptist; others that he is Elijah the O.T. prophet. But when asked who they thought he was, Peter answered "Thou art the Christ (i.e., Messiah)." Jesus enjoined them to tell no one of himself.

33. JESUS SPEAKS OF THE FUTURE AND OF THE COST OF DISCIPLESHIP (8:32-38): Jesus said to the people and his disciples that to follow him they must deny themselves and take up the cross. He who loses his life for Jesus' sake and the gospel's will not lose it but save it. He who is ashamed of Jesus and his words "in this adulterous and sinful generation, the Son of man also shall be ashamed of him, when he cometh in the glory of his Father with the holy angels." Some of the disciples

will not even die, at least not before the arrival of the kingdom of God.

COMMENT: The second miracle of the loaves is a duplicate of the first one. Its purpose may be a symbol of the Christian communion rite. The twelve baskets signifies Israel and corresponds to the Twelve who first governed the early Jewish-Christian community in Jerusalem after the crucifixion. The seven baskets corresponds to the group of Gentile believers in the Hellenist dispersion (cities other than those in Israel) governed by *seven* Church leaders. This indicates a late addition to the gospel of Mark. The sign asked for by the Pharisees to prove that Jesus is sent from God could be the sign of Jonah (resurrected from the whale's belly at the O.T.), a sign common in Christian belief. The scolding of the disciples (they are more harshly treated in Mark than in Luke or Matthew) for their stupidity in not understanding the meaning of the miracle of the loaves and fishes (they took it in the material sense of food-giving) is explained by the fact that the miracles mean Christian salvation through blessed bread (communion); a message easy enough for any Christian. Salvation is inexhaustible, just as the bread and fishes were! The cure of the blind man points to the opening of the eyes of the disciples and other believers. Mark, the germinal gospel, shows much evidence of later doctoring. Beginning with the confession of Peter in the true Christ, we have the second part of the gospel catechesis (religious instruction) known as the cycle of the Last Supper and Crucifixion. Note that the announcement is made publicly of the Passion (trial and crucifixion of Christ) and resurrection, which contrasts with his wish to keep his messiahship secret. The Son of Man redeems man by his death on the cross, saves man from damnation, and opens the possibility of paradise to him. Peter's density may reflect the Pauline (Paul, the writer of epistles in a time *before* the gospels were composed) dislike of the disciples—who were considered Judaizers—too much centered in Judaism for Paul's liking.

CHAPTER 9

34. JESUS FORETELLS HIS GLORY (9:1-13): Jesus brings Peter, James, and John to a high mountain and is transfigured before them—clothes and all became dazzling ("glistering") white, "so as no fuller (bleacher) on earth can whiten them." Elijah and Moses also appeared, and Peter said, "Let us make three tabernacles (shelters)" for the three, "for he wist (knew) not what to answer, for they became sore afraid." From a cloud came a voice: "This is my beloved Son: hear ye him." Jesus again enjoins them to secrecy until the time when the Son of man "should rise again from the dead." The disciples wondered what this "rising" meant. Jesus refers to Elijah and how the people did what they wanted to him and made him suffer.

35. JESUS HEALS AN EPILEPTIC BOY (9:14-29): A man approached Jesus from the crowd and told him that he had brought his son who had a "dumb spirit" (epilepsy) which made him fall and foam at the mouth, grind his teeth, and "pineth away" (wears him out). The boy was brought forward and the dumb spirit "tare" (convulsed) the boy terribly and he fell to the ground, wallowing and foaming at the mouth. The father said that often the boy was made to fall into fire or water, and he asked for pity on the boy. Jesus said that all things were possible "to him that believeth." Straightway the father of the child cried out and said, "I believe; help thou mine unbelief." The Christ rebuked the spirit, commanding him to come out, which the spirit did, "and the child became as one dead," but Jesus took him by the hand and the boy arose, alive

and well! When the disciples asked him why they were not able to cure the boy, Jesus said that this kind of spirit can "come out by nothing, save by prayer."

36. JESUS PRIVATELY WARNS HIS DISCIPLES OF HIS OWN DEATH (9:30-32): Jesus tells them he will be betrayed, killed, and will rise to life again in three days, "but they (the disciples) understood not the saying, and were afraid to ask him."

37. JESUS DEFINES THE NEW "GREATNESS" (9:33-37): At the house in Capernaum the disciples argue over which of them was the greatest disciple. Jesus took a little child into his arms and said, "Whosoever shall not receive the kingdom of God as a little child, he shall in no wise (way) enter therein."

43. ENTERING THE KINGDOM MAY MEAN PAINFUL SACRIFICE (9:38-50): When told of a man who cast out devils in Jesus' name, Jesus said that he who is not against them, is therefore with them. Beware those who were against them! They shall be cast into hell, "where their worm dieth not (decay never stops), and the fire is not quenched. For everyone shall be salted with fire . . . Have salt in yourselves, and be at peace one with another."

COMMENT: The transfiguration of Jesus in glorious light with only the three disciples as witnesses is a prelude to the glorious assumption of the Christ (God's Messiah) into heaven after the crucifixion. We already know the reason for the secrecy injunction. The denseness of the disciples is obvious here again. Peter's rather ludicrous offer to build tent-shelters for Elijah, Moses, and Jesus can be looked upon as an over-enthusiastic gesture of hospitality on Peter's part. The cure of the epileptic shows the power of true faith and the impotence of the disciples without that power. The description of the epileptic in the powerful, if primitive, descriptions of Mark is a masterpiece. Note the tenderness of Jesus in taking the child into his arms, and note too the vivid description of hell "where their worm dieth not."

CHAPTER 10

39. THE DIVINE PURPOSE OF MARRIAGE (10:1-12): Some Pharisees test Jesus while teaching to crowds by asking him whether divorce of man from wife is right. Man and wife are one flesh, said Jesus, and hence divorce is wrong. Later in the house his disciples question him on this matter. Jesus said that a divorced man who remarries is adulterous and the same is true of the wife.

40. HE WELCOMES SMALL CHILDREN (10:13-17): When the disciples chase children away, Jesus "is moved with indignation" and tells them that children are of the kingdom of God, "and he took them into his arms, and blessed them, laying his hands upon them."

41. JESUS SHOWS THE DANGER OF RICHES (10:17-32): A man kneeled before Jesus begging to know the way to "eternal life," and addressing him as "Good Master." To him Jesus said, "Why callest thou me good? none is good save one, even God." The man said he had kept the commandments of Moses on adultery, killing, stealing, defrauding, etc. "And Jesus looking upon him loved him," and told him to give his wealth to the poor and to follow Jesus. The man's face fell, for he was rich. And Jesus said it is hard "for them that trust in riches to enter into the kingdom of God." The disciples say they have given up all to follow him. The man who leaves family and home "for my sake, and for the gospel's sake" will be rewarded a hundredfold with eternal life, and even in this time (now) they will have many houses and brethren "and lands, with persecutions" (i.e., for being Christians).

42. THE LAST JOURNEY TO JERUSALEM BEGINS (10:32-35): Finally they are on their way to Jerusalem (the holiest of holy cities, where the Temple is located. Jesus walked on ahead of them while the disciples, dismayed and afraid of what lay ahead, lagged behind. Again he told them of his betrayal into the hands of chief priests and scribes (the chief priests head the temple administration and chief law bodies of the temple—the Sanhedrin), who will condemn him to death and hand him over to the pagans (the Romans) "and they shall mock him, and shall spit upon him, and shall scourge him (whip him), and shall kill him; and after three days he shall rise again."

43. AN ILL-TIMED REQUEST (10:36-52): James and John begged Jesus for the favorite seats upon his right and left hand when the new kingdom came. Jesus refused, telling them they were not able to "be baptized with the baptism" that he had been baptized with, nor were they able to drink from his cup (suffer). They assure him they are able, to which Jesus agreed, but to sit on his right or left hand was not in his power to determine, "but it is for them for whom it hath been prepared." The other ten disciples were indignant at the two asking for special favor, but Jesus calmed them by saying that he who wants to be first among the disciples must first be the slave of all men, just as the Son of Man will give his life to set others free. On their way to Jericho (city in the lower Jordan valley) the son of Timaeus called Bartimaeus, a blind beggar, was sitting on the side of the road. He begged for mercy in spite of the rebuke of the disciples, and Jesus told him to rise and cast away his garment and come to him. "Rabboni (master), that I may receive my sight," he begged of Jesus. Jesus cured his blindness and Bartimaeus became his follower.

COMMENT: The early Christians were dead set against divorce, perhaps because they had attracted so many women to their standards. Equality for women was more or less a powerful impetus in the early Church. The unquestioning innocence and simplicity of children is required of the true Christian convert. The special favor requested by James and John reflects a tradition that in the new kingdom the disciples would each be ensconced in a special throne, making twelve thrones in all; naturally, the thrones on the left and right of Jesus would indicate superior positions. Note that in Matthew (20:20-28) the *mother* of James and John makes the request, thus softening the denigration of the two disciples. Matthew also omits "none is good save one, even God" (see 19:17). Note again Jesus' love for little children. Matthew even omits the (perhaps ignoble) detail of how Jesus shall be spat upon! Matthew increases the blind men to two instead of one, perhaps to magnify the miracle, and he omits the casting away of the garment (a vivid detail) and the springing up to Jesus. Jesus as teacher and the Christ and the founder of Christianity are beautifully reflected in Matthew, but Mark puts in the vivid *human* details that reflect reality—many such details are omitted in Matthew.

CHAPTER 11

44. JESUS ARRANGES FOR HIS ENTRY INTO THE CITY OF JERUSALEM (11:1-19): At the borders of Jerusalem near the Mount of Olives Jesus sends two disciples into the village to obtain "a colt tied, whereon no man ever yet sat." They find the colt, and when they say the Lord has need of it, they are allowed to take it. Entering Jerusalem, Jesus finds his way strewn with garments and "branches, which they had cut from the fields"—and he was cheered by great crowds: "Blessed is he that cometh in the name of the Lord: Blessed is the kingdom that cometh, the kingdom of our father David: Hosanna (God save him!) in the highest." Jesus entered the temple and drove out the money-changers, "and he would not suffer that any man should carry a vessel through the temple." Jesus called it the house of prayer "for all nations," which they have made a den of thieves. The chief priests and scribes now sought how they might destroy Jesus, for they were afraid of him. In addition, his teaching had captured the interest of the people.

45. JESUS TALKS OF FAITH, PRAYER, AND FORGIVENESS (11:20-26): The next morning Jesus was hungry and found a leafy fig tree bare of fruit, since it was the wrong season. "No man eat fruit from thee hence forward for ever" said Jesus, and the tree died immediately. To Peter he said all things were possible with faith.

46. JESUS' AUTHORITY IS DIRECTLY CHALLENGED (11:27-33): In answer to the chief priests, elders, and scribes as to the source of his authority (to perform miracles, teach, speak as a prophet, etc.), Jesus countered with a question as to the source of John the Baptist's authority. Afraid to give an answer, they said they knew not, so Jesus likewise would not give an answer.

COMMENT: The miracle of the fig tree is a symbolic act really (see Luke 13:6-9) and represents that the Jews in the very heart of Jewry will reject Christ, and he in turn will curse them, causing their death and rejection by others. The reference in his cleansing of the temple to not allowing the carrying of vessels has to do with the use of the temple as a shortcut—which the Talmud (religious law) later forbade (cf. Berakoth 9:5); this detail is not in Matthew. Jesus' use of rabbinical cunning in outwitting the questioners of his authority is interesting. Some scholars say that here is proof of a link between the sect of the Baptists and Christ's. Incidentally, Matthew also omits the phrase about the temple's being a house of prayer "for all the nations," as does Luke. The meaning is obvious—Christianity will be available to all.

CHAPTER 12

47. JESUS TELLS A STORY WITH A POINTED APPLICATION (12:1-17): Jesus began speaking in parables to his opponents. He told the parable of the vineyard, how the master rented it out to farmers who kept beating and killing the servants the master had sent to pick up the harvest: one servant, for example, was "wounded in the head, and handled shamefully." Even the master's son was killed by the greedy farmers. But the master of the vineyard will come and kill all the farmers and give the vineyard to others. When the opponents saw the meaning of his anecdote, they "left him and went away." In another trick question about paying tribute (tax) money to the Romans, Jesus saw through their hypocrisy, and taking a coin he showed Caesar's face on it (Caesar, Emperor of Rome) and said, "Render unto Caesar the things that are Caesar's, and unto God the things that are God's." The priests, elders, and scribes were struck with astonishment at his answer.

48. JESUS REVEALS THE IGNORANCE OF THE SADDUCEES (12:18-27): Then came the Sadducees (an aristocratic group of Jews who collaborated closely with the Romans), who deny the resurrection of the body, and they put a trick question to him: whose wife will a woman be in heaven when on earth she had married seven times? Jesus said in heaven there is no marriage, for "they live like angels in heaven."

49. THE MOST IMPORTANT COMMANDMENTS (12:28-34): In another trick question he is asked by a scribe which commandment of Moses comes first, and Jesus replied that to love the Lord entirely "with all thy strength" and to love thy neighbor as thyself are number one and two in importance. Thenceforth, no man dared ask him any more trick questions.

50. JESUS CRITICIZES THE SCRIBES' TEACHING AND BEHAVIOR (12:35-44): The common people listened gladly to Jesus' teachings in the temple, and he told them to beware of the scribes who like to parade in their long robes and strut about; yet they grow fat on the property of widows and cover up their sins with prayers in public. They shall be punished more! Then Jesus watched the people dropping money into the almsbox. Rich people put in large sums, but a poor widow could only put in a nickel ("two mites"). Jesus told his disciples she had put more in the box than all the others, for she had given away everything, even her whole living!

COMMENT: The parable of the wicked husbandmen is a short apocalyptic story (the end of the world is coming, a new judgment by God, etc.) and signifies the fall of Jerusalem (the wicked farmers are killed), new farmers (pagans will be made Christians) will be given the vineyard, and Jesus will rise. The tribute money to Caesar was inserted to show that the Christians were not Jewish Zealots (anti-Roman revolutionaries). The answer to the Sadducees, believers in non-resurrection, implies a mystical and incorporeal type of resurrection, a belief which later conflicts with Christ's own resurrection. The essence of Christianity lies perhaps in Jesus' statement to love God and neighbor. In an important reply Jesus shows that David was not necessarily the father of the Christ (Messiah), since David himself had addressed Christ, his supposed son, as "My Lord." This is told to show that Jesus need not have been the son of David, but surely he was the son of God—"he was Lord Christ, not by filiation to David, but became so by resurrection from the dead" (Loisy, p. 111).

CHAPTER 13

51. JESUS PROPHESIES THE RUIN OF THE TEMPLE (13:1-11): While sitting on the slope of the Mount of Olives facing the Temple, Peter, James, John, and Andrew asked him for signs of the new Kingdom. Jesus told them of such signs as wars, earthquakes, famines, persecutions of the disciples, the spread of the gospel. Not a single stone of the Temple will be left standing!

52. JESUS FORETELLS UTTER MISERY (13:12-20): Brother will betray brother, children their parents, the whole world will hate the followers of Christ. The judgment day will come suddenly, surprisingly, and without warning!

53. HE WARNS AGAINST FALSE CHRISTS, AND COMMANDS VIGILANCE (13:21-27): False messiahs will appear and false prophets—so the disciples must keep their eyes open! The sun and moon will darken, the stars will fall—then shall the Son of Man appear in the clouds with power and glory. Then Christ will send out his angels to summon the good from everywhere. The end of the world will happen during your lifetime! But no one knows the day, time, or hour; not even the Son— only the Father. Keep on the alert!

COMMENT: This apocalyptic discourse is based on a short Jewish apocalypse story some time before the fall of the city of Jerusalem in 70 A.D. All three gospels give special emphasis to the destruction of the Temple. The meaning is obvious. The Temple destroyed is Jewry; the Day of Judgment will be filled with great, unusual natural phenomena, and in its midst Christ will appear with angels to rejudge the living and the dead. Mark is vividly descriptive as to the suddenness of the onslaught

— without warning. The alertness warning meant to practice fervently the teachings of Christ in prepara- tion for the Day. Note that in such expectations, property, family, chil- dren can mean little.

CHAPTER 14

54. AN ACT OF LOVE (14:1-9): Now the chief priests plot to kill Jesus, but not during the feast of the Passover. While in Bethany in the house of Simon the leper a woman with a bottle of ointment of spikenard perfume, very costly, broke the bottle and poured the oil on his head. The disciples murmur at the waste, saying the money could have been given to the poor, the money amounting above "three hun- dred pence" (about $30). Christ said she had done well: she had anointed him before burial! He predicted the memory of this woman would never be erased, wherever the gospel is preached. Now Judas Iscariot, a dis- ciple, promised to deliver Christ to the chief priests; they were glad "and promised to give him money."

55. THE PASSOVER SUPPER PRE- PARED (14:12-16): Jesus sends two disciples into the city where they will meet a man with a pitcher of water; they are to follow him into the house in which he enters; the landlord of the house will show them a large upper room ready and fur- nished for the Passover supper. The disciples found Jesus had foretold correctly, and they made ready for the Passover supper.

56. THE LAST SUPPER TOGETH- ER: THE MYSTERIOUS BREAD AND WINE (14:17-28): While eating the Passover, Jesus said that one of them would betray him, "even he that eateth with me." It would be the one who is dipping his bitter herbs in the bowl at the same time Jesus is doing so. Such a betrayer, he said, is better off dead! Taking bread and wine and blessing both, he told them to eat and drink both, saying, the wine is the blood and the bread is the body of Jesus. He tells them he will drink no more wine "until that day when I drink it new in the king- dom of God."

57. PETER'S BOLD WORDS—AND JESUS' REPLY (14:29-31): Peter promises he will never lose his faith in Christ, but Jesus tells him before the night is over—before the cock crows twice—Peter will deny him three times (deny: = claim he does not know who Jesus is). But Peter vehemently swore: "If I must die with thee, I will not deny thee" and all the other disciples spoke in the same manner.

58. THE LAST DESPERATE PRAY- ER IN GETHSEMANE (14:32-42): In a place called Gethsemane (geth SEM uh nee) he is accompanied by Peter, James, and John to keep watch for him so that Jesus could be alone to pray. In his prayer he begged God to remove his suffering (i.e., his cup), but God's will comes first. Upon re- turning to the disciples he found them fast asleep; this occurred two more times—and after repeated warnings! "The spirit indeed is willing, but the flesh is weak" said Jesus . . . "and they wist (knew) not what to answer him." After the third time he tells them to continue sleeping, for the betrayers were at hand. But then he tells them to arise "and let us be go- ing: behold, he that betrayeth me is at hand."

59. JUDAS BETRAYS JESUS (14: 43-52): Indeed, Judas was at hand with an armed mob, and he kissed Christ affectionately, thus putting the "finger" on him. The disciples deserted him and fled, but a certain young man had his linen garment torn off, "but he left the linen cloth, and fled naked."

60. JESUS BEFORE THE HIGH PRIEST (14:53-72):

When Jesus is brought bound before the Sanhedrin, Peter follows and sits with the officers "warming himself in the light of the fire." Perjured testimony states that Jesus had threatened to destroy the Temple and in three days build another "made without hands." Jesus after some silence admits to the High Priest that he is the "Son of the Blessed." He is condemned to death for his blasphemy. They begin to spit at and beat him and mock him. Meanwhile Peter denies to the maids of the High Priest that he knew Jesus—and the cock crew. In all, he made three separate denials before the cock had crowed twice. At this thought the repentant Peter wept.

COMMENT: For us the date would be the evening of the twelfth of Nisan (Jewish month), and Passover (Jewish feast celebrating the escape from Egyptian bondage) would fall on the fourteenth of Nisan, which comes about the time of Easter. The high Priests and scribes wanted to arrest Jesus before the festival, since such action would have provoked the wrath of the people, especially on the day of holiness. Oddly, a scene of anointing is inserted in a meal that should have been the Last Supper; in this scene we have the disciples railing against the anointer, thus showing them again in a bad light. Mark indeed was no great admirer of the Twelve! Note that Jesus has to explain the mystic significance of the anointing to them. Note the slip of the writer (v.9) in saying her memory will be maintained wherever the gospel is preached throughout the world. This assumes Jesus already crucified, a written gospel, and a worldwide missionary, thus indicating a date sometime after the crucifixion! The Judas story is largely fictitious, largely legendary; for example, he could not have been one of the Twelve since the college of the Twelve was not initiated by Jesus. Are we to believe that Judas was to occupy one of the twelve thrones in the New Kingdom? Of course not. This simply means that the Judas legend is a later addition. The Last Supper of course forms the base for the Christian holy communion, with Jesus at his death to be man's redeemer from sin. In actuality the Last Supper might originally have been an eschatological one—the last one before meeting in heaven, as Jesus himself indicates. Peter's triple denial indicates especial dislike of that disciple, not to mention the flight of all the disciples at Jesus' arrest, and not to mention the thrice-sleeping Gethsemane disciples! Note the purely Marcan episode of the fleeing naked young man whose linen garment had been torn off. A tradition associates the man with Mark, the writer of the gospel—a way of signing his name.

CHAPTER 15

61. JESUS BEFORE PILATE (15:1-2):

Jesus is brought bound before Pontius Pilate for judgment, who marvelled at his silence in the face of charges of kingly ambitions; the people demand Barabbas "lying bound with them that had made insurrection, men who in the insurrection had committed murder" be given his freedom instead of Jesus. Indeed, stirred up by the chief priests, they call for his crucifixion, and the unwilling Governor is forced to have him whipped (scourged) in readiness for crucifixion. The soldiers torture and mock him, smiting his head "with a reed," clothing him in mock royalty and then putting on his old garments again. Simon of Cyrene, "coming from the country, the father of Alexander and Rufus," is compelled to bear the cross destined for Jesus.

62. THE CRUCIFIXION (15:22-41):
Jesus is brought to Golgotha, offered wine mingled with bitter myrrh (which he rejects), and is crucified. His garments are divided after the soldiers cast lots for them, and a superscription over his head reads THE KING OF THE JEWS. Two robbers are also crucified, one on his right and one on his left. He is mocked and told to come down from the cross if he is the Christ; even the robbers "reproached him." At the ninth hour (3:00 P.M.) Jesus cried out, "My God, my God, why hast thou forsaken me?" and died; and when the centurion (Roman captain) saw his noble death, he

said, "Truly this man was the Son of God." The women looking on from afar are Mary Magdalene, Mary the mother of James the Less and of Jesus, and Salome, "who, when he was in Galilee, followed him, and ministered unto him," and there were many other women, who had previously followed him to Jerusalem.

63. THE BODY OF JESUS IS REVERENTLY LAID IN A TOMB (15:42-47):
In the evening of the same day, the day before the sabbath, Joseph of Arimathea, "a councillor of honourable estate, who also himself was looking for the kingdom of God," boldly asked for Jesus' body from Pilate. Pilate, surprised that Jesus was already dead, called the centurion on the length of time Jesus had been dead. When told (about three hours) he "granted the corpse to Joseph," who took him (Jesus) down from the cross, wrapped him in linen, and laid him in a rock-hewn tomb with a stone rolled against the door. Mary Magdalene and Mary, "the mother of Jesus beheld where he was laid."

CHAPTER 16

64. EARLY ON THE FIRST LORD'S DAY THE WOMEN ARE AMAZED (16:1-8):
When the sabbath was past, the three women bring spices to annoint the dead body; the hour is very early "when the sun was risen," and they were discussing how to move the stone before the door, but looking up they see the exceedingly great stone had already been rolled aside. Entering the tomb, they saw a white-robed young man sitting who said, "Be not amazed (astonished): ye seek Jesus, the Nazarene," the crucified. He told them that Jesus "is risen; he is not here: behold, the place where they laid him!" He tells them to tell the disciples "and Peter" that Jesus will see them in Galilee as he had promised them. They fled

from the tomb and said nothing to anyone out of fear.

65. AN ANCIENT APPENDIX (16:9-18):
Jesus first appears to Mary of Magdala, "from whom he had driven out seven evil spirits." She told what she had seen to the disciples "but they did not believe it." Later Jesus showed himself to two of the women "as they were on their way to the country." Still they were not believed. Still later Jesus appeared to the eleven disciples "as they were sitting at table" and he scolded them for their lack of faith in him and their skepticism of the women. Then he told them to go out to the whole world and preach the gospel. Those baptized will be saved, those disbeliev-

ing will be condemned. The believers will be able to drive out evil spirits "in my name," to speak with new tongues, to pick up snakes, to drink poison without being harmed, and to cure the sick by the laying on of hands.

66. JESUS, HIS MISSION ACCOMPLISHED, RETURNS TO HEAVEN

(16:19-20): After these words to the Eleven, the Lord Jesus was taken up into Heaven and enthroned at God's right hand. The disciples went out and preached everywhere, "the Lord working with them, and confirming the word by the signs that followed. Amen."

COMMENT: Note that Mark has Barabbas guilty of revolutionary activity, a Zealot very likely. Mark also adds the reed "smiting" and the details of Simon of Cyrene, "coming from the country, the father of Alexander and Rufus." Such details point strongly to the basic truth and historicity of Jesus, since, in a historical sense, the gospel of Mark is the most important of the gospels and the one upon which the others are based. In Mark the superscription differs from Matthew ("This is Jesus the king of the Jews") and Luke ("This is the king of the Jews"). The precise details of the two Marys and Salome are also pure Mark. Note the interest and importance of women in Mark. Joseph of Arimathea is merely called Jesus' disciple in Matthew but in Luke he is called "a good man and a righteous who had not consented to their counsel and deed, a man of Arimathea, a city of the Jews, who was looking for the kingdom of God." These differences in the synoptic gospels are part of their fascination. Only Mark mentions the spice-bearing Marys and Salome. The differences in the episode of the visit to the empty tomb among the three synoptic gospels are interesting: in Matthew "Mary Magdalene and the other Mary" behold a great earthquake and an angel came from heaven, rolled away the stone and sat upon it. In Luke two angels tell them Jesus is risen after the women have found the stone rolled away and an empty tomb. The gospel of Mark actually ended at verse 8: "for they trembled and were amazed: neither said any thing to any man; for they were afraid." The ending is abrupt. The so-called lost ending of Mark is still an almost insoluble research problem today. An attempt to supplement Mark (verses 9-20) is not in the original manuscripts, and its authorship dates from the second century. Amazing—but the gospel of Mark ends without a resurrection, the very scene for which the whole gospel is headed!

LUKE: A PREFACE

WRITER: Luke, called by Paul "the beloved Physician" (Col. 4:14), was Paul's frequent companion in his missionary journeys. Luke was a Jew of the Dispersion (not of Palestine, but a settler in some other Mediterranean area), and his polished and correct Greek indicates his non-provincial background. Tradition has it that he came from the cosmopolitan city of Asia Minor called Antioch.

DATE: Around 90 A.D. During this time the number of accounts (gospels) of Jesus' acts and sayings which, if taken along with the oral, memorized gospel still in use, "might well confuse the ordinary believer by their variety and differences" (Goodspeed tr., p. 128), multiplied greatly. Meanwhile, Christianity had spread over a large part of the Greek-speaking world with incredible speed. The new religion was threatening to overwhelm the old national cults and mystery religions so abundant throughout the Empire.

SOURCES: Mark's gospel, the oral gospel, a "proto-Luke" possibly, and one or two other sources. Luke follows Mark's order much more closely than did Matthew.

THEMES: Luke felt an urgent need to unify the varied and scattered accounts of Jesus' life and teachings as well as to enter into the written rec-ord the rise and spread of Christianity. The result was two volumes: the Gospel of Luke and the Book of Acts. The first, like Mark's and Matthew's, is a description of the life and words of Jesus Christ, and the latter is an account of the rise and growth of the Faith. Luke's work is filled with social, humanitarian, and historical interest, for much of our specific knowledge of early Christianity comes from him. He is literary-minded too, what with his prefaces, dedications, and accounts of sources. Hitherto men of Jewish blood had written of Jesus and the Church; we will now be treated to a man purely Greek in his instincts and pen.

DETAILED REVIEW AND COMMENTARY ON THE GOSPEL ACCORDING TO LUKE

CHAPTER 1

1. PREFATORY NOTE (1:1-4): This prefatory note is in the form of a letter addressed to Theophilus ("lover of God:" very likely a pseudonym; Thee OFF uh luss); Luke tells he has decided to trace the course of the events in the life of Christ "from the beginning" and to set them down in the proper order so that the Christian reader may have reliable information "concerning the things wherein thou wast instructed."

2. A VISION COMES TO AN OLD PRIEST OF GOD (1:5-25): Once there was a priest named Zacharias (in the days of Herod of Judea) whose wife was named Elisabeth, both of them "stricken in years," but good and just people. While in the temple burning incense Zacharias was frightened by the appearance of an angel who told him to fear not, for his childless wife would at last bear a son, "and thou shalt call his name John"; at whose birth there will be great rejoicing, "and he shall drink not wine nor strong drink; and he shall be filled with the Holy Ghost" (Holy Spirit). He will prepare the people for the appearance of the Lord. Zacharias mentions their old age and his barren wife, but the angel Gabriel afflicts him with dumbness of tongue (for his scepticism) until the appearance of the child itself. His wife did become pregnant ("conceive") as the angel had predicted.

3. A VISION COMES TO A YOUNG WOMAN IN NAZARETH (1:26-55): Six months later the same angel appeared in Nazareth to the virgin Mary, who was engaged to Joseph, descended from King David. "Hail, thou that art highly favoured, the Lord is with thee." The anxious girl is told that she will conceive in her womb, "and bring forth a son, and shalt call his name JESUS." The angel predicts greatness for the child, the son of God, who will be given the throne of King David (ruler of Israel) "and of his kingdom there shall be no end." The virgin wants to know how pregnancy will be effected since she has lain with no man, and the angel tells her that the Holy Ghost (God-Spirit) "shall come upon thee, and the power of the Most High shall overshadow thee." The angel tells her that her cousin Elisabeth is already in her sixth month of pregnancy; to which Mary replies, "Behold the handmaid (servant) of the Lord; be it unto me according to thy word. And the angel departed from her." Mary visited her cousin, and at Mary's greeting, the baby "leaped in her (Elisabeth's) womb." Elisabeth asks why the mother of her Lord has come to visit her and tells Mary how her baby still in the womb had "leaped" at Mary's salutation. Elisabeth predicts fulfillment of Gabriel's prophecy. In reply Mary said, "My soul doth magnify (this reply is often called the 'Magnificat') the Lord," and she predicts how all generations to come shall call her blessed. She tells how the Lord is merciful to all; how he scatters the proud in heart; how he has "put down the princes from their thrones"; how "he hath exalted them of low degree" (social status); how he satisfies the hungry and sends the rich away with nothing. Mary stays at her cousin's for three months and then returns home to Nazareth.

4. THE OLD WOMAN'S SON, JOHN, IS BORN (1:56-80): Elisabeth's son is born and on the eighth day the child is circumcised (Jewish religious rite with all male children to this day). The neighbors say he ought to be called after his father, but she insists that he be called John. The mute father himself settled the dispute by writing on a tablet "His name is John." Instantly Zacharias could speak and he blessed God! "And the child grew, and waxed strong in spirit, and was in the deserts (countryside) till the day of his shewing (showing) unto Israel."

COMMENT: We do not know who this Theophilus was; perhaps he was some notable and wealthy Christian at the time. A few critics date this gospel from the second century for various reasons, especially from the linguistic and religious factors mentioned in the introduction. Here the largely legendary birth-stories are more restrained in their element of the marvellous so incredible in the Matthew parallel. There is more concrete and precise detail in Luke; the tone is more anecdotal and soft. The purpose of the birth stories here is to show that John the Baptist prepares the way for the Lord even to the timing of his birth, he being six months older than Jesus. Another purpose is to show that Jesus is born in a thoroughly Jewish tradition. The annunciation to Elisabeth resembles the incident in Malachi (3:1; 4:6); resemblances to scenes in births of Isaac, Samson, and Samuel are also evident. The annunciation (announcement) of Jesus' birth is one of the most frequently painted scenes in art. The visit of Mary who is pregnant to her cousin Elisabeth is a preliminary story to the later announcement of John of the coming of Jesus to baptism and the Messiahship. John recognizes the Messiah while still in his mother's womb! The Magnificat is imitated from Hannah's song in I Samuel 2:1-10. Zacharias' long blessing is often known as the Benedictus.

CHAPTER 2

5. THE CENSUS BRINGS MARY AND JOSEPH TO BETHLEHEM (2:1-7): The Emperor Augustus calls for a census of the population; this was when Quirinus was governor of Syria, and all were required to return to their birthplaces for registration. The pregnant Mary and her fiancé Joseph go to Bethlehem, the town of the house of David. Here Jesus is born and is wrapped in swaddling clothes and laid in a manger "because there was no room for them in the inn."

6. A VISION COMES TO SHEPHERDS ON THE HILLSIDE (2:8-20): Shepherds watching their flocks of sheep see an angel standing by them clothed in light (glory). He tells them not to fear; he has good news, "for there is born to you this day in the city of David a Saviour, which is Christ the Lord." He tells them of the babe in the manger. Suddenly a heavenly choir sings, "Glory to God in the highest, And on earth peace among men in whom he is well pleased." Quickly the shepherds visit the babe and then return spreading the miraculous news.

7. MARY AND JOSPEH BRING THEIR NEWLY BORN SON TO THE TEMPLE (2:21-40): Jesus is circumcised on the eighth day and named Jesus, the name given to him by the angel. His parents visit Jerusalem to present him to the Lord (God) and offer as sacrifice to God two pigeons. Now a man named Simeon, upright and good, living in hope of the salvation of Israel (by a messiah), had been told by the Holy Spirit that he would not die before having seen the Lord's Christ (messiah or saviour of Israel). In the temple he saw Jesus and took him up in his arms and blessed God, saying that he had seen God's servant of salvation for the people, "a light for revelation to the Gentiles, And the glory of thy people Israel." He tells Mary that the child will cause the fall and rise of many in Israel, "And for a sign which, is spoken against; and a sword shall pierce thine own soul" (the crucifixion?). A prophetess called Anna, a widow for eighty-four years who stayed constantly in the temple praying and fasting, saw the child and gave thanks to God and told all how Jerusalem will be redeemed by him. Then Jesus, Mary, and Joseph returned to Nazareth. Jesus grew up strong and wise and with God's blessing on him.

8. TWELVE YEARS LATER: THE BOY JESUS GOES WITH HIS PARENTS TO JERUSALEM: Every year at Passover Jesus' parents went to Jerusalem. In Jesus' twelfth year they went, and when returning home they missed the boy. Three days later he was found in the Temple sitting with the religious teachers and asking them questions. His understanding and wise questions amazed all. He asked his worried parents, "How is it that ye sought me? wist ye not (did you not know) that I must be in my Father's house?" His parents did not understand what he had just said. He was obedient to his parents and as he grew in body and mind he also grew in his love of God.

CHAPTER 3

9. SEVERAL YEARS LATER: JOHN PREPARES THE WAY OF CHRIST (3:1-20): John the Baptist, son of Zacharias and Elizabeth, in the area around the Jordan river preaches baptismal repentance and washing away of sins. He is asked by the crowds what they must do to wipe out sin, and John tells the owner of two coats to share one with him who had none; the same would be true of food. To the tax-collectors (publicans) he said cheating is to be avoided; to soldiers he preached non-violence and non-graft and to "be content with your wages." They think John is the Christ, but he tells them of the greater might of Jesus, who will baptize them with fire. Herod arrests John for his criticism of Herod's religiously illegal marriage to Herodias.

10. JESUS IS HIMSELF BAPTIZED (3:21-23): Jesus is baptized by John in the Jordan and the heavens open; the Holy Ghost descends "in a bodily form, as a dove" upon Jesus and God says, "Thou art my beloved Son; in thee I am well pleased."

11. THE ANCESTRY OF JESUS TRACED TO ADAM (3:23-38): Jesus at the age of about thirty begins to preach and teach. He was the son "as was supposed" of Joseph whose genealogy goes back many, many generations, back to Noah, Adam and God!

COMMENT: Most of our Christmas and Easter stories come from the charming stories told in Luke. It is Luke who says there was no room for the Christ child in the inn and had therefore to be put in a manger. Matthew tells of the Magi led by a a star; Luke tells of adoring shepherds led by an angel. Simeon's joy is symbolic of a Jewish prediction of his reception by the Gentiles (the *Nunc dimittis* as it is called). Anna too functions similarly. John's teaching about sharing is missing in both Matthew and Mark. Luke's genealogy, unlike Matthew's, begins in the present and works its way backward to the original father, God himself! Women are not counted in genealogies generally, and the discrepancies and errors in the table have consumed much scholarly candlelight.

CHAPTER 4

12. JESUS FACES TEMPTATION (4:1-13): In the wilderness for forty days Jesus is tempted by Satan to command stone to become bread, to take over vast kingdoms, and to jump from the top of a temple. All these Jesus resisted, and the devil "departed from him for a season."

13. JESUS BEGINS HIS MINISTRY IN GALILEE (4:14-30): Jesus preaches in Galilee and finally in his hometown of Nazareth he teaches in the synagogue and reads from Isaiah 61:1-2: "The Spirit of the Lord is upon me / Because he appointed me to preach good tidings (= the gospel) to the poor"; and Jesus closed the book and sat down telling the congregation that "Today hath this scripture been fulfilled in your ears." The people asked if this were not really only Joseph's son. Jesus tells them they will no doubt ask him to heal his own self ("Physician, heal thyself"), and require the same healing miracles of Jesus that he had effected elsewhere. But no prophet is acceptable to his own countrymen, says Jesus, and he tells of the days of the great prophet Elijah when in a three-and-a-half-year drought there was great famine and many widows in Israel, "but Elijah was not sent to any of them." In the prophet Elisha's time one Naaman the Syrian was healed of leprosy. The crowd got furious and drove Jesus out of town, even threatening to throw him down from a high cliff, but he walked straight through the crowd and went on his way.

14. JESUS HEALS IN CAPERNAUM (4:31-41): In the city of Capernaum in Galilee he cured a man of an unclean spirit (illness). The devil causing the illness had thrown the man down in the midst of the crowd while coming out of the man. Jesus' authority and powers of curing amazed all in that region. He cured Simon's mother-in-law of the fever, and made many other cures, the devils always recognizing in Jesus the Son of God; but Jesus would rebuke the devils, telling them not to broadcast that he was the true Christ.

15. JESUS ATTEMPTS TO BE ALONE—IN VAIN (4:42-4): Jesus tells the crowds, who bar him from private prayer, that he must preach of the kingdom of God in other towns as well: "that is my mission."

COMMENT: This chapter is much like that dealing with similar cures in the other two gospels. The same is true of the temptations except that the order of the last two is reversed by Luke in order to bring Jesus back to Galilee instead of leaving him stranded in Jerusalem. The ministry of Jesus begins properly in Galilee and Luke adds the quote from Isaiah which states the Messianic program. The "physician heal thyself" parable seems forced and inapplicable in the instance in which Jesus quotes it. The prophet unacceptable in his own

country may refer to Jews who discard Jesus—the Gentiles know the prophet, the Jews do not. Jesus' miraculous escape has the thrill of an old-fashioned "cliffhanger" serial.

16. SIMON, JAMES, AND JOHN BECOME JESUS' FOLLOWERS (5:1-11): At Lake Gennesaret Jesus climbs aboard Simon's boat and teaches the crowds from there. Then he tell Simon to go out into deep waters and let down his nets. Simon complains of how all night they have caught nothing, but he lets down his nets and they came up so filled with fish the nets began to rip. Friends come and two boats are filled to the sinking point. Simon Peter falls on his knees before Jesus and says, "Depart from me; for I am a sinful man, O Lord," for he and the others (his partners) James and John, the sons of Zebedee, are staggered at the great haul of fish. To Simon Peter, Jesus says, "Fear not; from henceforth thou shalt catch men." They beach their boats and follow Jesus.

17. JESUS CURES LEPROSY (5:12-16): A leper fell on his face before Jesus and asked for cure. The man was cured and the news spread rapidly and great crowds came to Jesus, "but he withdrew himself in the deserts, and prayed."

18. JESUS CURES A PARALYTIC IN SOUL AND BODY (5:17-26): A paralytic ("palsy") borne on a bed was let down through the roof of the house Jesus was in (this because of the crowds). He forgave the sins of the paralytic (to the horror of the Pharisees and scribes), who then took up his bed and went home—cured! The crowd was struck with amazement and holy fear.

19. JESUS CALLS LEVI TO BE HIS DISCIPLE (5:27-32): Levi the tax collector (publican) left his office desk and followed Jesus who had

said, "Follow me." Jesus dined at Levi's house with other publicans and friends of Levi. The Pharisees muttered indignantly at his dining with publicans and sinners, but Jesus said the sick need the physician—not the well. So the same is true of sinners.

20. JESUS HINTS AT WHO HE IS (5:33-39): At the complaint that his disciples violate the fast, Jesus tells of the bridegroom who will be gone from them, at which time there will be days enough for fasting. Then two parables are told about new and old garments and new and old wineskins:

"new wine must be put into fresh wineskins."

COMMENT: The calling of the first four disciples is not related in Mark in this way. It is a vividly told tale, the import of which is the great spread of Christianity via the apostles, chief of which, as we see, will be Simon Peter, or just plain Peter. The cure of the leper, the calling of Levi, the question of fasting are all found in various ways in Mark and Matthew (for which see the Harmony table). The parables too are given fully in Mark and Matthew.

CHAPTER 6

21. JESUS SPEAKS OF THE SABBATH (6:1-5): Jesus' disciples pick wheat on the Sabbath and eat the grains, at which the Pharisees remind Jesus that this violates the law. Jesus illustrates from David's life and says, "The Son of Man is lord of the sabbath."

22. —AND PROVOKES VIOLENT ANTAGONISM (6:6-11): A man enters the synagogue with a withered right hand, and in spite of the Sabbath, Jesus cures him, telling his critics, the scribes and Pharisees, that it is lawful to do good on the Sabbath. "But they were filled with madness; and communed one with another what they might do to Jesus."

23. AFTER A NIGHT OF PRAYER JESUS SELECTS THE TWELVE (6:12-19): Jesus chose from among his disciples twelve select ones whom he termed *apostles*. Among the twelve were Simon the Zealot (revolutionary) and Judas the son of James, and Judas Iscariot, "which was the traitor." Great crowds came to learn and be cured, from "all Judea and Jerusalem, and the sea coast of Tyre and Sidon."

24. JESUS DECLARES WHO IS HAPPY AND WHO IS TO BE PITIED, AND DEFINES A NEW ATTITUDE TOWARD LIFE (6: 20-49): And Jesus preached a discourse on righteousness: the poor own the kingdom of God and are blessed; but woe to the rich, the full-bellied, the laughers—for they shall weep and mourn soon! Love and do good to your enemies, he told his apostles. Give to those who ask, and if stripped of goods, ask not for them back. Be merciful as God is; condemn not others and you will not then be condemned; "give, and it shall be given unto you: . . . For with what measure ye mete (weigh) it shall be measured to you again." The disciple is not like his master, but when perfected he shall be like his master. Each tree is known by its fruit; a house is no better than its foundations.

COMMENT: In the apostles' list Thaddaeus' name is absent here, although cited in Matthew and Mark. Judas the son of James is not mentioned in Matthew and Mark. The long sermon is a repeat (most of it) of Matthew's Sermon on the Mount.

The Beatitudes (Blessed are . . .) are followed by Woes (Woe to . . .). For the parable of the house on sand see the Harmony Table. Luke omits the Lord's Prayer, which is contained in Matthew's Sermon. Luke omits over half of the contents of the Sermon as seen in Matthew. Antithesis between gospel and Jewish law is seen Matthew's sermon, but Luke omits that part, since he is primarily interested in showing how Christianity *developed* and *extended* from Old Testament teaching.

CHAPTER 7

25. A ROMAN CENTURION'S EXTRAORDINARY FAITH IN JESUS (7:1-10): A Roman captain (centurion) sent Jewish elders to Jesus to ask that he cure his beloved servant who was ill; the master loved Israel and himself had helped build a synagogue for the Jews. Jesus cured the servant from a distance and exclaimed on the captain's great faith, greater than any he had found in Israel.

26. JESUS BRINGS A DEAD YOUTH BACK TO LIFE (7:11-17): In the city of Nain (NAH een) near Nazareth some people were carrying out of the town a dead man, "the only son of his (widowed) mother." Jesus told her to weep not and touched the bier, telling the dead young man to arise. The man sat up, began to speak. Amazement seized the crowd, who glorified God and called Jesus a great prophet, saying God had visited the people. The news spread wide.

27. JESUS SENDS JOHN A PERSONAL MESSAGE (7:18-35): John the Baptist sent two of his disciples to Jesus to ask if he is the one "that cometh" (the Messiah). Jesus answered by telling of his cures and of the good tidings he had brought to the poor. The disciples returned to John. Jesus says to the crowd, "Behold, they which are gorgeously apparelled, and live delicately, are in kings' courts"—but instead they had gone to see the prophet John. But John, although greatest of women-born men, "yet he that is but little in the kingdom of God is greater" than John. Men today are children who call John crazy and Jesus a bosom friend of tax collectors and the outsider. Wisdom is in the hands of children, says Jesus.

28. JESUS CONTRASTS UNLOVING RIGHTEOUSNESS WITH LOVING PATIENCE (7:36-50): A Pharisee invites Jesus into his house to dine. While there a sinful woman of the city, bringing with her an alabaster flask ("cruse") of perfume, weeps upon his feet and then dries them with her hair. Then she kisses his feet and perfumes them. The Pharisee tells Jesus she is a bad woman and in reply Jesus tells Simon the Pharisee a parable: A man cancelled the debts of two men, one owing ten times more than the other. Which loved the debt-forgiver more? asked Jesus. The one owing more, said Simon. So, says Jesus, this woman has washed my feet with her tears, kissed them, anointed them— all of which you did not do. Her sins are forgiven her, for she has shown me much love. He then forgives her sins, tells her her faith has saved her and adds, "Go in peace." Jesus keeps preaching the good news of the kingdom of God in the towns and villages, accompanied by the Twelve and Mary "the woman from Magdala" who had once been torn by seven evil spirits, Joanna, the wife of Chuza, Herod's agent, Susanna, and many others who looked after the men.

COMMENT: The cure of the dead youth is peculiar to Luke. Both John and Jesus are rejected; John who lived the ascetic life, and Jesus who came wining and dining with publicans and sinners are rejected, both of them. The captain's friends represent believing Gentiles. The incident is related to indicate that Jesus will not come into direct contact with Gentiles. The raising of the widow's son will prove to John's messengers that Jesus is the "one who cometh." That is why the story is where it is. The anointing sinful woman (Mary Magdalene?) is basically from Mark, but there are some delightfully typical Lucan touches. The mention of Mary Magdalene, Joanna, and Susanna prepares us for their appearances later at the empty tomb. The specificity of their names is again typically Lucan!

CHAPTERS 8-9:20

29. JESUS' PARABLE OF THE MIXED RECEPTION GIVEN TO THE TRUTH (8, 9:1-20): We have the parables of the sower, the disciples' request for an explanation, the double answers of Jesus. Also from Mark are the calming of the sea tempest, the cure of the demoniac of Gadara, the cure of the woman with the issue of blood, the raising of the daughter of Jairus, the mission of the Twelve, the talk in Herod's court on John's death, the miracle of multiplied loaves and fishes, and the confession of Peter (consult Harmony Table for parallels).

30. JESUS FORETELLS HIS OWN SUFFERING: THE PARADOX OF LOSING LIFE TO FIND IT (9:21-27): Jesus warns his disciples to secrecy and tells them of the son of Man, his suffering, his death, his resurrection on the third day. Men must give up all to follow Jesus. In losing one's life, one really saves it in God's kingdom. Men standing before Jesus will not taste death until they will have seen the kingdom of God.

31. PETER, JOHN, AND JAMES ARE ALLOWED TO SEE THE GLORY OF JESUS (9:28-36): (Transfiguration scene from Mark.) Luke adds that as Jesus was praying "the fashion of his countenance was altered." Moses and Elijah speak of Jesus' death soon in Jerusalem. Peter and John were asleep at first but awoke in time to see Moses and Elijah and Jesus.

32. JESUS HEALS AN EPILEPTIC BOY (9:37-51): A man from the crowd begged a cure for his only child, an epileptic "who suddenly crieth out," who foams at the mouth, and his evil spirit which bruises him sorely. Jesus cured the boy (see Harmony Table for Mark and Matthew parallels). Jesus told his apostles that he will be betrayed; they are to let the words sink in their ears. They do not understand him and are afraid to ask for more information. When they started arguing who was the greatest of the disciples Jesus showed them a little child and taught them how the least is the greatest (see parallels in Matthew and Mark).

33. JESUS SETS OFF FOR JERUSALEM TO MEET INEVITABLE DEATH (9:52-62): Jesus complains that the son of Man "hath not where to lay his head." He tells the man to leave the dead to bury their own dead and to follow him.

COMMENT: A significant omission is Christ's fiery scolding of Peter (see parallels in Matthew, Mark). This betrays an effort on Luke's part to soften the harsher portrait of Peter in the other two gospels. The same is true in the treatment of the disciples' reaction to the Transfiguration.

CHAPTER 10

34. JESUS NOW DISPATCHES THIRTY-FIVE COUPLES TO PREACH AND HEAL THE SICK (10:1-21): Jesus chose seventy disciples in couples to preach the new kingdom of God: "I send you forth as lambs in the midst of wolves." They get instructions on travel (see parallel in Matthew) and dress. A malediction is ready for those towns that turn the seventy away. They returned from their travels with joy and tell how they had power over devils. Jesus assures them nothing can hurt them, not Satan, serpents, nor scorpions: "but rejoice that your names are written in heaven."

35. JESUS SHOWS THE RELEVANCE OF THE LAW TO ACTUAL LIVING (10:22-38): Jesus tells of a certain lawyer who tried to trap Jesus with a question on eternal life: what shall he do to inherit it? In reply to a counter-question from Jesus he learns to love God and neighbor for eternal life. In another parable a man on the way to Jericho (JAIR' ih koh) was robbed, stripped, beaten, and left half dead. A priest, a Levite (special priests) passed him by, but a Samaritan (despised by Jews) pitied the man and took care of him. When the lawyer replied to a question that the one who took care of his neighbor the best was the Samaritan, Jesus said, "Go, and do thou likewise."

36. YET EMPHASIZES THE NEED FOR QUIET LISTENING TO HIS WORDS (10:39-42): On his way he was entertained by Martha and her sister Mary, who both sat at his feet. Martha is busy working while Mary sits listening to Jesus. Martha complains and is told that Mary has chosen "the good part, which shall not be taken from her."

COMMENT: Instead of Mark's twelve, Luke has seventy apostles on this mission; this symbolizes all the known world (*seventy* nations in the world; *twelve* tribes of Israel). The lack of Jesus' success in Galilee must indicate that Christianity was not too popular in that area. Note the success of the seventy after returning from their mission. The parable of the Good Samaritan is one of the most famous in Christian literature —the brotherhood of man. The story of the two sisters symbolizes the following: Martha = Judaism or Jewish Christianity, and Mary = the Gentile believer.

CHAPTER 11

37. JESUS AND PRAYER AND SENTIMENTALITY (11:1-28): Jesus teaches his disciples the Lord's Prayer and tells them of the friend who will help if earnestly requested to do so. "Ask and it shall be given you; seek, and ye shall find; knock, and it shall be opened unto you," he says to them. What man will give back a scorpion if asked for an egg? How much more then will God give of the Holy Spirit to those who ask of him? Then he cures a dumb man; following that he is asked by enemies to show some sign he is heaven sent. Jesus defends himself from the charge of being in league with the devil by telling of the strong man who is conquered by a still stronger one; hence, "anyone not with me is against me." A woman calls out what a blessing it would have been to have nursed Jesus as a babe; a far greater blessing is to hear the word of God and obey it, he answers her.

38. HIS SCATHING JUDGMENT ON HIS CONTEMPORARY GENERATION (11:29-32):

To the crowds he preached that this generation is evil! It wants a sign—but only the sign of the son of Man will be given them as Jonah's was to the Ninevites (O.T. prophet who reformed Nineveh). Now there is something more than Jonah's preaching!

39. THE NEED FOR COMPLETE SINCERITY (11:33-44):

No lamp should be hidden under a bushel; make the light in you bright: "therefore the whole body be full of light, having no part dark." A Pharisee asked him in to dine and saw that Jesus had not washed first before dinner. Jesus said not the outside of the platter and cup must be clean, but the inside. If one is clean within, all is clean. But woe unto the Pharisees who lose sight of God's love and justice and fret over petty things. You love the front seats in the synagogues and bow in public. You are like unmarked graves—men walk over you without knowing the rottenness underneath!

40. JESUS DENOUNCES THE LEARNED FOR OBSCURING THE TRUTH (11:45-54):

Alas for the experts in the Law, for you have taken away the key of knowledge, he tells them. You never have known things yourselves and still you prevent others from knowing. The scribes and Pharisees want more than ever to trap him. But Jesus denounces the pretense of the Pharisees. All private corruption will be exposed. He warns the disciples to be alert and on guard.

COMMENT: The tale of the importunate friend following the Lord's prayer sounds rabbinical in its tradition and seems to carry no particular point. Note Luke avoids the three days and nights of Jonah as in the other gospels. for he knows they do not tally with Christ's death and resurrection. In Matthew the great and vitriolic denunciation of the Pharisees is here reduced to dinner talk! The whole thing is watered down, as if Luke were attempting to show a greater interest in Judaic-Christian continuity than either Mark or Matthew.

CHAPTER 12

41. FEAR GOD AND BEWARE LOVE OF MATERIAL SECURITY (12:1-34):

Jesus teaches: the market price of sparrows is two cents, yet not one bird is forgotten in God's sight. Those who recognized the son of Man will be rewarded; others who do not will be disowned. He warns his disciples against covetousness by telling the parable of the rich man who hoarded and yet was not prepared for God. The good life is more important than daily food, the body, clothes. Set your heart always on the kingdom of God; sell what you own, give your money away. and store inexhaustible treasures in heaven.

42. JESUS' DISCIPLES MUST BE ON THE ALERT (12:35-59):

Jesus tells the parable of the faithful steward and the unfaithful steward. One must be ever on the alert for the coming of the son of Man! His coming is bound to bring division, father against son, etc. Intelligence should be used not only about the weather but the times in which men live. Learn to interpret the meaning of the times.

COMMENT: The feeling that the new age is imminent is so strong that the disciples must at any time in their own lifetime be ready to expect the end of the world and the coming of the son of Man to rejudge mankind and usher in the New Era of justice. Thrift and security are useless in such times: spend all the time you have in readiness for the Coming! The leaven of the Pharisees, the exhortation to proclaim the gospel boldly, blasphemy against the Holy Spirit, the promise of the Spirit's aid for persecuted disciples, the parable of the rich fool, the warning against concern for things of this world, the comforts of real treasure in heaven, the vigilance for the Judgment (comparable to the allegory of wise and foolish virgins), the simile of the night robber, the contrast between the good and wicked servant (comparable to the parable of the talents), the family divisions produced by the new teachings, etc., are all to be found in either Mark or Matthew or both. (See the Harmony Table for appropriate passages in the synoptics.)

CHAPTER 13

43. ON DISASTERS, ON SABBATARIANS, AND ON THE KINGDOM (13:1-31): Some people told Jesus how Pilate (the Governor of Judea) had mingled the blood of Galileans with his sacrifices. He warns them they are as bad sinners as the Galileans and will die just as miserable a death. He reminds them of the eighteen people at Siloam killed by a collapsing tower, and tells them they will die as tragically unless their whole outlook is changed! Jesus hints at God's patience with the Jewish nation in a parable of a man who had a fig tree which bore no fruit. He orders it cut down, but the gardener tells him to delay until it is manured, "and if it bear fruit thenceforth, well; but if not, thou shalt cut it down." Jesus rebukes the ruler of a synagogue for criticizing Jesus for making a cure of the doubled-up woman. Jesus denounces the ruler (i.e., president) for hypocrisy, since they release their oxen and asses to bring them to water on the sabbath. How much more right it is to help this woman doubled-up for eighteen years! His opponents were reduced to shame, but the congregation was thrilled. He compares the kingdom of God to a mustard seed and to yeast. Later when asked who is to be saved, Jesus replies that they may find them barred from the narrow door to the master's house. The master will chase them off the premises. Some who are sitting in the rear shall be seated in the new kingdom in the front.

44. THE PHARISEES WARN JESUS OF HEROD; HE REPLIES (13:32-35): Jesus is warned that Herod intends to kill him; Jesus replies that the "old fox" will see that in three days his work will be finished, and for that he must be in Jerusalem, a city for which he predicts woe, a city which is to see Jesus for the last time until *that Day!*

COMMENT: The slaughtered Galileans and the tower victims foreshadow the ruin of the Jewish nation! The fig tree allegory (see Harmony Table for the barren fig tree parallels) signifies that the Jews will surely die unless they accept the "manure" of Jesus' teachings. The cure in the synagogue signifies the salvation of the Gentiles, perhaps. The parables of the mustard seed and the leaven (see Harmony Table) signify the rapid progress of Christianity in the Roman world. The allegory of the narrow gate, the caution to those disciples that nearness to Jesus insures comfort in Heaven, the saying of how the elect will come from the four corners of the world to replace the Jews all hint at a wide popularity of Christianity, well on its way by the time Luke was writing his gospel—these stories are all eschatological in character (the coming Judgment stories). The lament over Jerusalem (there is no historical basis for Herod's threat) is a splendid peroration to the eschatology.

CHAPTER 14

45. JESUS AGAIN REBUKES STRICT SABBATARIANISM AND TEACHES A LESSON IN HUMILITY (14:1-35): At a Pharisee's house for a meal Jesus healed a paralytic (dropsy) and asked if it were right to heal on the Sabbath. He received no reply then, and no reply to his question whether they would rescue an ass or cow if it fell into a well on the sabbath. When he saw the guests choosing the best seats, he told them to choose the inconspicuous seats so that the host can graciously invite them into the best seats: "For every one that exalteth himself shall be humbled; and he that humbleth himself shall be exalted." Jesus told the host to invite the poor and the lame to his meals and he shall be blessed, "for thou shalt be recompensed in the resurrection of the just." He told a guest the parable of the man who made a great supper, but when the guests made excuses, the furious host invited the poor and lame to the meal and even the hedge-thieves: "For I say unto you, that none of those men which were bidden shall taste of my supper." Later great crowds followed Jesus, and he told them sacrifice of family and comfort is necessary for his followers. Which of them would build a tower without first counting the cost? What king will fight a war without first planning the strategy and size of his forces? Unseasoned salt (flavorless salt) is fit neither for land nor dunghill. "So, therefore whosoever he be of you that renounceth not all that he hath, he cannot be my disciple."

COMMENT: Sometimes Luke becomes incoherent in his jostling of stories: we have here a sabbath story woven around an argument (verse 3) without symbolic background, etc. Advice about behavior at a feast is turned into allegory not quite appropriate to the original intent. The parable of the great supper means that the poor and disinherited of this world will be saved, as well as the pagan, but pompously conceited Jews will perish!

CHAPTER 15

46. JESUS SPEAKS OF THE LOVE OF GOD FOR "THE LOST" (15: 1-32): In answer to the criticism that he dines with sinners, Jesus tells the parable of the man who owned a hundred sheep, lost one, and left the ninety-nine to find the lost sheep, which is finally brought home with great joy! Heaven, too, shows more joy at the reformation of one sinner than over ninety-nine righteous people who have no need of repentance.

He tells the parable of the woman who had lost one of ten silver coins she had owned. And lastly he tells the parable of the Prodigal Son: a man with two sons divides his property between them; the younger squanders his property in a foreign land and is forced to eat with pigs during a famine. He is finally contrite and decides to return home. While still some distance off, his father runs up to him to embrace him, while the son begs his forgiveness. The father orders a huge celebration, fine clothes, and food for the lost prodigal. When the good elder son hears that his younger prodigal brother has returned and is being treated with the fatted calf, etc., he becomes furious and tells his father of his many years of good service. "Son, thou art ever with me, and all that is mine is thine. But it was meet (proper) to make merry and be glad: for this thy brother was dead, and is alive again; and was lost, and is found."

COMMENT: The three parables of divine mercy and forgiveness (the one on the lost drachma seems weak) are Jesus' defense against the Pharisees. The jealous elder brother may represent Christian Jews jealous of pagan converts.

CHAPTER 16

47. A CLEVER ROGUE, AND THE RIGHT USE OF MONEY (16:1-17): Jesus tells his disciples the story of the unrighteous steward: the steward of a certain rich man is about to be fired for inefficiency and waste, whereupon the steward very cleverly reduced debts owed his master by half so that all debts were immediately paid off. "And his lord commended the unrighteous steward because he had done wisely: for the sons of this world are for their own generation wiser than the sons of light." He tells them to gain friends "by means of the mammon (greed) of unrighteousness; that, when it shall fail, they may receive you into the eternal tabernacles." After he told them that one cannot serve God and mammon, the greedy Pharisees scoffed. Such greed is an abomination in heaven; every man enters the kingdom of God violently!

48. JESUS SHOWS THE FEARFUL CONSEQUENCES OF SOCIAL INJUSTICE (16:18-31): Jesus tells the story of the beggar Lazarus and the rich man: Lazarus, covered with sores and fed from scraps of the tables of the rich, his sores licked by dogs, dies before a rich man's gate and is carried into heaven ("Abraham's bosom"). The rich man dies and goes to hell ("Hades") and is tormented. From there he glimpses Lazarus embraced by Abraham (the first great Jewish patriarch) in heaven and begs) that Lazarus be sent down so "that he may dip the tip of his finger in water, and cool my tongue; for I am in anguish in this flame!" Abraham tells that on earth the rich man had all the good things, but now the situation is reversed; besides, the gulf separating them is impassable. The rich man then asked that Lazarus be sent to warn his brothers about hell. "They have Moses and the Prophets; let them hear them."

COMMENT: Jesus' advice to use tainted money to make friends as in the case of the steward is decidedly immoral, his worst parable—and inappropriate! Next to it is one of the most beautiful and touching of all parables; his sympathy for the poor and hostility to the rich is an outstanding trait in Luke. The fact that the gospel is the fulfillment of the

Jewish Law is what this parable really teaches, besides telling us of the eternal happiness of the poor and the everlasting torment of the rich. The brothers of Lazarus are also unable to see Moses and the Law fulfilled in Christ: hence, heaven is unattainable to them. See the resurrection of Lazarus in John (11:1-46) for a different treatment.

CHAPTER 17

49. JESUS WARNS HIS DISCIPLES ABOUT SPOILING THE SPIRIT OF THE NEW KINGDOM; WORK IN THE KINGDOM (17:1-10): Jesus teaches forgiveness and faith. He illustrates a teaching by telling of the servant coming in from work on the farm, who is given a series of tasks instead of being bidden to eat. It is the same with the disciples: "when ye shall have done all the things that are commanded you, say, We are unprofitable (not much good as) servants," and have done our duty.

50. JESUS HEALS TEN MEN OF LEPPROSY: ONLY ONE SHOWS HIS GRATITUDE (17:11-19): They meet ten lepers crying for mercy and Jesus cures them. One of the lepers who was cured glorified him and thanked him, even falling on his face at his feet. He was a Samaritan, and Jesus praises him who, unlike the nine who had left, returned to give glory to God.

51. THE KINGDOM NOW AND IN THE FUTURE (17:20-37): Jesus tells the Pharisees that the kingdom of God is "within you." Then to his disciples he said they shall expect to see the day of Judgment, but like the days of Noah and Lot there will be destruction of the evil ones and the sinners, and the Day will come unexpectedly: two men in one bed—one will be taken to God, the other left.

COMMENT: In teaching forgiveness the number seven means really an infinite number, and *brother* means all mankind. The story of the grateful Samaritan is still another example of how an outcast shows more humanity than the other nine men (very probably meant to be all Jews). The Kingdom of God being within you signifies inward peace, content, and spiritual harmony—a very popular thesis with preachers nowadays, but the following passages contradict this psychological definition by picturing a specific day of the coming of Christ, bringing with it peace, justice, and happiness to the virtuous livers and destruction for the evil-doers.

CHAPTER 18

52. JESUS ON PRAYER AND THE SELF-RIGHTEOUS (18:1-17): Jesus tells the parable of the judge and the persistent widow who annoyed the judge so that he finally took over her case and rendered his judgment in her favor to be rid of her. But God will dispense *true* justice to his chosen who are persistent in his worship. "Howbeit (yet) when the Son of man cometh, shall he find faith on the earth?" To some people who thought they were righteous (proud and contemptuous of others) he tells the parable of the Pharisee and the publican. The former preened himself on his unlikeness to the unjust, the extortioner, the adulterer, and the publican. The publican in his turn was humble and asked for mercy as a sinner. He is more holy in God's eyes than the Pharisee "for every one that exalteth (who sets himself up as "somebody") himself shall be humbled; but he that humbleth himself shall be exalted." When little children are brought to Jesus, he teaches that to enter the kingdom of God one must be like a child in attitude and mind.

53. JESUS AND RICHES: A FORECAST (18:18-34): Jesus tells a rich man to give to the poor, but he is unwilling to give all. He foretells his death and resurrection to the non-comprehending disciples. Finally, in Jericho he encounters a blind beggar and cures him.

COMMENT: The story of the widow and the judge has the same unethical import as the story of the importunate friend. Nagging persistence, however unethical, seems to win God's favor! The parable of the Pharisee and the publican contrasts Christian humility (Gentile publican) with Judaic incredulity and stubborn refusal to accept the true Christ. The rest of the chapter is already available in Matthew and Mark, for which see the Harmony Table.

CHAPTER 19

54. ZACCHEUS; A PARABLE ON THE USE OF GIFTS (19:1-28): In Jericho Jesus met Zaccheus, a rich publican, short of stature, who was forced to climb a sycamore tree in order to get a good look at Jesus. When Jesus saw him up there, he said, "Zaccheus, make haste, and come down; for to-day I must abide at thy house." Zaccheus tells Jesus how he gave half his goods to the poor, and restored extorted sums fourfold. Jesus promised him salvation, "For the Son of man came to seek and to save that which was lost." He related the parable of the ten servants who were given ten dollars each to invest and use well. All did well except one who presented the king, his master, with the original ten dollars, "which I kept laid up in a napkin (handkerchief)." The king condemned the servant for not having put the money to good use as the others had; he was forced then to give his money to the more investment-wise servant. "Everyone that hath shall be given; but from him that hath not, even that which he hath shall be taken away from him."

55. JERUSALEM AT LAST (19:29-48): Jesus gives his disciples orders on how to obtain the colt for his entry into Jerusalem. He makes a triumphant entry, but later he weeps at the thought of the city's future destruction as a result of its not having accepted the Christ. He then drives the money-changers out of the temple.

COMMENT: The lament over Jerusalem is vividly related, as if Luke had written *after* the destruction of that city. Luke's parable completely transforms Matthew's parable of the talents (15:14-30), with its theme of divine retribution, into an apocalyptic (coming Judgment) allegory. The crowd listening to Jesus telling the parable of the ten servants were supposing that the kingdom was immediately to appear since Jesus was nearing Jerusalem, the place where many of the early Christians supposed that the Messiah would appear. Christ's weeping over Jerusalem replaces the blasted fig-tree story in Mark; the replacement is not accidental.

CHAPTERS 20-21

56. JESUS TELLS A POINTED STORY (20:1-26): Jesus is questioned by the chief priests, scribes (lawyers of the Law), and elders as to the source of his authority in teaching, but he outwits them with a counter-question. He then tells them the parable of the wicked husbandmen who slew both the servants and the son of the landowner. The Pharisees try to trick Jesus on the paying of taxes, but he outwits them by displaying a coin, pointing to the face on it and saying "Render unto Caesar the things that are Caesar's," and unto God his things. This leaves his enemies nonplussed.

57. JESUS EXPOSES THE IGNORANCE OF THE SADDUCEES (20: 27-47) (21:1-37): Jesus says that the widow who cast two cents into the temple treasury did more than the wealthy. Again he predicts the destruction of the temple; of war, earthquakes, plagues, which shall be a sign of the coming of the son of Man again. The disciples will be persecuted in Christ's name—but they must have patience in order to win heaven. They must be alert and ready at all times for the Coming. Every morning Jesus preaches to the people of Jerusalem in the Temple.

CHAPTER 22

58. JUDAS ISCARIOT (22:1-30): "And Satan entered into Judas who was called Iscariot"; and the betrayer communed with the chief priests and captains, how he could "put the finger on" Jesus. They were glad and covenanted (arranged) to give him money. Judas sought an opportunity to betray Jesus when there was no crowd present. Jesus sends Peter and John to arrange the Passover meal, at which meal he tells his disciples how he has desired to eat this meal with them before he shall "suffer." He takes the cup of wine and tells them to divide it amongst them: "I will not drink of the fruit of the vine, until the kingdom of God shall come." He broke bread and gave it to them, calling it his body "which is given for you: this do in remembrance of me." After supper he took the cup, saying, "This cup is the new covenant in my blood, even that which is poured out for you." The hand of his betrayer was with him on the table; Jesus then predicted woe to his betrayer. The

disciples dispute as to which of them is the greatest, and Jesus teaches them that the greatest must act the most humbly. He tells them they have stood by him in all that he has gone through, and as surely as God has given the Kingdom to Jesus, so as surely will Jesus give his disciples the right to eat and drink at his table in that kingdom: "and ye shall sit on thrones judging (ruling) the twelve tribes (Israel was thought to have arisen from the descendants of twelve brothers) of Israel."

59. SIMON PETER; ARREST AND CAPTURE OF JESUS (22:31-54): Peter vows he will face death and prison before failing Jesus, but Jesus predicts thrice-betrayal. He tells them swords are necessary now, at which they present him with two swords. "That is enough," Jesus says. On the Mount of Olives he prays in agony so that his sweat was like falling blood, only to return to find the disciples sleeping out of sheer grief. "Rise and pray, that ye enter not into temptation," he told them. A crowd arrives at that point, led by Judas, who steps out to kiss Jesus. "Judas, betrayest thou the Son of man with a kiss?" said Jesus to him. The disciples ask him if they could use their swords to resist, one of them even striking off the right ear of the servant of the high priest. "Suffer (endure it) ye thus far," said Jesus to them and touching the servant's right ear, he healed him. To the chief priests, captains of the temple, and elders out to arrest him he said, why carry swords and sticks as if he were an ordinary thief; "but this is your hour, and [this is] the power of darkness (evil)." And he was seized and led into the high priest's house.

60. JESUS IS ARRESTED: PETER FOLLOWS BUT DENIES HIS MASTER THREE TIMES; THE INTERROGATION OF JESUS (22:55-71): Peter followed his master from afar, "and when they had kindled a fire in the midst of the court and had sat down together, Peter sat in the midst of them." After the third denial that he had known Jesus, "the Lord turned, and looked upon Peter . . . and he (Peter) went out, and wept bitterly." Jesus is then mocked and beaten; then blindfolded and ridiculed. At the council in answer to whether he was the messiah, he replied, "If I tell you, ye will not believe: and if I ask you, ye will not

answer. But from henceforth shall the Son of man be seated at the right hand of the power of God." When asked if he is the Son of God, he replied, "Ye say that I am." No more witnesses are needed, claim his enemies, and he is brought before Pilate, the Governor of Judea.

COMMENT: In proto-Luke (the early Luke version) the last meal was not probably the paschal (Passover or Easter) meal but a kind of last meal before meeting his followers again in the new Kingdom, a kind of memorial supper to see the master off. Verse 32 indicates Simon Peter is perfect in faith, but later he proves imperfect. The two versions are in contradiction—one of the remarks being interpolated very likely. The scene in Gethsemane (39-46) omits Mark's hostility towards the three disciples. Interesting too is that the blood-sweat passage is omitted in certain manuscripts, seemingly a fact added later. Compare the arrest of Jesus in Mark and note Luke's correction of certain items. The small miracle of the restored ear is new to the gospels, and Luke does not have the disciples fleeing town, another softening of his attitude towards the disciples. New and starkly dramatic is the piercing look directed at Peter at his third denial, Jesus being present, and by that look arousing Peter's penitence.

CHAPTER 23

61. THE TRIAL (23:1-25): Jesus is accused before Pilate of "perverting" the Jews, "and forbidding to give tribute to Caesar, and saying that he himself is Christ a king." He stirs up the mobs he teaches throughout Judea, they said. Pilate, upon discovering Jesus to be a Galilean, sends him to be tried before Herod, the Governor of that province. Herod was delighted to see him, hoping to

view some miracle, but Jesus remained silent to all questions. He is mocked, arrayed in gorgeous clothes, and returned to Pilate. From then on Herod and Pilate are fast friends, whereas they had formerly been enemies. Pilate can find no fault in Jesus; he is not guilty as charged; nor did Herod find fault in Jesus, since he had sent Jesus back to Pilate. Therefore he is to be merely chastised (taught a sharp lesson) and released. The people call for the release of Barabbas: "one who for a certain insurrection made in the city, and for murder, was cast into prison." In spite of Pilate's protests, the mob yells, "Crucify, crucify him!" A third time Pilate goes through the same plea and receives the same reply from the hostile crowd. So Barabbas is released and Jesus is to be crucified.

62. CRUCIFIXION (23:26-56): Simon of Cyrene, "coming from the country," was made to bear the cross after Jesus. Great crowds followed him, especially weeping and lamenting women. To them Jesus said, "Daughters of Jerusalem, weep not for me, but weep for yourselves, and for your children." For much harm and destruction is to befall the city. On a place called "The Skull" they crucified Jesus between two criminals ("malefactors"), and Jesus said, "Father, forgive them; for they know not what they do." They cast lots for his clothes after this. The soldiers mock him, offering him vinegar, and telling him to save himself. Above his head a sign: THIS IS THE KING OF THE JEWS. One of the crucified criminals rails at Jesus, saying, "Save thyself and us." The other rebukes the railer, saying, "Dost thou not even fear God" seeing that you are in the same condition. He adds they are justly punished for their evil deeds, "but this man hath done nothing amiss." And he asked Jesus to remember him when he should come into his Kingdom. "Verily I say unto thee, To-day shalt thou be with me in Paradise" was Jesus' reply to the "good" criminal. The sky darkens, the veil of the Temple is rent, and with a loud voice Jesus cries, "Father, into thy hands commend my spirit," and dies on the cross. The onlooking Roman captain (centurion) saw what had happened and said, "Certainly this was a righteous man." All the crowds looking on beat their breasts in sorrow, and all his followers to Jerusalem from Galilee, and the women too, "stood afar off, seeing these things." Joseph, a good man who "had not consented to their (high priests') counsel and deed, of Arimathea (AIR ih muh THEE ah), "who was looking for the kingdom," asked Pilate for the body of Jesus. The body is taken down, wrapped, and laid in a tomb hewn from stone, "where never man had yet lain." The Galilean women saw this, and returned to prepare burial spices and ointments. On the next day they rested (the sabbath) according to the Law.

COMMENT: The completely unnecessary trial of Jesus before Herod (only in Luke) might be an attempt to lay responsibility for Jesus' death in Herod's lap. See the gospel of Peter (apocryphal = outside the canon) for direct blame of Herod. Luke is very strong and over-insistent in indicating Pilate's innocence and sympathy. Luke shows Pilate passing a sentence of death as the product of Jewish venom and hate. The crucifixion details do not differ much from Mark, but note the centurion's change from "this was the Son of God" in Mark to "righteous man" in Luke. Other differences from the other gospels: the women of Jerusalem prophesy, insults of the "bad" criminal, praise for the "good" criminal, (note he says they will pass into Paradise—not the tomb, not Hades; Jesus says the same), Jesus' last words, less harsh than in the other gospels of Mark and Matthew, the great number of witnesses and their mourning, the woe of the women (see Zechariah 12). The whole picture is more pathetic, more vivid and striking in Luke—if a bit over-sentimental. We must assume the disciples have been witnesses of the crucifixion too. For parallels in Mark and Matthew see Harmony Table.

CHAPTER 24

63. THE FIRST DAY OF THE WEEK: THE EMPTY TOMB (24:1-12): At dawn on the first day of the week they returned to the tomb, only to find the stone rolled away from the door and the two angels, who tell them that Jesus is risen. The women report the news to the disciples (eleven of them). Mary Magdalene, Joanna, Mary the mother of James, and other women had reported all this, but the disciples called it idle talk. Peter ran to the empty tomb and saw the linen cloths—empty, and he wondered at it all.

64. JESUS AND HIS DISCIPLES (24:13-53): Two of the disciples on their way to Emmaus (eh MAY us: 4 miles from Jerusalem), deep in talk over what had happened, are joined by Jesus in their walking, but they do not recognize him. He inquires on the subject of their talk, and the amazed Cleopas (one of the two) exclaims he must be the only stranger in Jerusalem who has not heard of what has happened. Jesus asks what has happened, and they tell him. After this recital Jesus explains how Christ should suffer and find his glory; he explains to them everything in the Scriptures that referred to himself. They invite him into the house for supper, and while sitting at table with them he took the loaf of bread, gave thanks, broke it, and passed it to them. They recognize him, but Christ vanishes from their sight. They discuss how he had made the Scripture so plain to them while on the road. They tell the story to the other disciples and their friends after they had hastily returned to Jerusalem. They tell them the Lord is really risen—"and hath appeared to Simon." Suddenly Jesus appears amongst them saying, "Peace be unto you." They are terrified at what they take to be a ghost. Jesus reassures them by telling them to look at his hands and feet, to feel him and see for themselves: "for a spirit (ghost) hath not flesh and bones, as ye behold me having." Jesus asks for something to eat and is given a piece of broiled fish, which he eats before their eyes. Jesus tells that all that is written in Moses, in the prophets, and in the Psalms must come true. Christ must inevitably suffer and "rise from the dead on the third day." They must proclaim his name to all nations, beginning with Jerusalem, and bring about a change of hearts of the people, which will lead to forgiveness of sins. He hands over to them the command "of my Father," and they are told to stay in the city until invested with power from God. Then he led them as far as Bethany, where he blessed them with uplifted hands, and while doing so, he "was carried up to heaven." The disciples spent their waiting time in praising and blessing God.

COMMENT: It is odd to see Luke putting in the mouth of Christ the typical system of Christian-theological-rabbinic demonstration by citing scripture! Nevertheless the Emmaus story is vivid, touching, and highly dramatic—full of theatricality. Why should the two disciples have said the Lord had appeared to Simon? Why not "to *us*"? There is confusion here indeed. The final apparition of Jesus at Bethany is also a confused story, crowded with incident, seemingly without connection between the incidents. Luke, who is also the author of the Acts, will introduce a wait of forty days before Jesus ascends, unlike this version where he ascends on the night following the morning of the resurrection. *Ascension* refers to the rising of Jesus into heaven after having appeared in the flesh to various people.

JOHN: A PREFACE

WRITER: A Greek Christian of Ephesus. A scholarly minority, slowly dwindling in size, insists that the apostle John was the author.

DATE: About 110 A.D., the fourth and last of the canonical gospels.

THEMES: The entire New Testament was written in Greek, but the synoptic gospels and the still earlier letters of Paul are basically very Jewish and hence provincial in their outlook. The largest public and the readiest acceptors of the Faith were the Greeks, and a gospel was needed to appeal to their tastes and sophisticated interests. Jesus is related not simply as the Jewish Messiah but as the Messiah to the whole world, its Light and Saviour. It is this Messiah that remains with mankind today: Jesus as Light, Life, Love, Truth, and Freedom is the Jesus of our churches. John the Theologian is "the Divine among the evangelists, and he did set Christian thought upon the rails on which it ran for centuries" (Goodspeed tr., p. 209). John is a mystic too; his Christ is essentially one of *inner* experience, a Christ of the heart, mind, and soul —an almost ineffable experience. But the human being, the gentle, kind, passionate, and even sometimes violent Jesus of the synoptics is missing here. John's gospel searches into the very mystery of Christianity with great insight, but the historical Jesus is lost in all this dazzling light. Needless to say, this gospel can not in any sense be "harmonized" with Mark, Matthew, and Luke—hence, its absence in the Harmony Tables.

DETAILED REVIEW AND COMMENTARY ON THE GOSPEL ACCORDING TO JOHN

CHAPTER 1

1. PROLOGUE (1:1-5): "In the beginning was the Word, and the Word was with God, and the Word was God." (At the beginning God expressed himself. That personal expression ("Word") *was* God himself. It existed with God from the very beginning of all things. He ("Word") is the beginning and source of all creation — no creation took place without him. In God was life itself, and this life was the light of all mankind itself. This light still shines and never has nor ever will be put out by darkness.

2. THE GOSPEL'S BEGINNING ON EARTH (1:6-18): As a witness to the truth of this light, a man called John was sent by God so that those hearing his testimony could then believe in the truth of the light (God). Now John was not the light himself, but he was sent simply as a personal witness to the holiness of that light. This light shines upon every man when he is born into this world. God came into the world himself (Christ)—into the very world he had created—and the world failed to recognize him. Even his own people (the Jews) refused to accept him; yet wherever he was accepted in the world, he gave them power to become the sons of God! These people who accepted "which were born, not of blood, nor of the will of man, but God" (their birth in God depended not on the course of nature nor on any impulse or plan of man, but on God). "And the Word was made flesh, and dwelt among us" (the word of God became a human being and lived among us = Jesus Christ). We saw his splendor—the splendor of the father's only son (Christ)—full of grace (mercy) and truth. And it was about this Light and Word become flesh (Christ) that John the Baptist stood up and testified, exclaiming, "This (Jesus) was he of whom I spoke, He that cometh after me is preferred before me; for he was before me." Indeed, we all have shared in his riches—there is grace in our lives because of his grace ("And of his fulness have all we received, and grace for grace"). For although Moses handed down the commandments and the Law, grace (i.e., merciful love in this context) and truth came only through Jesus. Although it is true that no man has ever seen God, yet his divine Son, who is most intimately close to God, has made God known to man.

COMMENT: This prologue contains within it the chief doctrines of the entire book of John. It very likely might have been at one time a fervid theological poem attached here as a "preface" or "prologue," for example. It is not a summary of the chief themes of the book but a profound and penetratingly thought-out explanation of the entire book. God = Logos or Word: a term taken from the Stoic school of philosophy (Greece from fifth century B.C.), in which it meant divine reason inherent in nature and man. In John "the universe becomes rational to men by the revelation of the divine creative principle in a truly human life . . . it (Logos) is both life and light. Grace means God's free and unmerited favor . . . nothing else than love in action. Wisdom and creative energy in one God are essential to the Logos." (Quotes from *The Interpreter's Bible*, p. 442). The Logos doctrine was spread widely by the

Philo, a Jew of Alexandria (30 B.C. -50 A.D.): the Word (God) = Logos = the intermediary between God and man. The Logos is "pre-existent, incarnate, rejected, yet revealer of God and giver of sonship to those who believe in his divine mission" (*I.B.*). Logos is eternal, fellowed with and in God, and is divine in God. More of these concepts will arise later in the text, at which time further clarification of various Johannine (referring to gospel of John) meanings will be attempted.

3. JOHN'S WITNESS (1:19-34): When "the Jews" sent priests and Levites (priests) to ask John who he was, he admitted with complete frankness, "I am not the Christ (Messiah)." They asked if he were Elijah or the Prophet—to which he answered negatively. "I am the voice of one crying in the wilderness. Make straight the way of the Lord," as Isaiah (O.T. prophet) had said. They then asked John why he baptized if he were not these people, and John answered that he baptized with water, "but there standeth one among you, whom ye know not"; "He it is, who coming after me is preferred before me." The next day John saw Jesus walking toward him and said, "Behold the Lamb of God, which taketh away the sins of the world!" And John bore witness to the fact that the Spirit abode upon him from above, "And I saw, and bare record that this is the Son of God."

COMMENT: Reference to "the Jews" shows an author not a Jew himself, and by the constant use of the term, revealing himself as implacably hostile to Jewry in general. Note that John the Baptist denies he is the Messiah for good reasons. The author is making sure that John witnesses to the true Messiah, Jesus, because historically there is evidence that Jesus was one of the baptized followers of John who later broke with him (see Goguel). Most important is John the Evangelist's omission of a baptism of Jesus by John the Baptist! The Spirit descending from heaven is a sign for John to recognize the Christ, but in the synoptics it is a sign of God's divine choice of Jesus while being baptized by John. Christ as Logos obviously would not need purification by water or remission of sins! The gospel writer finds such an action on excrescence and demeaning to the Logos-God-Christ concept he urgently preaches.

4. MEN BEGIN TO FOLLOW JESUS

(1:35-51): John the Baptist with two of his disciples sees Jesus walking along and says, "Behold the Lamb of God," and the two disciples hear this "and they follow Jesus." Jesus asks them, "What seek ye?" They call him Rabbi (Master) and ask him where he dwells. He tells them to come and see, and they do and stay with him. One of the disciples is Andrew, who seeks his brother Simon Peter and tells him of having found the Messiah. As soon as Peter is brought to Jesus, Christ says, "Thou art Simon the son of Jona: thou shalt be called Cephas (a stone)." The next day Jesus seeks Philip and tells him to follow also. In turn Philip finds Nathanael (Nah THAHN ah ell) who says to him, "Can any good thing come out of Nazareth?" And Philip says, "Come and see." Jesus on seeing Nathanael says, "Behold an Israelite indeed, in whom there is no guile!" Jesus tells him he recognized him "when thou wast under the fig tree." Nathanael calls him the Son of God, the King of Israel. Jesus says that his having recalled the fig tree is no cause for worship—"thou shall see greater things than these!" Jesus tells him that he shall see heavens open and the angels "ascending and descending upon the Son of man."

COMMENT: The disciples are sent to Jesus by John to indicate that John was a willing admitter of the true Messiah, but this seems an editorial gloss (addition or change of text) to conceal former disciple-rivalry between John and Jesus. The anonymous first disciple with Andrew, he who is a follower before Simon Peter himself, will later be designated as Jesus' beloved disciple (13:23). The stone = Peter pun (Cephas in Aramaic) will signify Peter as the Rock upon which Jesus will build his Church. Philip, who receives an individual call from Jesus, is well known to Asiatic Christianity, and Nathanael, who gets fullest notice of all, is perhaps from Cana near Nazareth, which explains his incredulity as to the Messiah's being his countryman. He is unmentioned, however, in the synoptics. The aim of the entire passage is to indicate that the Christ and the son of Man of the synoptics are the same as this son of God.

CHAPTER 2

4. THE SON OF GOD AND A VILLAGE WEDDING

(2:1-11): Jesus and his disciples attend a marriage at Cana near Nazareth. His mother tells him they have run out of wine, to which Jesus replies, "Woman, what have I to do with thee? mine hour is not yet come." Now six waterpots of stone, each holding two or three firkins (20 or 30 gallons) apiece if filled to the brim, are ordered by Jesus. He orders the pots filled with water; then he tells the servants to draw from the pots and bring the liquid to the governor (master of ceremonies) of the feast. The governor found the drink was real wine and was puzzled (but not the servants). The M.C. called the bride-groom and marvelled how he had replenished the supply of wine.

5. JESUS IN THE TEMPLE (2:12-25):

Jesus goes to Jerusalem and drives the money-changers and deal-ers out of the temple with a scourge (whip) made of small cords. The Jews asked for a sign of his authority and Jesus said, "Destroy this temple, and in three days I will raise it up." The Jews reply that 46 years of work is not done in three days, "But he spake of the temple of his body," says the evangelist (gospel writer). When Jesus had risen from the grave, they re-membered his saying and believed the Scriptures.

COMMENT: In the synoptics Jesus generally refuses to perform miracles for the sake of proving he is the Messiah ("the sign"), but here such proofs will be common. Also in the synoptics the driving-out of the mer-chants occurs just before the Pas-sion, but here it occurs at the be-ginning of his ministry. The epiphany (manifestation) of Christ begins here at Cana, the place where Jesus first reveals his glory in this gospel. This miracle is borrowed, say some com-mentators, from the Bacchic ritual. The meaning is clear: the Jewish law with its rules of outward purification must give way to the Christian sac-rament in Christ's blood (the new wine). His mother represents the Jew whose wine (Law) has run out.

CHAPTER 3

6. JESUS AND A RELIGIOUS LEADER (3:1-21):

A Pharisee named Nicodemus came to Jesus at night and told him that he must have come from God since he has shown via his miracles that God is with him. "Verily, verily, I say unto thee, Ex-cept a man be born again, he cannot see the kingdom of God," replied Jesus. Nicodemus is puzzled about the term "be born again," and Jesus re-plies, "Except a man be born of water and the Spirit, he cannot enter into the kingdom of God." Nicodemus shows disbelief, and he is told that disbelief of earthly things would bar his being told of heavenly things. Whoever believes in the son of Man will have eternal life, "for God so loved the world, that he gave his only begotten Son, that whosoever believeth in him should not perish, but have everlasting life." God did not send his Son to condemn the world but to save it. The unbeliev-ers are condemned already since they prefer darkness to God's light.

7. JESUS AND JOHN AGAIN (3:22-36):

Jesus baptizes in Judea while John was baptizing in Aenon (near

Salim, both places unknown), since John had not yet been imprisoned. A discussion arose between John's dis-ciples and a Jew over purifying. The disciples tell John how all are going to Jesus to be baptized, and John again emphasizes that he is not the Christ, "but that I am sent before him . . . He must increase, but I must decrease."

COMMENT: Jesus is sent from God to *save* mankind—not to judge it. Bap-tism by water will bring about a spir-itual regeneration and cleansing of sin (through repentance) which, along with God's love and mercy, will ad-mit the baptized one to eternal life with God in Heaven. The good life, unlike in the synoptics, is here more spiritual, more abstract, less tangible. The new era will not be a physically new world but a spiritual and psy-chological one. What a disappoint-ment to the more materialistic para-dise of the New Kingdom in the synoptics! Evidently by John's time, the apocalyptic visions were receding, since the world obviously was deter-mined not to come to an end. So John substitutes the New World of the Christian Spirit, less material but more exalted. This is really a didactic piece by the evangelist tacked on to a weak framework of a dialogue with Nicodemus, a habit that will become almost fixed in John. Nicodemus is told that the Kingdom is an inner possession of the believer, "realized in the Church, to which the believer is initiated by a symbolic act (baptism) effecting the spiritual regeneration of the individual performing it, and in keeping with the faith in him which the Son, come from God, claims for himself" (Loisy, p. 230-1).

Note the odd scene of Jesus and John baptizing at the same time, and not far from each other! The discussion between the disciples and "a Jew" is really an editorial substitution for Jesus. The "discussion" was between John's disciples and *Jesus*—the "a Jew" just does not make sense here. The disciples of John must have thought Jesus was being disloyal to his former master, but John makes his passionate disclaimer of any rivalry. We see here editorial glossing, concealing what must have been an interesting rivalry!

CHAPTER 4

8. JESUS MEETS A SAMARITAN WOMAN (4:1-42): In Sychar (a Samaritan city) a Samaritan woman wonders why a Jew like Jesus would ask her for a drink (the scene is Jacob's well). He tells her that if she knew his true nature she would be asking for a drink of "living water" from him. She is puzzled and asks if he is greater than "our father Jacob" who gave them the well as well as having drunk from it himself. Jesus tells her that one could be thirsty again after having drunk from Jacob's well, but "whosoever drinketh of the water that I shall give him shall never thirst." She asks for such a water, but he denounces her for having had five husbands and living in adultery with a sixth! He tells her that "you Jews" need the Temple, or Jerusalem, as a place of worship, but we Jews are worshipping with our eyes open. God is Spirit, and those who worship him can only worship in spirit and in reality. The woman says she believes that the Messiah is coming, and when he comes he will make everything plain to them. "I that speak unto thee am he," says Jesus. She left her waterpot and went into the city saying, "Is not this (Jesus) the Christ?" Later the disciples urge Jesus to eat, but he assures them that his meals

are "to do the will of him that sent me, and to finish his work." He points out that the harvest is already ripe for the picking. Meanwhile, many of the Samaritans in that city believed in Jesus the Christ after hearing the woman tell her story.

9. JESUS IN CANA AGAIN (4:43-54): Jesus left Samaria and went to Cana, in Galilee, and cured the son of a certain nobleman by his word alone. When the man got home he found out that his son had recovered just at the time Jesus had spoken to the father. So the whole house believed in Christ. This is Jesus' second miracle in Galilee.

COMMENT: Again we have the theme of the Water and the Spirit. The disciples' passages look interpolated to give added force to the message. The woman's remarks are fine dialogue, albeit a bit irrelevant at times. The Water and Spirit = the gift of immortality. The laborers in the harvest are of course Jesus and the apostles and the reapers are the contemporaries of the gospel writer himself. The sudden conversion of the city of Samaria = Gentiles converted into Christians.

CHAPTER 5

10. JESUS HEALS IN JERUSALEM (5:1-47): Jesus goes to Jerusalem to a pool called Bethesda Pool (bee THEHZ dah) circled by five porches (arches). Under the arches are found many blind, lame, and ill people. They are in the habit of waiting for the water to "move," for at certain times an angel would come down into the pool and disturb the water, and then the first person who stepped into the pool would be healed of his sickness. One man has been lying there for 38 years, and Jesus asks him if he wanted to be well again. The man complains that someone ·always beats him to the pool after the angel disturbs the water. "Rise, take up thy bed and walk," Jesus says to the man, and the man does so—cured! The day was the sabbath, and the Jews complained and asked the man who had cured him. The man did not know, for Jesus had by now gone away. Later the Jews found out it was Jesus who had made the cure and "did persecute Jesus, and sought to slay him" for violating the sabbath and for saying he was God's Son. Jesus tells them the Son can only do what the Father does, for the Father has given the judgment authority to his Son: "He that honoreth not the Son honoreth not the Father which hath sent him." The believers who are dead shall be raised to life and the evil condemned. Jesus simply executes his Father's will, who had sent him to save mankind. Jesus again tells of John the Baptist's witness to the true Messiah. "But I have greater witness than that of John," and no one has seen the voice or shape of the Father. The Scriptures will also witness the truth of Jesus' Messiahship, but Jesus knows that the Jews "have not the love of God" in them. "I am come in my Father's name, and ye receive me not: if another shall come in his own name, him ye will receive." Moses wrote of Jesus in the Torah and believed and wrote of Jesus, "But if ye believe not his writings, how shall ye believe my words?"

COMMENT: This gospel dwells almost unendingly on doctrine and creed and abstraction: Jesus is concerned with his relationship to his Father, with the mission to mankind, with the fulfilling of God's will, with the Christian message of light-truth-immortality, etc. His cure of the paralytic on the sabbath points to the life-giving work that is Jesus' mission in life. Jesus scolds the Jews for not hearkening to Moses and John the Baptist about his Messiahship. One reason for much of this inserted material is to show the Jews that their temples and pools and synagogues are ineffective in the face of the Christian Spirit. This is the second time the feast of the Passover is mentioned (see also 2:13), and the third time will be at the loaves and fishes miracle (6:4). The reader need not worry: even the chronology of this gospel is symbolic! The pool cure, at Capernaum in the synoptics, and the symbolism by now will be quite evident to the reader: God's power in Jesus works miracles, to the bafflement of the uncomprehending Jews!

CHAPTER 6

11. JESUS SHOWS HIS POWER AND TEACHES ABOUT THE TRUE BREAD (6:1-71): At the shores of the Sea of Galilee Jesus is faced with a worshipping but hungry crowd. Taking five small barley loaves and a couple of fishes from a boy (the only food) he multiplies them into enough food for five thousand people with twelve basketfuls left over! The crowd calls him a Prophet and wants him as their king, but he retires into the hills alone. In the evening the disciples are in heavy seas in a small boat when to their amazement they see Jesus walking on the water toward them! He reassures them while he climbs on board. The crowd on the next day discovers Jesus after a long search and asks how he had arrived at that place. Jesus accuses them of searching for material food when they should be seeking the food of eternal life, the food the son of Man will give them. Their work in God is to believe in the one God has sent to them, the *true* bread from heaven (unlike the manna of Moses)—the bread that gives life to the world. They beg him for that kind of bread and he replies, "I am the bread of life: he that cometh to me shall never hunger; and he that believeth on me shall never thirst." Those who believe in the Son will have everlasting life. The Jews mutter against his blasphemy in saying he had come from heaven, and say, "Is not this Jesus, the son of Joseph, whose father and mother we know?" Jesus tells them to desist: "No man can come to me, except the Father which hath sent me draw him (draw: God in his grace, mercy, and love must first *accept* the sinner before he can be saved): and I will raise him up at the last day (i.e., Judgment Day)." He tells the Jews that unless they eat the flesh of the son of Man and drink his blood they will not have everlasting life: "he that eateth me, even he shall live by me." Even his disciples murmur at his teaching, and he tells them that his words, "they are spirit, and they are life!"

COMMENT: Note that the enemies of Jesus in this gospel are not the synoptic Pharisees, Sadducees, Scribes, or elders, but are Jews as a class, some few of whom see the light—the rest have blinders and more. The flesh-and-blood-eating = the Christian sacrament of the mass. By partaking of the actual or symbolic flesh and blood of Christ at the mass, the eater thereof sheds his guilt and sin by partaking of the sacrifice of Christ, himself given by God to redeem mankind. The miracle is used to symbolize the new faith and the mystery of salvation. The rejection of kingship means that Christ refuses to be a Jewish Messiah and also refuses to become the Messiah of the synoptics —the eschatological Christ. Rather he is to be the Messiah of the Christian Church at about the time the gospel was written in the early second century; the Christian Christ of John strongly resembles that of the Church today: no end of the world, peace-and-plenty, reign-of-God New-Kingdom in John, but a mystery, a mystical union with Christ in Spirit and holy communion. In a way, there is a substitution of a mystical paradise for a landed utopia. The doctrine of predestination (God *selects* those of the elect predestined to be saved, as distinguished from those doomed from the beginning not to be selected by God and hence not saved) is implicit in verses 39, 40, and 44. The sacramental system tradition is largely from First Corinthians (11:24-25), which see. Peter's famous confession that Jesus is the Christ "the Son of the living God" and his choice of the twelve (69, 70) soften the hard blows delivered to the Jews as a lot. *Meaning*: the Jews are blind and certain Judaizing Christians are also blind: even Judas Iscariot personifies the Jewish hatred of Jesus. Certainly he is much less individualized here than in the synoptics.

CHAPTER 7

12. JESUS DELAYS HIS ARRIVAL AT THE FESTIVAL (7:1-13): Jesus' brothers tell him to go to Judea and "work" publicly, for not even his brothers have any faith in him. Jesus replies that the time is inappropriate for him to go, but he urges his brothers to go ahead to the festival of the "Tabernacles" (autumn festival of eight days, very sacred to the Jews). Later Jesus enters furtively into the city of Jerusalem. The Jews enter into dispute about Jesus, whom they do not recognize.

13. JESUS DECLARES HIS AUTHORITY AND MAKES MORE CLAIMS (7:14-53): At the height of the festival Jesus begins openly teaching in the Temple. The Jews wonder at the unlearned man who teaches with such authority, and Jesus says he is taught by God himself. He accuses them all of violating the Law of Moses. "Why are you trying to kill me?" he asks them, and they reply that he must be mad. Jesus tells them that Moses had given them the custom of circumcision (a custom really inherited from their primitive forefathers), and they would even circumcise a man on the holy Sabbath. Then why criticize Jesus for violating the Sabbath? They must judge things not by appearances but by the reality! But the Jews do not see Jesus as the Christ, since they know where he comes from—unlike the origin of the true Messiah, which will be unknown. Jesus says that he has been sent by one who is true but the Jews do not know him. They try to arrest him, but the right time is not yet. Jesus tells the arresting officers, "Yet a little while am I with you, and then I go unto him that sent me." The Jews are puzzled as to his Messiahship. There is division amongst them; some would arrest him, but they do not dare touch him. Even the officers tell their superiors, "Never man spake like this man," and their superiors (the Pharisees) tell them that they and the people are deceived. Nicodemus (a secret night-follower of Jesus) defends Jesus, telling his colleagues not to judge Jesus before trying him. The Pharisees end the session by saying that out of Galilee no prophet could arise.

COMMENT: Jesus is often difficult to understand, a bit haughty, and too often so complexly obscure in his teachings that small wonder his hearers are too often puzzled at his riddle-like doctrines. This chapter is the second phase of Christ's combat with the Jews—the scene now set in Jerusalem. The brothers of Jesus represent unbelieving Jewry. Note his denial that his place of origin is really known—not from Nazareth (Mary and Joseph) but from God. See the contradicting synoptics.

CHAPTER 8

14. JESUS DEFLATES THE RIGORISTS AND MAKES BOLD CLAIMS (8:1-58): A woman adultress is brought before Jesus by the scribes and Pharisees. She had been caught in the "very act." The law of Moses requires that she be publicly stoned (rocks are hurled at the victim until dead) for her crime. Wishing to trap Jesus, they ask him his opinion. But Jesus stoops down, "and with his finger wrote on the ground, as though he heard them not." Then he adds, getting up from the ground, "He that is without sin among you, let him first cast a stone at her," and again he writes on the ground. From the eldest onlooker to the youngest they file out, conscience-stricken at his words, until Jesus is left alone with the adultress. To her he says, "Woman, where are those thine accusers? hath no man condemned thee?" She says, "No man, Lord." And Jesus says unto her, "Neither do I condemn thee: go, and sin no more." Then Jesus calls himself the light of the world, that he attests to the truth of his divinity as well as his Father. Still they could not arrest Jesus, since the time was not yet come. Jesus tells them he shall be sought and killed for their sins, but they shall not be able to follow him later. "Ye are from beneath; I am from above: ye are of this world; I am not of this world." Some believe in him and to them he says, "And ye shall know the truth, and the truth shall make you free." The Jews protest they love God, but Jesus says if they loved God they would love Jesus. The Jews remain uncomprehending as usual. "Why do ye not understand my speech?" asks Jesus. The Jews are of the devil their father, murderers, liars, incapable of belief in the true God-Messiah. "Ye are not of God," Jesus adds. Jesus promises eternal life to believers in him, but the Jews point out how even Abraham and the prophets are dead. "Before Abraham was, I am," Jesus tells them, and they cast stones at him, but Jesus escapes in time.

COMMENT: The story of the woman taken in adultery is not to be found in most of the older manuscripts of the gospel; certainly it was not originally a part of the gospel of John —perhaps it once was part of Luke's gospel. Anyway, it is a fine story indeed, vivid, terse, dramatic. What Jesus wrote in the sand is unknown, but tradition has it that he listed therein the sins of the accusers. This story is one of the most popular in the history of the Church. To this day it is well-thumbed on ministerial and priestly lecterns. In most of the quarrel scene with the Jews, Jesus is merely telling them in so many ways that he comes from God and returns to God. Note that this indicates no earthly existence before epiphany (manifestation as Christ) nor a bodily resurrection after death! Note that verse 29 says that God does not forsake Jesus—in spite of Psalm 22 and Mark (15:34)! This is an intentional contradiction of Mark for obvious reasons. Remember that John writes much later than the synoptics and makes many doctrinal and factual changes in the life of Jesus. Item: verse 57: "Thou art not yet fifty years old" = John's fact on Jesus' age, another piece of unfounded "fact," inserted for propagandistic reasons to establish a careful time schedule befitting John's plan.

CHAPTER 9

15. JESUS AND BLINDNESS, PHYSICAL AND SPIRITUAL (9:1-41): Jesus cured a man who has been born blind by applying a clay-spit pack to the man's eyes. The blind beggar then went home and told of the miracle of Jesus. The Pharisees were told how Jesus had cured the man on the sabbath. The cured man praised Jesus even in face of false charges of conspiracy to deceive. He insisted Jesus is from God since he had cured a case of congenital blindness—unheard of in the history of cures! The Pha-

risees threw him out nevertheless. Later the cured beggar tells Jesus he believes in the son of Man, "And Jesus said, For Judgment I am come into this world, that they which see not might see: and that they which see might be made blind."

COMMENT: This sign-cure brings out how blind the Jews really are to spiritual things. A man *born* blind makes the cure more dramatic and symbolic than similar cures in the synoptics. Born blind = man ignorant of the blessings of revelation of Christ. The Pharisees = Judaism and its disbelief in the Christian gospel. Verse 39

contradicts 3:17-18: Christ came to save man—not to judge him.

CHAPTER 10

16. JESUS DECLARES HIMSELF THE TRUE SHEPHERD OF MEN (10:1-40): Only thieves and rogues enters a sheepfold by some other way than the door. But the shepherd of the flock enters by the right door; his sheep follow his voice only—and not that of a stranger's. The Jews still do not understand his parable. Jesus explains: he is the door for the sheep. Those entering by the door will be safe and sound; those entering otherwise come to kill and steal. I come to bring life; "I am the good shepherd: the good shepherd giveth his life for his sheep." Other sheep Jesus has who do not belong to this fold (i.e., the Gentiles), but there shall soon be "one fold, and one shepherd" (Church and bishop?). Some Jews believe and some not. Later, walking on Solomon's Porch in the Temple, Jesus is asked to prove he is the Christ. Jesus replies that his words and deeds have not yet convinced

them, "But ye believe not, because ye are not of my sheep." The Jews prepare to stone him for blasphemy in making himself God. At least believe in the works of Jesus, is what Jesus tells them, even if you do not believe in Christ Jesus. Jesus again escapes from them and flees to the Jordan.

COMMENT: The poem of the Good Shepherd seems quite distinct from the story of the blind beggar, and very likely was a separate parable simply stuck in at this point. Just who are the "false shepherds" who came before Jesus had come, and are thieves and killers? Perhaps the Jewish teachers or the false messiahs, or perhaps false religions, etc. Finally Jesus retreats to the province of Perea (40-42) where John the Baptist had cleansed people of their sins.

CHAPTER 11

17. JESUS SHOWS HIS POWER OVER DEATH (11:1-44): In Bethany (BETH uh nee) the brother of Mary and Martha, whose name was Lazarus, was ill. This was the same Mary who had anointed the Lord and wiped his feet with her hair. Jesus was notified of the illness, and loving Martha, Mary, and Lazarus very much, he hastened to Bethany (but only after a two-day stay in the place where he was) in spite of the danger to his life; and so his disciples warned him. Jesus went anyway: "I go, that I may awake him out of sleep." He told his disciples that Lazarus was by now dead, and added that he was glad he was not at Lazarus' bedside

when he was merely ill, "to the intent ye may believe." Thomas, called Didymus, said, "Let us go, that we may die with him." Martha scolded Jesus for arriving four days late, Lazarus being by now a four-day corpse in the grave. Jesus comforted Martha: "Thy brother shall rise again." She replied that she knows he will rise on the Judgment Day—but not now. "I am the resurrection, and the life: he that believeth in me, though he were dead, yet shall he live: And whosoever liveth and believeth in me shall never die," replied Jesus. Martha's reply was a statement of her belief in Jesus as "the Christ, the Son of God, which should come into the world." At the grave, around which were relatives and friends, Jesus wept for Lazarus; then he told them to remove the stone from the cave-tomb. Martha protested that by this time the four-day corpse should be stinking, but Jesus prayed in a loud voice and "Lazarus came forth," bound in deathcloths from hand to foot; even his face was covered with a cloth ("napkin"). Jesus gave orders to loose the man and "let him go."

18. JESUS' MIRACLE LEADS TO DEADLY HOSTILITY (11:45-57):

Some of the Jews now, because of the miracle, believed in Jesus, but others reported to the chief priests and Pharisees, who feared that soon he would convert all men to Christ, and as a result the Romans would take their homeland from them. That year Caiaphas (KYE uh fuss: high priest from 18 A.D. to 36 A.D.), called his colleagues know-nothings: he told them that it would be better that one man die rather than the whole nation be destroyed. He was inspired to say that Jesus was going to die for the Jewish nation and for all mankind. From that day on they planned to kill Jesus. Jesus fled to the town of Ephraim (EE fray um). The Jewish Passover (freedom from Egyptian bondage festival of the Jews, which was required to be celebrated by all Jews in the Temple in Jerusalem at about our present Easter time) was approaching and many Jews were arriving in Jerusalem early; and many looked for Jesus

but saw him not. An order had been issued that anyone seeing Jesus should report it to the authorities so that he could be arrested.

COMMENT: This is the greatest miracle of them all, the most spectacular and most well-known of any in all the gospels! It is this miracle that precipitates the crisis between the Jews and Christ—the climax of the Johannine gospel. The only way to prevent conversion of all Jews is by putting him to death instantly. Jesus flees because his hour for death can only come on the Passover and not before it (see 11:1-57). This miracle redoubles the intensity of similar miracles in Mark and Matthew (Jairus' daughter, and the young man of Nain). The two sisters in Luke (10:38-42) are here made the sisters of Lazarus, and Mary incorporates the sinful woman in Luke (7:37) and the anointing woman in Mark and Matthew. Verses 1-2 reveal a superaddition by some commentator to an original story without the sisters. Was the loud cry Jesus uttered at the funeral an outraged groan? Interesting speculation. The main import of the entire story is the symbolism: mankind's possibility of attaining immortality and escaping death by belief in the Spirit. Now, why is little said of Lazarus after issuing from the cave in grave cloths? The answer seems to be that the evangelist was no longer interested in earthly imports of the story now that the symbolic intention had been realized.

CHAPTER 12

19. AN ACT OF LOVE AND A TEMPORARY TRIUMPH (12:1-50):

Six days before the Passover, Jesus dined with Lazarus and his sisters. Then Mary anointed Jesus' feet and wiped them with her hair, using in the process a very expensive perfume. The betrayer complained at the waste

of the perfume, his name being Judas Iscariot. He really cared not about the poor (for whom the perfume could have been sold as money for them) but about stealing the money for himself, since he was accustomed to stealing money from the common purse of the disciples. Jesus told him to let her alone, for the poor are with us always, but Jesus is not. Many Jews were converted by the Lazarus miracle after seeing him alive and well. The enemies of Jesus resolved to kill him also. The next day Jesus was met by a great crowd with palm branches in their hands, shouting, "Blessed is the King of Israel that cometh in the name of the Lord!" Jesus entered, seated on a young ass, as it is written (Zechariah 9:9). The disciples did not understand these things at first, but after the resurrection they recalled the truth of what the scripture had said of Jesus. Now certain Greek travelers came to Philip the disciple and asked to see Jesus; Philip told Andrew and they both reported to Jesus. To the Greeks Jesus said that the hour for the son of Man to be glorified was come, and "he that loveth his life shall lose it; and he that hateth his life in this world shall keep it unto life eternal." A voice from heaven replied saying, "I have both glorified it (Jesus' name), and will glorify it again." The onlookers reported a thunderous voice, and others said an angel had spoken to Jesus. The voice came for the sake of the Jews, was Jesus' reply, and

"Now is the judgment of this world: now shall the prince of this world be cast out." Then Jesus left to go into hiding again. Yet the Jews did not believe in him in spite of the miracles; just as Isaiah had prophesied, the messiah would be spurned by the Jews (Isaiah 6:10). Nevertheless, many of the chief rulers believed in Christ but did not dare to admit it because of the hostility of the Pharisees.

COMMENT: Episodes from Mark and Matthew are here given a typical Johannine turn for their symbolic intent: 1. the anointing at Bethany is symbolic of Christ's death, a prelude to the actual death on the cross and the anointing required after death, as well as the anointing of an Israelite king as in the O.T. 2. The triumphal entry into Jerusalem symbolizes the glorious return of Christ to God. 3. The last teachings (discourses) symbolize the future conversion of the Gentiles (note the message to the Gentile Greeks) and the damnation of the Jews who showed unbelief. The quotation from Isaiah, as usual with messianic Christianity, is distorted from its context in order to apply favorably to Jesus.

CHAPTER 13

20. JESUS TEACHES HUMILITY AND FORETELLS HIS BETRAYAL (13:1-38): At the Last Supper the devil put it into the heart of Judas Iscariot (Simon's son) to betray Christ. Then Jesus tied a towel around his waist and proceeded to wash and wipe his disciples' feet with a basin of water and the towel around his waist. Peter protested being washed by Jesus, but Jesus said that if he does not wash Peter's feet, Peter can never share Jesus' lot. Peter then told him to wash his hands and face as well, but Jesus replied he is clean all over through merely washing his feet. And the disciples are clean, but not all of them, for Jesus knew who would

betray him. Jesus sat and told them that now they also ought to wash "one another's feet. For I have given you an example, that ye should do as I have done to you." He went on to indicate that one disciple sharing the meal with him "hath lifted up his heel against me . . . one of you shall betray me." Now "leaning on Jesus' bosom" was one of his disciples whom Jesus loved, and Peter beckoned to him to ask Jesus who the betrayer was. The beloved disciple "lying on Jesus breast" asked who the betrayer was, to which Jesus answered, "He it is, to whom I shall give a sop, when I have dipped it (sop = morsel)." And after dipping his morsel in his bowl he gave it to Judas Iscariot, the son of Simon. After the morsel entered Judas' mouth, Satan too entered into him, and Jesus said to Judas to do quickly that which he is going to do; yet no one else understood what Jesus meant. Judas left immediately—and it was night, and as soon as Judas had left, Jesus said that now is the Son of Man glorified. He then tells his disciples to love one another and show they are true disciples of Jesus to all men. Peter wishes to follow Jesus and swears fidelity; but Jesus predicts that Peter will deny Jesus three times before the cock crows in the early morning.

COMMENT: The period of Jesus' ministry on earth is now over, and the Last Supper portrays the beginning of his Passion (arrest, trial, and crucifixion). This scene illustrates the law of love by 1. the humble washing of feet by Jesus 2. the love shown for the beloved disciple 3. the love he instructs them to show for each other. Some critics say that the feet-washing (a later addition to the synoptic account) acts as a memorial of Christ as the suffering servant who lives and dies with his beloved disciples. The act is a kind of purification rite like that of baptism. In fact, Jesus may well be symbolizing his own death in the washing rite, which explains Peter's objection here, and at the Passion crisis. The threat to Peter should he not be washed = 1. baptism 2. the eucharist (Christian holy communion through eating and drinking Christ at the mass), both necessary for Christian salvation. Note the life-giving water and Jesus' later death, which brings greater life for all. That the rites of the Church are vital to salvation seems prefigured here. The "sop" given to Judas is symbolic of his damnation, and we see the devil enter him a second time. The incident of the beloved disciple's favored position, superior even to that of Peter's, is unique— it is John, the supposed writer of the gospel carrying his name. It is from him that Peter learns the traitor's name, and it is to him that Jesus will later entrust the care of his mother.

CHAPTER 14

21. JESUS EXPLAINS AND PROMISES THE SPIRIT (14:1-29): Jesus delivers an extended discourse to his disciples: "In my Father's house are many mansions (heaven) . . . I go to prepare a place for you." When Thomas asks which is the way, the Christ replies, "I am the way, the truth, and the life: no man cometh unto the Father, but by me (one attains immortality in heaven only through Christianity)." To Philip he explains that those who have seen Jesus have seen and known the Father (God), and he instructs them to love him and keep his commandments: "He that hath my commandments, and keepeth them, he it is that loveth me; and he that loveth me shall be loved of my Father, and I will love him, and will manifest (show) myself to him." The manifestation will be through the Holy Spirit (Ghost), "whom the Father will send in my name."

COMMENT: In a sense then the Spirit is a substitute for Jesus; it will continue the work and revelation of the Father and the Son, and will be present in the Church to manifest the presence of Jesus Christ. In the book of Acts the miracle of Pentecost takes place ten days after Christ had risen to heaven—Pentecost is God's presence shed into the persons of the apostles. This Spirit-Helper, or *Paraclete*, functions as Christ would in person. It is the Paraclete that Jesus promises his apostles and that scene of the Pentecostal bestowing will occur in Acts, which see. This chapter ends as if all were to arise and prepare for the Passion, but three chapters will now intervene before the actual Passion commences—Chapters 15, 16, 17.

CHAPTER 15

22. JESUS TEACHES: ON UNION AND ON HATE (15:1-27): "I am the true vine, and my Father is the vinedresser" (these are the beginning words of a long discourse); Jesus tells his disciples that he is the vine and they are the branches " . . . for without me ye can do nothing." He exhorts them to love, to keep his commandments: "Greater love hath no man than this, that a man lay down his life for his friends." Whatever they shall ask in God's name will be given them. If the world shall hate them, remember Christ was the first hated. Because they are not of this world, the world will hate them. "But when the Comforter (Spirit of God's truth; the Paraclete) is come, whom I will send unto you from the Father, even the Spirit of truth, which proceedeth from the Father, he shall testify of me."

COMMENT: These are Christ's last instructions to his disciples—and they are fervid and effective! However, they may be taken in the sense not only of Christ addressing his disciples but also his own Church. The allegory of the vine and vinedresser is based upon similar allegories in the synoptics, but the eucharistic symbolism is much more beautifully stated here. The gardener must tend the vine, and the branches must remain united to the main stem if the Church is to survive. Note too that Love is the theme between disciples, but Hate is the world's reaction to them—a vivid contrast. Of interest: try to follow the metaphor of the vine and vinedresser through—if you can!

CHAPTER 16

23. JESUS GOES ON TEACHING AND EXPLAINING (16:1-33): Jesus goes on to explain how they will be driven from the synagogues, how he must go away, how he will send the *Comforter* who will guide them in all truth and in glorifying Christ. He tells them that when Christ is gone, they will be sad but will again rejoice, for he will see them again; and "Whatever ye shall ask the Father in my name, he will give it you." Finally the disciples say they understand it all; that Christ is from God, that they now believe, but Jesus predicts they shall be scattered, "and shall leave me alone: and yet I am not alone, because the Father is with me."

CHAPTER 17

24. JESUS PRAYER FOR HIS DISCIPLES—PRESENT AND FUTURE (17:1-26): Jesus prays to his Father: he asks for glorification, that man might know the only true God, "and Jesus Christ, whom thou hast sent." He tells how his work is finished, how God's name was made manifest, his words made manifest, how he is praying for his disciples but not for the world, and how he is glorified in his disciples. "And I have declared unto them (the disciples) thy name, and will declare it; that the love wherewith thou hast loved me may be in them, and I in them."

COMMENT: Noteworthy slip: 16:4: "And these things I said not unto you at the beginning, *because I was with you.*" In the words I have underlined we see strange words coming from Jesus, who has been with the disciples from the very beginning. Obviously these are the words of a later writer who was so busy inserting material that he lost his perspective and began talking as if he were addressing the Church of the second century (see Loisy, p. 255). Note that the disciples will abandon their master as Jesus predicts—but not in the Johannine account (it occurs only in the synoptic gospels)—as flat a contradiction as exists anywhere. Perhaps the gospel writers missed this very important point (see 16:32); see also Loisy, p. 255. Chapter 17 is Christ's final prayer, the summation of all his teachings, the epitome of glorious Christian prayer displaying supreme confidence in the future victory over evil; a prayer of great thanksgiving to the Father, a prayer of great love! It is a supreme piece of verse, a hymn of joy.

CHAPTER 18

25. THE ARREST AND THE DENIALS OF PETER (18:1-27): Judas led the guard, officers, and others that the chief priests and Pharisees had provided for him to a certain garden at night where Jesus was found. Twice Jesus told them that he was the man they were looking for, adding that the others should be let free. Peter cuts off the right ear of the high priest's servant, whose name is Malchus; but Jesus said to Peter, "Put up thy sword into the sheath: the cup which my Father hath given me, shall I not drink it?" Then Jesus was taken and bound and led away to Annas, the father-in-law to Caiaphas, the high priest. Behind Jesus followed Peter and one other disciple known personally to Caiaphas. He went in with Jesus to the high priest's courtyard, but Peter was left standing at the door outside. So this other disciple spoke to the doorkeeper and brought Peter inside. The young woman at the door asked Peter if he were Jesus' disciple, which Peter denied. To the high priest inside Jesus declared he has always taught openly, so why not ask his listeners what he has taught? Here an officer slapped Jesus, saying, "Answerest thou the high priest so?" The kinsman of Malchus then asked Peter in the courtyard (the second time Peter had denied Christ to those in the courtyard with him) if he is a disciple of Jesus, and there is a third denial—immediately the cock crowed. The Romans led Jesus into the hall of judgment, but the Jews would not go there lest they be made unclean for the Passover feast in coming in contact with Gentiles. Pilate asked Jesus if he is the King of the Jews, to which the reply was, "My kingdom is not of this world." Was that why his servants had put up no fight for him? "Thou sayest that I am a king. To this end was I born, and for this cause came I into the world; that I should bear witness unto the truth," added Jesus to the same question from Pilate. Then Pilate said, "What is truth?" and told the Jews outside that he found no fault in Jesus at all. Instead of the release of Jesus, the Jews yelled for release of Barabbas the robber.

COMMENT: Jesus seems to be in perfect control of things from the very start. This is a kind of orderly and systematic progression of the Passion, more so than in the more primitive synoptics. Note that the garden is *not* called Gethsemane, but remains unnamed. Note, too, that

Jesus advances to meet his captors and inquires their errand, nonplusses them for a while, and then gives himself up—at the same time demanding freedom for his disciples! John adds to the synoptics the name Malchus, the *right* ear, and the sword-striker as being Peter. Peter's sword-play takes the place of the bitter denunciation he gets in the synoptics. The Judas kiss too is omitted. In sum: the scene is given great dignity; Peter is still "stupid" enough not to understand the mystery of the Passion, and Judas the "fingerman" is omitted—he simply leads the captors to the garden! The episode before the high priest is most confused; in the primitive story base to this episode there is only one high priest known —Annas. Nothing was known of Caiaphas; he is inserted to agree with Matthew's account; and this is done by making him the son-in-law to Annas. "All these precisions reveal the compiler of our Gospel as a man of lively invention. It is abundantly clear that in the original account not one of his disciples followed Jesus after his arrest" (18:8; 16:32; from Loisy, p. 259). Note that all the abuse Jesus receives is a mere slap in the face in contrast to the vile abuse he receives in the synoptics. The slapper stands for the murderers of Jesus, the unbelieving Jews! Note the care taken to indicate that the time is the *morning* of the Passover. In the evening the paschal lamb will be sacrificed, and this will symbolize the sacrifice of Jesus on the cross. This will fit neatly into the Easter rites of the Christian church. Friday eve = Crucifixion; Resurrection — Sunday at dawn.

CHAPTER 19

26. THE CRUCIFIXION (19:1-42): Jesus is scourged, crowned with thorns, dressed in royal purple, and is beaten and mocked as the King of the Jews. Pilate, proclaiming Jesus' innocence, presents him to the mob outside: "Behold the man!" (*Ecce homo!*) The Jews insist on his death, but within Pilate pleads with him. Jesus is fearless, saying, "Thou couldst have no power at all against me, except it were given thee from above." The mob even threatens to report Pilate as inimical to Augustus Caesar the Emperor of Rome: "Whosoever maketh himself a king speaketh against Caesar!" Now it was about midday ("the sixth hour") of the Passover, and Pilate calls out to the Jews, "Behold your King!" And Pilate adds, "Shall I crucify your King?" But the chief priests answer, "We have no king but Caesar." They insist on crucifixion for Jesus, and he is finally led away to be crucified. He bore his own cross to Golgotha (Skull Hill) where he was crucified between two other victims. Pilate inscribed a title for the cross: JESUS OF NAZARETH THE KING OF THE JEWS, and it was written in three languages: Hebrew, Greek, and Latin. The soldiers divided his clothes among them; his coat was without a seam from top to bottom. Lots were cast for the undivided cloak to fulfill the scriptures which say, "They parted my raiment among them, and for my vesture they did cast lots." Near the cross stood his mother Mary, his mother's sister, Mary the wife of Cleophas, and Mary Magdalene. When Jesus saw his mother and his beloved disciple (John) standing by, he said to her, "Woman, behold thy son." and to the disciple he said, "Behold thy mother!" And from that time the disciple took Jesus' mother into his care. When Jesus says, "I thirst," a sponge is filled with vinegar (sour wine) and put on a spear and pushed toward his mouth. Jesus takes it and cries, "It is finished!" and dies, his head lolling forward. The Jews want the bodies removed before the Passover sabbath, and so they asked

Pilate to have the victims' legs broken and the bodies removed. The legs of the other two were broken, but not Jesus', since they (the soldiers) saw he was already dead. But one soldier did pierce his side with a spear, and at once there was a flow of blood and water. And "he that saw it bare record, and his record is true: and he knoweth that he saith true, that ye might believe" (this is the gospel writer John affirming his veracity as a witness). The scriptures say that no bone of the lamb shall be broken and his side shall be pierced (Exodus 12:46; Zechariah 12:10). Now the disciple, Joseph of Arimathea (secretly a disciple for fear of recrimination from the Jews), took the body down from the cross with Pilate's permission, along with the help of Nicodemus, who had brought along spices of myrrh and aloes weighing about a hundred pounds. They wound it in linen with the spices, as is the custom of the Jews in burial. Now in the same place (Golgotha) was a garden with a new sepulchre, never used before, and there Jesus was laid.

COMMENT: Note how Pilate is brought to heel when the Jews confront him with possible political subversion in Jesus. Some translators even have Jesus sitting down in the judgment seat—to impress more strongly that he is the *King* of the Jews. That seems the more apt translation, more befitting the context. There is no doubt in this gospel that the Jews are responsible for the crucifixion of Christ. Note the care with which Pilate absolves himself from blame! Note too the grandly dramatic and tragic irony in the spectacle of the Jews calling for the blood of Christ, who (say the Christians) really was their true Messiah. Observe too that Jesus carries his own cross. It is quite clear, however, that the Romans perform the actual crucifixion. The reason for the omission of the Simon of Cyrene episode is that greater dignity and greatness is added if Christ bears his own cross. (Perhaps also there is the intention

of answering certain gnostic heretics like Basilides, who maintained that Simon was crucified in Christ's place! See Loisy, p. 262.) John omits mentioning *thieves* as Jesus' companions on either side so as to put his Christ in better company. The inscription on the cross, in spite of Jewish protests, is indeed symbolic = Jesus was truly the divine King of the Jews. Pilate's triple-tongued translation of the motto signifies the universal appeal of the Christ salvation for all mankind. The unseamed cloak may (a guess) represent the solid, unified-in-one Christian Church. Jesus addressed his mother as "Woman," not to deny her but to symbolize that converted Jews (his mother) should accept Christianity ("beloved disciple") as the legitimate issue of the Old Testament. On the other hand Christianity (John) must accept as its mother the Judaic-Christian Church with its Old Testament tradition. The "hyssop" mixed with vinegar must refer to the Passover ritual in which hyssop is used to splash lamb's blood on housedoors (see Exodus 12:22). Note finally the manner of Jesus' death: it is peaceful, accepting, and unprotesting—unlike his death in the synoptics. No darkness, earthquake, etc., but a simultaneously joyful death-resurrection at that very moment (so believe the "quartodeciman" Christians of Asia; "quartodeciman" has to do with the fact that they accept John as to the date of crucifixion, the 14th of Nisan; Westerners accept the synoptic date, the 15th of Nisan. The fires of this date-quarrel have raged for centuries, and there is not time to search these flames now). Note that Jesus died on the evening of a Friday and must be buried before the sabbath, the next day. The leg-breaking is not in the synoptics, nor is the quick removal of all three bodies for common burial. Most important, the reader should be aware of the water-blood symbolism in the last spear-thrust of the Roman soldier: the Christian sacraments are signified. The unbroken bones refers to the Passover lamb of the Jews, which must be in an unbroken state before eating. In John, Jesus = the *Lamb* of God (as John the Baptist had witnessed) sacrificed to atone for man's sins, and to make possible Paradise again through partaking in the Lamb's sacrifice in the Christian sacraments. The reader should note the rather naive affirmation of the veracity of the gospel writer that he had witnessed it all and could swear to the truth of it all—that is, John "the beloved disciple" is the author of this gospel, his Apocalypse, and his three Epistles (which see). As a matter of fact there has been much editing, changing, interpolating, and even adding of elements in this gospel. Not *one* author alone—but one author with many "helpers" who came later.

CHAPTER 20

27. THE RISEN LORD (20:1-31): The first day of the week at dusky dawn Mary Magdalene sighted the empty tomb; she told Peter and "the other disciple" the news, and they both ran, but the "other disciple did outrun Peter, and came first to the sepulchre." They saw the empty linencloths; and "that other disciple" saw and believed. They left, but Mary wept and, looking in, saw two angels in white who asked her why she weeps; to which her answer was that she missed her Lord. Turning back she saw a man who asked her why she wept, and she, thinking him the gardener, asked where he has laid the body. Jesus simply said, "Mary," and her reply is simply "Master." He told her not to touch him, "for I am not yet ascended to my Father." She told the disciples as Jesus had bade her. That very evening within closed doors (for fear of the Jews) the disciples saw Jesus in their midst saying, "Peace be unto you." He showed them his pierced hands and side, and they were glad. "Receive ye the Holy Ghost (Spirit)," said Jesus to them—and he "breathed on them." He gave them the power to forgive sins. Only the disciple Thomas was absent at this time, and upon returning he expressed scepticism about their story: "Except I shall see in his hands the print of the nails, and put my finger into the print of the nails, and thrust my hand into his side, I will not believe." Eight days later Jesus marched through closed doors to accost Thomas and give him his chance to feel for himself the truth of the resurrection. After testing for himself, the (doubting) Thomas said, "My Lord and my God." Jesus replied, "Blessed are they that have not seen, and yet have believed." Jesus gave them many other signs of his resurrection, many of which are not recorded in "this book." But these things are written (says the author) "that ye might believe that Jesus is the Christ, the Son of God; and that believing ye might have life through his name."

COMMENT: Nicodemus is not in the synoptics, and the hundred pounds of spices for embalming would take a long time to use—too long for the quick burial required before the sabbath began. The garden near the cross = the Church (the new Eve); Christ = the new Adam from whose side (remember the wound) the new Eve-Church is born. Jesus makes three appearances: 1. to Mary Magdalene 2. to the disciples 3. to the disciples-Thomas, two appearances on the same day and the last on the following Sunday. Note how the beloved disciple beats Peter in the footrace to the tomb, and how he is the first to believe in the resurrection! This does great harm to the Peter of the synoptics, where his status and dignity is much higher. One must be aware that the "beloved" disciple so divinely treated, so tenderly given the care of Jesus' mother is the author of the gospel himself— John; if one accepts his authorship, which, as already stated, is quite doubtful itself. The doubting Thomas episode was inserted perhaps by some compiler to convince us of Jesus' *material* resurrection in *body* as well as spirit. This doctrine seems to conflict with John's entire outlook throughout this gospel. Verses 30, 31 come from the original editor of the gospel who speaks of the disciples in the third person—another slip, if this person were John. Verse 31 is a farewell verse, the end of the gospel —but Chapter 21 follows! Conclusion: Chapter 21 is an afterthought or an unnecessary addition by some other writer, the effect of which does harm to the economy of the entire book.

CHAPTER 21

28. PETER AND THE RISEN JESUS (21:1-25): Jesus again showed himself to Peter, Thomas, Nathanael, the sons of Zebedee, and two others. They had gone fishing overnight and had caught nothing. He told them to cast their net again, and it came up heavily loaded with fish. The beloved disciple was the first to recognize the Lord. At this news Peter put his coat over his naked body and jumped into the sea, and along with the others hauled in the fish, 153 of them, and the net was not torn! They dined on fish then, and Jesus told Peter to "Feed my lambs" on three distinct occasions; and each time Peter swore to feed the lambs of Christ (i.e., Christians of the Church). Then Jesus told Peter to follow him, and Peter did so, noticing that the disciple Jesus loved followed behind them. "Yes, Lord," said Peter, "and what shall this man do? (i.e., What about him?)," to which Jesus replied that the beloved disciple must stay behind and that Peter must follow as directed. This gave rise to the saying "among the brothers" that this disciple (i.e., the beloved one) would not die. Yet, of course, Jesus did not say, "He will not die," but simply, "If it is my wish for him to stay until I come, is that your business?" ("If it is my will that he remain until I come, what is that to you"). This same disciple is hereby giving testimony to what is in this gospel, and he has written it down. We know that he is a reliable witness. There are many other things that Jesus did, and I suppose that if "they should be written every one, I suppose that even the world itself could not contain the books that should be written. Amen."

COMMENT: Note that the beloved disciple recognizes Jesus first in the miraculous draught of fishes. The prominence given to Peter is designed to win acceptance for this particular gospel in the Church of Rome, where Peter is especially beloved. The fish = Christians taken in by the Church. Peter plunging into the sea reminds us of Matthew (14:25-33) when Peter attempts to join Christ on the water. The meal of bread and fish is sacramental also and reminds us of Emmaus. The thrice repeated request for love from Peter and admonitions to care for the Christian sheep (the Church of Rome) would be bound to joyously accept such primacy of Peter, since he is recognized as the first Bishop of Rome and the first Pope. Peter's death is even predicted—his martyrdom. The last words of the author signify 1. John the Old, a "well-known figure long resident in Asia" as author of the Gospel and 2. convey a hint — no more than a hint is given—that he is the same person as the apostle John, son of Zebedee. Who are the "we" who guarantee his testimony (24)? They are "the Elders" who had known this John and had brought out under his name the collection of Johannine books. "We thus see that this supplement to the Gospel, intended to make it acceptable to all the Churches, was also intended to give it apostolic authority and value" (Loisy, p. 270).

ACTS: A PREFACE

WRITER: Luke—this is his second volume on Christian beginnings, his gospel being the first. The book of Acts continues without interruption where his gospel had left off, at Jesus' ascension into heaven, or (depending upon which manuscript you read) at the point where he promises to clothe his apostles with the Holy Spirit.

DATE: About 90 A.D., at the point when Luke realized what a massive force Christianity would be *outside* the small state of Judea. So he tells the story of the birth of the missionary movement and its rapid spread throughout the Roman Empire. When Luke was in Palestine he had received from the imprisoned Paul material about the early Church, and his travels with Paul from city to city over Asia Minor and across the wide Mediterranean had supplied Luke with the rest of the fascinating story.

THEMES: The rise of Christianity from a Jewish sect to a world-wide religion ending in the great city of Rome itself. The story is filled with drama and even melodrama, what with shipwreck, riots, arrests, deaths, murders, tortures, escapes, and martyrdoms! Above all the Holy Spirit makes all things possible for the salvation of the human race. Halfway through the story, Paul takes the center of the stage and carries the Faith successfully to the Gentiles. The Acts is the foundation stone of church history.

DETAILED REVIEW AND COMMENTARY ON THE GOSPEL OF ACTS

CHAPTER 1

INTRODUCTION (1:1-3): The author (Luke) continues to address Theophilus and tells him that in his first volume (treatise) he had dealt with the life, death, and resurrection of Jesus. The volume ended where Jesus was taken up into heaven (ascension), but not until he had given his chosen apostles their instructions. Jesus had shown himself alive to them (after his crucifixion) in many convincing ways ("by many infallible proofs") and had remained with them forty days, all the time speaking of the kingdom of God.

JESUS' PARTING WORDS BEFORE HIS ASCENSION (1:4-14): Once while dining with them ("being assembled together with them"), he told them not to leave Jerusalem, but to "wait for the promise of the Father." John baptized only with water, but you (the Twelve) "shall be baptized with the Holy Ghost (Holy Spirit)" in a few days. They will not know the time or place of bestowal of the Holy Spirit, but once bestowed upon them "ye shall receive power," and they shall preach his word in Palestine and "unto the uttermost parts of the earth." "And when he had spoken these things, while they beheld, he was taken up; and a cloud received him out of their sight." Two angels in white appeared and told the Twelve that this same Jesus who ascended into heaven will one day return "in like manner." They returned to Jerusalem to their "upper room" where dwelt Peter, James, John, Andrew, Philip, Thomas, Bartholomew, Matthew, James the son of Alpheus, Simon Zelotes, and Judas the brother of James. Among the women there were Mary, Jesus' mother, and his brothers.

JUDAS' PLACE IS FILLED (1:15-26): Peter addressed about 120 of his fellow disciples of Christ ("brothers") and tells them how Judas the betrayer had bought a piece of land with his bloody money, and "falling headlong," he had burst asunder in the midst (his body swelled up and burst open in the middle), and "all his bowels gushed out." The place became known as "the field of blood." Lots were drawn to fill Judas' place and Matthias is chosen as the twelfth apostle.

COMMENT: Nothing is known of Theophilus, to whom both the gospel

of Luke and Acts is dedicated. At the beginning of Acts the apostles still expect the kingdom of God on earth, like the kingdom of David but far more full of peace, riches, and glory; by the end of Acts they realize the kingdom is spiritual—not temporal. The ascension of Jesus is often pictured in the more realistic church windows by showing a worm's-eye view of two gigantically naked feet protruding from a cloud! The cloud represents the "glory" in which Christ ascends to heaven. The two angels predict the Second Coming of the son of Man in trailing clouds of glory. The "upper room" was probably Mary's, the mother of Mark —some say the room of the Last Supper. As usual the words of David had nothing to do with the Judas situation, but all such prophecies, whether relevant or not, are deemed to apply as part of the direct aims of the Holy Spirit. The account of Judas' death is really Luke's interpolation but ascribed to Peter; he often interpolates his own "footnotes" into the fabric of the story. Judas Isacariot is in the place where he belongs—hell! Lots were cast by putting stones into a jar and shaking it until one jumped out; the stones would have had names inscribed on them.

CHAPTER 2

PENTECOST AND PETER'S SPEECH (2:1-47): While they were all together, there came "a sound from heaven as of a rushing mighty wind, and it filled all the house where they were sitting." The flames darted above the heads of each of them ("it sat upon each of them"); and they were all filled with the Holy Spirit and began to speak in foreign languages at the promptings of the Spirit. A crowd gathered in great excitement ("were confounded") because the crowd heard each speaking in his own language. Some thought they

were drunk, but Peter spoke to the crowd in the following manner: We are not drunk since it is only 9:00 A.M. (the third hour). What is happening is what the O.T. prophet Joel had predicted; in the last days God will pour out his Spirit upon all mankind: "and your sons and your daughters shall prophesy, and your men shall see visions, and your old men shall dream dreams." God sent Jesus his son in your midst, but you crucified and slew him. But he arose! Neither did his flesh see corruption (decay)! We the apostles of Christ are the witnesses to his resurrection; we have just received his Spirit, "which ye now see and heard." This Jesus, whom you crucified, God has declared to be both Lord and Christ. (The reader should bear in mind that the above is a paraphrase and not a direct quotation of Peter's speech; this will be the usual practice henceforth.) Stung to the quick, the Jews asked what to do; Peter told them to repent their sins and be baptized in the name of Jesus Christ for forgiveness of sins, "and ye shall receive the gift of the Holy Ghost." That same day three thousand Jews were converted to Christ. They (the Christians) owned all their goods in common, each according to his need.

COMMENT: The Feast of Pentecost celebrates what happened here, a great spiritual experience. The Holy Spirit like a flame filled them with ecstasy and a wonderful gift of languages as well as meaningless noises. A crowd collects, a polyglot crowd, since Jerusalem was polyglot in its inhabitants, especially at festival time.

The sudden ability to speak many languages seems pointless since Greek was a common language understandable to most. Luke very likely mistranslates the. Greek word *glossolalia* = speaking in ecstasy, and takes it to mean a literal speaking in many tongues. *Pentecost* means "fiftieth," and occurs fifty days after the Passover, the Jewish harvest festival known as "the feast of weeks." Specifically it celebrates God's giving the commandments to Moses at Sinai; here God gives a new Law: the Holy Spirit in the form of purifying flames. Jesus fulfills his promise of power to his apostles. One amazing proof of the effectiveness of the "power" is the sudden conversion of 3000 Jews, the first fruits of what will be a bumper crop of Christians. The Christian Pentecost occurs seven weeks after Easter (itself related to Passover). We have here a foreshadowing of an eventual evangelization of the entire world, and it is appropriately put here, before the disciples go on their missionary journeys. Note that communism was practiced by early Christians.

CHAPTER 3

PETER EXPLAINS ANCIENT PROPHECY; A PUBLIC MIRACLE AND ITS EXPLANATION (3:1-26): At three in the afternoon ("the ninth hour") Peter cures a man who had been congenitally lame since birth: "In the name of Jesus Christ of Nazareth rise up and walk." Peter speaks to the amazed crowd of Jews: the God of Abraham, Isaac, and Jacob glorified his son Jesus, but you chose a murderer (Barabbas) instead and crucified God's son. Repent then and be converted, "that your sins may be blotted out, when the times of refreshing (happier times) shall come from the presence of

the Lord." God first sent his son to you, the blessed children of God; and after he raised him from the dead; he had been sent by God "to bless you by making every one of you turn from his wickedness."

COMMENT: The cure of the paralytic since birth = first public display of followers of Jesus filled with his Holy Spirit of power to cure and convert. Why John is present in this story along with Peter will be explained later, since it happens often. Particularly delightful: "and immediately his feet and ankle bones received strength."

CHAPTERS 4-5

THE FIRST CLASH AND PETER'S BOLDNESS; THE YOUNG CHURCH (4:1-37) (5:1-42): And as they preached, the priests, the captain of the temple guard, and the Sadducees (the aristocrats, believers in conservatism, non-believers in spirits or angels or resurrection of the body) arrested them; yet the number of converts rose to 5000. The next day they were asked by what power or authority ("name") they did and said such things. Peter told them that the helpless ("impotent") man was made whole by the name of Jesus whom they had crucified. He is the cornerstone of the new salvation —nor is there salvation any other way! The authorities told them to preach no more in the name of Jesus, but the threats did not deter Peter and John, "for we cannot but speak the things which we have seen and heard." They were let go, since no cause for imprisonment was found —and besides there was fear of the people. The apostles returned to the others and prayed to God and asked for strength to continue their work. Now they were filled with the Holy Spirit and spoke the word of God fearlessly. Communal ownership of goods and brotherly love; all was distributed—each according to his need. A wealthy man named Ananias sold all his goods and property but kept a share secretly for himself, laying the rest at the disciples' feet. Peter accused him of a lie—not to men but to God, and Ananias collapsed and died on the spot! His wife, who also knew of the share kept from the common store, also collapsed at Peter's feet and died after he had said, "There at the door are the footsteps of the men who buried your husband, and they will carry you out also." People would bring out their sick and lay them down on stretchers so that Peter's shadow might fall upon their loved ones and cure them. All the sick were cured in one way or another. Again the apostles were arrested and put into a common jail, but an angel released them. They continued their teaching in the temple. The mystified guards again arrested the apostles, and again they were accused of preaching; "and ye have filled Jerusalem with your doctrine, and intend to bring this man's blood upon us." Again the apostles defied them and made counter-accusations of Christ-murder. The Jews grew furious and wanted to kill them, but a Pharisee named Gamaliel, a teacher ("doctor") of the Law highly esteemed by the people, ordered the apostles to be removed for a while ("to put forth a little space") and warned his fellows, citing the case of Theudas (THOH duhs) who in rebellion with 400 supporters came to a bad end; also there was Judas of Galilee (not Iscariot) who also perished for rebelling. Let the Christians alone (said Gamaliel), for if this movement is human in origin it will die out, but if from God, it would do no good to oppose it. His colleagues agreed. They called the apostles, beat them, enjoined them to silence, and let them go. The apostles departed, "rejoicing that they were counted worthy to suffer shame for his (i.e., Christ's) name." They continued their daily teaching and preaching.

COMMENT: The conversion of 5000 men by Peter is a fantastic number and ought to be considerably pared down to some kind of reality. Note the presence of the cured man in court—he had been cured formerly in the temple—he remains a living witness to Peter's power. The story of Ananias and his wife Sapphira seems incredible, and, in addition, puts Peter in a bad light. Mercilessness and cruelty, cunning and vindictiveness are not the traits we associate with Christ's chief follower. The purpose of the story is to impress with the power of apostolic authority. Gamaliel will later figure with Paul (22:3), and his intervention and speech indicate the better attitude of the Jewish authorities towards the Church, an attitude all too rare, according to the gospels.

CHAPTERS 6-7

STEPHEN (6:1-15) (7:1-60): A dispute arose as to what happened to the money for the poor, sick, and the widows. Seven disciples are selected as treasurers, and Stephen, a man full of faith and the Holy Spirit, was one of the seven deacons chosen. Thus the apostles could spread the word without dissension. Stephen performed miracles and cures and was unbeatable in his debates with synagogue teachers. Stephen was accused of blasphemy and marched off to court. The charge was that he said Jesus of Nazareth shall destroy the Temple and shall "change the customs which Moses delivered (handed down to) us." The onlookers looked at Stephen and saw that his face was like that of an angel. Stephen's defense relates the story of Abraham with the Chaldeans (kal DEE uhns) and his residence in Charran (Haran), the covenant with God, the bondage in Egypt, the covenant (contract with God) of circumcision, the story of Jacob and Joseph his son, the story of Moses and Mount Sinai, Moses and the golden calf, and how God turned away from his chosen people (Jews) for worshipping idols. Then Stephen told of David and how he wished to build a house of worship, but "the Most High dwelleth not in temples made with hands . . . Heaven is my throne, and earth is my footstool: what house will ye build me? saith the Lord: or what is the place of my rest? . . . Ye stiffnecked and uncircumcised in heart and ears, ye do always resist the Holy Ghost, as your fathers did, so do ye!" Stephen told of the Jewish persecution of their own great prophets, of their violations of Moses' law, etc. When the Jews heard these things, "they were cut to the heart, and they gnashed on him (raved at him) with their teeth." Stephen looks up and sees heaven open, with the son of Man on God's right hand. The Jews, however, shout and stop their ears, drag Stephen out of the city and stone him to death as Stephen kneels, saying loudly, "Lord, lay not this sin to their charge (i.e., don't blame them)!" Participating as an accuser was a young man named Saul.

COMMENT: Note the difficulty with the handling of funds for charity; their solution seems an admirable one: seven *spiritual-practical* men to oversee the charity funds. Stephen seems to have gone into an ecstatic trance when he saw the heavens open, but the purpose of his long speech is easily determined: 1. The history of the Jews revealed in their own Bible shows perpetual infidelity to God, a blindness and obstinacy revealed in the final evil act of the crucifixion. Joseph and Moses were prototypes of Jesus: both were rejected by their people and both were saviours. Canaan, Judea, and the Temple were not vital in the worship of God. He can be worshipped without constructing a building of worship. Joseph like Jesus was sold and delivered to the enemy and yet rose to the highest throne. Moses like Jesus saved his people from a foreign power, heard the voice of God (the Transfiguration), performed miracles, mediated between God and man, gave God's laws to man, etc. The tabernacle of the testimony was a tent containing a shrine, the Ark, in which the Law was kept. The trial of Stephen seems more like a lynching, but in all likelihood there was a legal trial. Stoning: an accusing witness shoves the accused over a precipice and then rolls a boulder after him. Then the other witnesses roll their stones, and often even the bystanders do so as well.

CHAPTERS 8-9

SIMON THE MAGICIAN; PHILIP AND THE EUNUCH; SAUL AT DAMASCUS (8:1-40) (9:1-43): Saul and many others persecuted the Church severely, Saul dragging with his own hands some of the Christians to jail. In Samaria (Suh MARE ee uh) a magician named Simon mystified the people with his magic; he was even said to have God's power, but he was converted by Philip after seeing Philip's even more remarkable demonstrations of power. Simon, seeing the remarkable curative display by the "laying on of hands" of the apostles, offered them money for similar power, but Peter said "To hell with you and your money!" (*King James*: "Go to destruction with your money!") and denounced him for trying to bribe them for the gift of God's Holy Spirit. Simon begs that none of Peter's curses come to pass.

Philip met on his journey an Ethiopian eunuch (EWE' nuck), a castrate, and the treasurer to Candace, queen of the Ethiopians. The eunuch was reading from Isaiah: "He was led as a sheep to the slaughter," etc. Philip was invited to tell the eunuch how to interpret the passage. The good news of Jesus was given and the Ethiopian was thereupon baptized with water, to his great joy. Philip continued on his way.

Saul went to the high priest for permission to go to Damascus to search for Christians to bring back as prisoners. On his journey to Damascus a light from heaven suddenly blazed around him and a voice said, "Saul, Saul, why persecutest thou me? . . . I am Jesus whom thou persecutest: it is hard for thee to kick against the pricks (go against the grain?)." The voice told Saul to go to the city where he will be told what to do; those with him stood speechless, hearing the voice but seeing nothing. Saul got up from the ground unable to see—blind from the light. He was led by the hand to Damascus, where he remained blind for three days, and without food or drink.

In a dream a disciple named Ananias (uh NAN ee uhs) was told to lay his hands on Saul to restore his sight. Of Saul the Lord said, "He is a chosen vessel unto me, to bear my name before the Gentiles (heathen), and kings, and the children (descendants) of Israel." The scales fell from Saul's eyes when Ananias put his hands on him, and immediately Saul preached Christ in the synagogues, that Jesus was the son of God. Soon the Jews decided to kill Saul, but Saul eluded the watch in this way: "Then the disciples took him by night, and let him down by the wall in a basket." Barnabas reassured the other disciples when Saul was introduced to them. For safety's sake, Saul was sent to Tarsus.

Peter cured a man called Aeneas who had been a paralytic for eight years. At Joppa a woman disciple called Tabitha (Dorcas in Greek) took ill and died. She had been a good woman and many mourned her, for she had been a good seamstress and worker. All were put outside the room and Peter told the body to get up, which it did! She was presented to the rest, well and alive! Many were converted by this feat.

COMMENT: Philip shows his originality by first converting the detested

Samaritans, and next by baptizing a eunuch! The Law of Moses forbade eunuchs to practice Judaism. Simon the magician might even have claimed to be the messiah to the naive and credulous Samaritans. Our word *simony* (buying Church office) comes from this incident; note that Simon, a Christian, had made the bribe. He is the first heretic in Christianity. The incident seems to teach that the Church has a monopoly of the Spirit, which is a rite after baptism, signified by the laying on of hands. Perhaps there were heretical groups (gnostics?) who claimed the Holy Spirit. The eunuch episode is (or seems to be) fabricated entirely from the Isaiah text (53:7-8) and Psalm 68:31.

Paul's (or Saul's) conversion is related three times (Chapters 9, 22, 26), with variations each time it is told. The tale, say some critics, might be legendary, since few if any Christians would have been in Damascus at that time. The tale is hinted at, however, in the Epistles of Paul, of an earlier date. Paul's hurrying to meet the old apostles in Jerusalem is contradicted in Galatians 1:15-17, 21-24. Other critics insist that Damascus would be a natural place for the disciples to flee after the slaying of Stephen. Note that here his companions do hear the voice. The three-day blindness and Pentecost = Christ after three days resurrected. The basket lowering became a popular gag in classic comedy. Paul smarted over that incident for a lifetime (see I Corinthians 29-32).

Peter's cure duplicates the raising of Jairus' daughter in Luke 8:41-56 as well as O.T. cures by Elijah and Elisha.

CHAPTER 10

CORNELIUS (10:1-48): Cornelius of Caesarea (sez uh REE uh) a Roman centurion (captain) and a good, God-fearing man, was commanded by an angel to send for Peter—which he did. At seeing Peter, Cornelius got on his knees, but Peter said, "Stand up; I myself also am a man." In spite of the Jewish prohibition of communion with Gentiles, Peter came to the centurion because "I should not call any man common or un-clean." God is no respecter of persons (shows no partiality), "but in every nation he that feareth him, and worketh righteousness, is accepted with him (i.e., Christ). While Peter taught, the Holy Spirit fell on all who were listening to the message. The circumcised (Jews) were astonished that the Gentiles too could receive the Holy Spirit (these are the *Christian* Jews who had accompanied Peter), but Peter reassured them it was so.

CHAPTERS 11-12

DISQUIET OVER PETER'S ACTION; PETER'S IMPRISONMENT AND RESCUE (11:1-30) (12:1-25): The "circumcision party" amongst the disciples protested Peter's co-habiting with uncircumcised men, but Peter explained how it had all come about: in a vision in Joppa he saw a great sheet lowered by its four corners from heaven. On it were birds, beasts, and reptiles of all types. A voice told Peter to kill and eat, but Peter protested that the food was unclean (according to the Law); the voice replied that he must not call what God has cleaned *common*. Three times this happened, and it was over.

Then he told them the centurion incident, which came right after the sheet-vision, and his brethren were satisfied that God had extended his gift to Gentiles also. The persecution following the death of Stephen dispersed the Christians to various cities; many were converted, but the persecutions continued. Barnabas (BAR nuh buss) and Saul stayed a whole year in Antioch, where the followers of Jesus were first given the name of *Christians*. Saul and Barnabas were sent to Jerusalem to bring relief to their brothers there.

King Herod executed by sword James, the brother of John, and then arrested Peter during the Passover festival. In the night an angel woke Peter, his chains fell away, and he was led to freedom. He hurried to the house of Mary, the mother of Mark, where many Christians were praying. As he knocked at the door, a young maid named Rhoda came but failed to open the door from sheer joy ("opened not the gate for gladness"). She announced the news to the company, who called her mad. The maid insisted, while Peter continued knocking: and when they had opened the door, and saw him, they were astonished." The angry Herod had the jailguards put to death for laxity on duty. While delivering an oration in royal apparel, he is hailed as a god by the people, at which point the angel of the Lord struck him down immediately, "because he gave not God the glory: and he was eaten of worms, and gave up the ghost."

COMMENT: Peter's conversion of the Roman officer Cornelius occurs, appropriately enough, in that most Roman of cities, Caesarea. Conversions portending big things—as in this case the first *uncircumcised* pagan convert—usually proceed from preliminary visions (10:1-23), to the meeting and mutual explanations (24-33), to the announcement of the discourse of universal salvation. The whole incident puts Peter before Paul as being the first to reach the Gentiles. Barnabas serves also to receive uncircumcised pagans into the fold. Note the foundation of the Church in Antioch. The famine might be the same as that mentioned by the contemporary of Jesus, Josephus the historian (*Antiquities*, XX, 5.2). The emperor Claudius urged a persecution of Jewish agitators and James is killed; but the reason John his brother is not killed along with him (which probably did occur) is to support the legend of his survival in the Ephesian legend that he was driven to the island of Patmos and wrote his *Revelation* there in his old age. Note that Luke in his gospel omits Jesus' prediction of John's martyrdom. A good theory about Peter's escape from jail is that he had fled to Antioch, but the city is not mentioned in order to cover the Peter-Paul conflict that beset the early Church in that city; 12:17 merely says that Peter went away to "another place." Not a word is mentioned of Peter after the meeting in Jerusalem. Might he not have been put to death by Agrippa I along with James and John, hence never reaching Rome? But Galatians shows him later in conflict with Paul in Antioch (2:11-21). See articles entitled "Simon Magnus" and "Simon Peter" in the *Encyclopedia Biblica*, vol. IV. Incidentally, the name *Christians* comes from the Greek *Christos* (messiah), which is very like the Greek word *chrestos*, meaning 'good, honest fellow, good guy,' with a note of contempt and a patronizing air. The people of Antioch heard so much of *Christos* (Christ) that they called the disciples Christians. Verse 17 of Chapter 12 refers to James, the brother of Jesus, the leader of the Church in Jerusalem. One final note: Roman Catholics insist that Peter had fled after his escape from jail to Rome.

CHAPTER 13

PAUL AND ELYMAS; PAUL PREACHES (13:1-52): The Holy Spirit sent Saul and Barnabas off on a special mission to Seleucia, Cyprus, and Salamis, where they came across a man named Bar-Jesus, a Jew who was also a false prophet and magician. This man served Sergius Paulus, the proconsul, a man of wit and intelligence. Paulus sent for Saul and Barnabas, for he was eager to hear their message; but Elymas the magician, the translation of his name Bar-Jesus, did his best to prevent the conversion of Sergius. Paul pierced him with his eyes and said, "O full of all subtilty (cunning) and all mischief, thou child of the devil, thou enemy of all righteousness, will thou not cease to pervert the right ways of the Lord?" Elymas was struck blind, "there fell on him a mist and a darkness," and he went about seeking some one to lead him by the hand. Sergius saw this and "believed." They came to Antioch and, entering the synagogue on the sabbath, were urged to speak to the congregation. So Paul (he is now called by his Christian name) began: he spoke of the past, of the Jewish exile in Egypt, of the winning of Canaan, of the judges, of Samuel, Saul, of David, of Jesus his descendant, of John the Baptist who prepared the Way and who said of Jesus that he was one "whose shoes of his feet I am not worthy to loose." Paul told them how the Jews of Jerusalem crucified Jesus, but how he arose from the dead. Paul brought them the good news (gospel) that the promise made to the forefathers of the Jews has come true, that Jesus is the fulfillment of all the prophecies in the Old Testament. The sermon aroused much interest. On the next sabbath almost the entire population of the city turned out to hear Paul and Barnabas, but they were abused publicly by jealous Jews. In disgust Paul and Barnabas told them that since they spurned God's message and refused eternal life, Paul and Barnabas would then turn to the Gentiles. The Gentiles in the audience were delighted at the good news! The Jews worked up feeling against the two apostles and had them expelled from the district. They shook off the dust of the city from their feet and went on to Iconium (eye KOHN ee uhm).

CHAPTER 14

PERSECUTION AND A MIRACLE (14:1-28): Securing many conversions in Iconium, they nevertheless are forced to flee. One day in Lystra a man "impotent in his feet, being a cripple from his mother's womb" (crippled since birth) is cured by Paul. As a result the people in their joy call Paul Mercury and Barnabas Jupiter. When the pagans prepare animal sacrifices in their name, the two apostles rend their clothes and tell them they are merely humans like them and that they should turn to the true God. Certain Jews from Antioch and Iconium come and persuade the people to stone Paul and leave him for dead outside the city limits. Paul nevertheless gets up and walks back into the city. The next day he preaches with Barnabas in Derbe (thirty miles away!) where they make many converts. They then return to Lystra, Iconium, and Antioch, and appoint elders for the congregations in each church. At Antioch they spend considerable time with the disciples.

COMMENT: Chapter 14 begins the account of Paul's great missionary journeys. The "work" to be done is of course to found the Gentile churches. Note that the church of Antioch commissions Paul—not Jerusalem. Remember Paul was a Roman citizen, and his great success with Sergius fires him to convert the entire pagan Roman world! Note too that from now on his name is the Roman Paul, not the Jewish Saul, and that henceforth the two apostles are referred to as Paul and Barnabas, not Barnabas and Saul. Bar-Jesus means "son of the saviour": that is why he is called the son of Satan. Elymas was very likely an oriental cultist-mystic-scientist; therefore the duel is a vital one. The proconsul is not really converted but is convinced Paul is the better man. Luke would certainly have made much more of a converted Roman proconsul at this early date. Paul's discourse seems a copy of Stephen's, and 26-41 seems a variant of Peter's to the Jews in Jerusalem. Ovid the Roman poet gives Lystra as the scene of the famous myth of Baucis and Philemon, where Zeus (Jupiter) and Hermes (Mercury) visited the town incognito. Paul was bald, slight, short, bow-legged, unimpressive looking, while Barnabas was tall, strong, and bearded like Jupiter. Zeus and Hermes were actually worshipped in this district. Paul's ability to endure stoning and still walk thirty miles the next day to Derbe is nothing short of amazing!

CHAPTER 15

THE GENTILE PROBLEM; TIMOTHY (15:1-41): Paul and Barnabas go to their brothers in Jerusalem to defend the accepting of Gentiles who are uncircumcised into the fold. Peter puts up his defense against the opposition made up of Jewish-Christians of Pharisee heritage (Pharisees were strict letter-of-the-Law men). Peter says God approves the Gentile as Christian. James quotes the scriptures "that the residue of men may seek after the Lord,/ And ask the gentiles, upon whom my name is called,/ Saith the Lord . . .". He adds that Gentiles should be made to avoid anything polluted by idols ("contaminated by idols"), sexual immorality ("fornication"), eating the meat of strangled animals, or tasting blood ("from things strangled, and from blood"). Judas and Silas are chosen to carry this message to the brothers in Antioch, Syria, and Cilicia. The brothers accept the message with delight (about the conditions of acceptance into the fold of Gentiles). Now Paul and Barnabas disagree about taking John (surnamed Mark) on their missionary journey. Paul disapproves of John's having at one time deserted them in Pamphylia (pam FILL yah). As a result Barnabas sails to Cyprus with Mark, while Paul chooses Silas to go with him. At Lystra Paul chooses the good Timothy, whose father was a Gentile Greek, as his companion also. To meet possible complaints Paul has him circumcised. Their journeys are quite successful in securing converts.

CHAPTER 16

CONFLICT, JAIL, AND AN APOLOGY (16:1-40): After choosing Timothy, the circumcised pagan-convert, as his companion, Paul went to Macedonia as the result of a vision he had had of a Macedonian man appealing for help. So "we" (the companions are grouped together as "we") went to Philippi, the chief city of Macedonia. At the riverside he preached and a woman named Lydia, a dealer in purple-dyed cloth, became a convert and was baptized along with her household. A certain young girl brought her owners a good deal of profit. It is she who harrassed Paul "and the rest of us" so much that Paul commanded the evil spirit to leave her "in the name of Jesus Christ." It left her immediately, but the profitless owners caused their arrest on the charge of proselytizing, and they were beaten and thrown into jail with their feet fastened securely in stocks. About midnight an earthquake broke open the gates and chains fastening the prisoners. At this the jailer started to commit suicide, but Paul yelled, "Do thyself no harm, for we are all here!" The jailer was converted along with his household, and he took the prisoners into his own house. The next morning the magistrates ordered the release of the prisoners, but Paul indignantly refused since they had been treated by the authorities in a wicked manner in spite of their Roman citizenship. "Let them come themselves and fetch us out!" Paul cried. Realizing they actually were Roman citizens, the authorities came in person and apologized. Finally Paul and Silas took their leave of the town after a final reassuring visit to Lydia's household.

COMMENT: In Chapter fifteen we have a constant narration of Paul's missions and captivity—but there is no mention of his death! The dispute and separation of Paul and Barnabas conceals a more fundamental dispute between Paul and the main body at Jerusalem. The travelers must have been Paul, Silas, and Luke (the narrator is Luke)—hence, the "we" passages. Note that the charge of the pythoness' owners (the pythoness = girl diviner) contradicts what Paul had actually done: exorcised an evil spirit; the charge should have been magic-practicing. The narrator often adds to and changes the facts of his source documents. For example, the earthquake business seems an invention of the narrator, perhaps Luke himself. Very likely the real facts were that Paul and his friends were allowed to leave the city after due security was given.

CHAPTERS 17-18

THESSALONICA, BEROEA, ATHENS; GALLIO AND APOLLOS (17:1-34) (18:1-28): At Thessalonica Paul argued for three days in the synagogue (three sabbath days), explaining and quoting scriptures to show them the true Christ as revealed in the Jewish testament. Some were convinced, but the Jews in a jealous fury hustled Jason and some of the brothers before the authorities. Jason was accused of harboring criminals who claimed fealty to another king called Jesus. That night Paul and Silas hurried to Beroea and at that synagogue many were converted; but trouble began anew and Paul alone was taken to Athens. In this idol-worshipping city Paul even took to preaching and arguing in the streets. Some Epicurean (epp ih CURE ee uhn) and Stoic philosophers called him a cock-sparrow ("babbler"); others ridiculed his outlandish gods. He was taken to the Areopagus (air ee OPP uh guss), the Athenian court, where he was told to preach to them his new teaching. The Athenians had an obsession for novelty.

Paul told the crowd how he saw

an altar inscribed: TO THE UN-KNOWN GOD, and how he is going to make that god known to them! He preached God's dislike of idols and the raising of his son from the dead. His reception was mixed, but Dionysus and Damaris were among those who joined him.

At Corinth Paul stayed with a Jew called Aquila and his wife Priscilla. They were tentmakers, as Paul had been. By this time Silas and Timothy had joined him. However, the Jews here turned against his preaching of the Christ and abused him. In anger "he shook his raiment (clothes) and said unto them, Your blood be upon your own heads; I am clean: from henceforth I will go unto the Gentiles!" Crispus, a synagogue leader, and many of the Corinthians believed and were baptized. Paul stayed there eighteen months, filled with the Holy Spirit while preaching. Again the Jews brought Paul before the governor of Greece, Gallio, but Gallio refused to intervene and chased the Jews from his court. Then the Gentile Greeks seized and beat Sosthenes, the Jewish leader of the synagogue. But Gallio paid no attention to this. Paul left for Syria with Priscilla and Aquila. At Cenchreae he had his hair cut because of a vow he had been under. Then he sailed to Ephesus (EFF ih suss) and then to Caesarea, to Jerusalem, to Antioch and throughout Galatia (gal LAY shee ah) and Phrygia (FRIDGE ee ah). Once at Ephesus a Jew named Apollos, eloquent and skillful in the use of the scriptures, listened to Aquila and Priscilla and was converted; he proved of great service to the brothers, especially in refuting his fellow-Jews.

COMMENT: Note that Luke is always interested in class distinctions; he is very class conscious, and is fond of citing conversions of upper-class figures, as in 17:12. Luke pictures Athens as a city without a soul; the Athenians are condescending. Paul did not appreciate the great art objects in the city, but he did act like Socrates and taught in the streets. Epicureans believed in happiness undisturbed by passion, superstition, or fear of an afterlife. Stoics believed in a God whose essence ran through the universe and man. They believed in the brotherhood of man and in reason, but it was the religion of the wealthy and aristocratic. "Babbler" means dilettante actually; literally, seed-picker. Note that Paul shows that he is cultured and knowledgeable. Why Paul prefers corrupt and prodigal Corinth to Athens is a mystery unless he feels the wickeder the city, the greater the converts! The Corinthians reveal themselves as gifted, passionate, and wayward. The beating of Sosthenes directly in front of Gallio leaves the governor indifferent to this lynch justice, conduct unbecoming a Roman governor. As for Paul's haircut—it was the Jewish custom to cut the hair at the commencement and finish of a vow. Paul's vow is unknown. Ephesus was a mighty and great city, the capital of the Roman province of Asia. It contained a world wonder—the gigantic temple of Artemis. It was the center of many mystery religions and hence filled with potential sinners waiting to be converted.

CHAPTERS 19-20

BOOKBURNING, DEMETRIUS; EUTYCHUS AND A FAREWELL

(19:1-41) (20:1-38): In Ephesus Paul discovered about twelve of the faithful who had not yet received the Holy Spirit and who had been baptized with the water of John the Baptist only. He explained that John's baptism signified repentance merely and duly baptized them, at which they too received the Holy Spirit. While staying for two years more at Ephesus he lectured in the hall of Tyrannus so that all who lived in Asia, both Greeks and Jews, could hear the Lord's message. Seven sons of a chief priest called Sceva tried dealing with evil spirits as did Paul, but the spirits would answer them, "Jesus I know, and Paul I know; but who are ye?" One man they attempted to cure attacked them, tearing off their clothes and wounding them. This incident awed many, many were convinced, and a number of those who had previously practiced magic collected their books, "brought their books together, and burned them before all men"; and the estimated value of the burned books was ten thousand dollars (50,000 pieces of silver). Now silversmiths, who made a good living making silver shrines for the goddess Diana (Artemis), were stirred up to wrath by one Demetrius who told them that Paul was changing the minds of many by telling them that gods made by human hands are not gods at all. This not only threatened their income but also the temple of Artemis and the great goddess herself. Furiously they shouted, "Great is Diana of the Ephesians!" The riotous people rushed into the theater and dragged out two of Paul's companions; Paul wanted to help them, but some high-ranking ones persuaded him not to. One Alexander tried to make a speech of defense, but the mob continued their rioting and shouting. The town clerk (recorder) finally quelled the riot by telling them to prefer their charges in court, for they were all in danger of being charged with rioting.

At Troas "we" were assembled for the ritual of bread-breaking while Paul addressed the group. Eutychus (EWE tih kuss), a young man, fell fast asleep during the very long sermon and fell out of the window from the third floor and was picked up for dead. Paul cured him and went upstairs to continue his discourse; the boy was taken home sound and well. After many travels Paul delivered a farewell message to the elders of the church at Ephesus: he told of his fidelity to God and Christ, of his trials with the Jews, how he had never shrunk from his mission, and how now feels compelled by the Holy Spirit to return to Jerusalem. In spite of warnings by the Holy Spirit of persecution he must continue to declare the good news. He told them they should never see him again and commended them to God's grace. He knelt to pray while the elders wept and kissed him.

COMMENT: The twelve Ephesian disciples rebaptized by Paul must have been converts of an inferior Christianity: hence the rebaptism. This reflects early church difficulties. The burning of the magic books is an ominous sign: this will not be the last time books will have been put to the torch, alas! Even Christian zealots will suppress the "heresies" by bookburning. Most of the traveling and appointing details have to do with the more solid realities of collecting funds for the church. The "resurrection" of Eutychus matches Peter's resurrection of Dorcas (9:36-42). Paul's oration (20:18-35) will serve as a model for Christian preachers who are giving their members instruction. Although Luke hints at Paul's death here, that fact is never recorded.

CHAPTERS 21-22

PAUL IS WARNED; A MURDER ATTEMPTED; PAUL'S DEFENSE (21:1-38) (22:1-30): At Tyre some disciples warned Paul that he should not go up to Jerusalem; but "we" nevertheless continued on "our" journeys to Cesarea (Caesarea), where Paul and his companions stayed at the home of Philip the missionary ("evangelist"), who had four virgin daughters gifted in prophesy. Now from Judea a certain prophet named Agabus took Paul's belt ("girdle") and tied his own hands and feet with it, signifying that the same will be done to Paul by the Jews at Jerusalem. "We" pleaded with Paul not to go to Jerusalem, but Paul said, "I am ready not to be bound only but also to die at Jerusalem for the name of the Lord Jesus." Upon reaching Jerusalem Paul was seized as one who preaches against the Law and one who had polluted the Temple by bringing a Gentile into it. Roman soldiers prevented Paul's being beaten to death by literally carrying him off (". . . he was borne of the soldiers for the violence of the people.") The mob followed cry, "Away with him!" The colonel asked if Paul were not the Egyptian who some time ago had raised the four thousand cutthroats ("murderers") and led them out into the desert ("wilderness"). Paul identified himself as from Tarsus in Cilicia and requested permission to speak to the people, to which the colonel consented.

(22:1-30) Paul spoke his defense in Hebrew and told the Jews that he had been trained in the Law under Gamaliel (guh MAY lee uhl) and had persecuted Christians until his vision on the road to Damascus, where those who accompanied him had seen the light but heard not God's voice. He told how Ananias cured his sight and how he was given his mission to the Gentiles by God. The crowd roared for his blood, whereupon the colonel took him into the castle to be bound and scourged, but the officer desisted when Paul told him that he was a Roman citizen by birth, which news amazed the colonel who had to pay "a great sum" for his freedom and citizenship (citizenship could be purchased as well as inherited by birth). Paul was unbound and brought before the Jewish Sanhedrin.

COMMENT: Chapter 21's reference to the thousands and thousands of Judaizing Christians in Jerusalem is very much an obvious exaggeration. Paul's presence in the temple (even though "disguised") is soon detected and he is brought into the barracks of Antonia (soldier site). Paul's method of declaring himself a Roman citizen is perhaps somewhat melodramatic and embellished; more likely he revealed his citizenship to escape Jewish justice for Roman. The Roman officer is Claudius Lysias, who is amazed that the puny man before him, battered and beaten and bloody, could possibly be his equal. His name derives from the Emperor under whom he had bought his citizenship, Claudius.

CHAPTERS 23-24

DANGER! PAUL IS SENT TO FELIX (23:1-35): Paul, who is about to be smitten on the mouth at the orders of the high priest Ananias (an uh NIGH us), cries out, "God shall smite thee, thou whited (whitewashed) walls!" Paul apologizes later when he is told that he had yelled at the high priest himself. In his speech he declares himself a Pharisee who believes in the resurrection of the dead, whereupon there arises a quarrel between the Pharisees and the Sadducees, who believe not in resurrection; and the tumult is such that the colonel, thinking Paul will be torn to pieces, brings him back to the castle (really the Antonia barracks). The next day forty Jews swear neither to eat nor drink until they have murdered Paul, but Paul's sister's son (his nephew) overhears their plot and tells his uncle. The nephew then tells the colonel, who writes a letter to Felix, the governor of Caesarea, in which he explains that the charges against Paul are groundless but that his life is in danger and that Paul should be tried before Felix. Paul is taken to Felix, who reads the letter and tells Paul that he will hear his case as soon as his accusers arrive in town.

(24:1-27) The accusers arrive and Tertullus, the prosecutor, charges Paul with being "a pestilent fellow, and a mover of sedition among all Jews throughout the world, and a ring-leader of the sect of the Nazarenes" who had also profaned the Temple. Paul's defense is that he was not guilty of insurrection, that he follows the Law, that he believes in the resurrection, and that he has done no evil. Felix, who is informed on the Christian Way (Christianity), puts Paul in custody to await a verdict. Later Felix and Drusilla, his Jewish wife, hear Paul on the way, but Felix becomes alarmed ("trembled") and dismisses him. Felix hopefully awaits a bribe for the release of Paul but meanwhile often hearkens to Paul's teachings. Two years later Porcius Festus succeeds Felix as governor, with Paul still in prison.

COMMENT: This is the fifth trial before the Sanhedrin; the others were those of Jesus, Peter and John, the Twelve, and Stephen. Luckily Paul is saved by a factional quarrel arising from the mutual hatred of Pharisees and Sadducees. Did the wily Paul deliberately precipitate the disturbance by claiming himself a Pharisee and believer in resurrection? Not without cunning is the noble Paul! The nephew seems brought out from nowhere—an invention? Certainly embellished is the great mass of Paul's military escort to Caesarea. An error: Ananias was not high priest in the time of Felix (see 24:1 and 23:2); and incidentally, the real issue is missed: which court is competent to try Paul's case? Felix is indeed a coward, since he did not wish to offend the Jews of the Sanhedrin and so adjourned the case on a pretext (that Claudius Lysias was not present).

CHAPTERS 25-26

FESTUS; AGRIPPA (25:1-27): Again there is a trial before Festus, and Paul again denies violating the Law, desecrating the Temple, or fomenting insurrection against the emperor, and appeals his case to the Emperor at Rome; Festus consents, but not before telling a certain king Agrippa and his wife Bernice about the entire case. Festus could find no wrong in Paul except that the Jews had some kind of internal quarrel over his claims "of one Jesus, which was dead, whom Paul affirmed to be alive." The King and Queen come in great pomp to hear Paul himself and to examine him and prepare charges so that Festus can send Paul on to

Rome for trial.

(26:1-32) Paul tells Agrippa how he had been raised a Pharisee, how he had persecuted Christians, how he was converted on the road to Damascus, how he found his mission in life among the Gentiles "to open their eyes, and to turn them from darkness to light"; and finally how he was seized by the Jews in the Temple and murder attempted upon his person—but God has been with him always. Festus calls out, "Paul, thou art beside thyself (raving); much learning doth make thee mad." Paul denies this before the King, "for this thing was not done in a corner"; to which King Agrippa replies, "Paul, Almost thou persuadest me to be a Christian." They declare Paul innocent, Agrippa adding, "This man might have been set at liberty, if he had not appealed unto Cesar."

COMMENT: Paul does not want to be tried in the Jerusalem court for fear of a "frame-up," like that handed to Jesus. *Caesarem appello* ("I appeal to Caesar!") were words carrying great authority in those days. A precious right of the Roman citizen was the right of appeal. Naturally, most Jews would have looked upon a Jew making such an appeal as a betrayer of his country, since Rome to the patriotic Jew was a tyrant-oppressor of Palestine. The emperor at this time was the young and still fairly innocent Nero, and it was to him Paul would be sent. Nero succeeded Claudius in 54 A.D. Agrippa was actually a petty Jewish king brought in by Festus to pad his official report—an excuse that seems ludicrous and very likely invented. The purpose is to show Paul's innocence in the eyes of Festus and Agrippa; the trial in Rome however will condemn Paul, and he will not say a word in his defense!

CHAPTERS 27-28

TEMPEST AT SEA; PAUL IN ROME (27:1-44): "We" set sail under the guard of the officer Julius for Italy, and while at sea after a series of stops, Paul predicted trouble and woe, but the officer believed him not. They were sailing for Crete when a violent wind called a northeaster ("Euroclydon") put them in peril; they began to throw cargo overboard and the ship's tackle ("tackling"); at this point Paul reminded them that he had warned them not to sail! He predicted no loss of life but loss of the ship only as a result of the storm. An angel (his guardian angel) had so informed him the night before. He also advised that they stay in the ship and not flee in boats, and in addition told them to break their fourteen-day fast and to eat. Paul himself broke bread first and gave thanks to God, after which all ate. There were about 76 (or 276) people on board when the ship ran aground and stuck fast, but the stern began to break under the strain. The soldiers wanted to kill the prisoners lest they escape by swimming to shore, but the officer in charge, "willing to save Paul, kept them from their purpose." He commanded those who could swim to jump in and swim for shore, and the rest to follow on planks or other pieces of wreckage. So they all got safely to land.

(28:1-31) The island was called Malta ("Melita") and the natives displayed much kindness. While he was laying sticks on a fire, a viper (poisonous snake) bit Paul's hand; Paul simply shook the animal into the fire with no ill effects whatsoever, so that the natives took him for a god. The chief's name was Publius, and it was his father whom Paul cured of a fever and dysentery ("a bloody flux") as well as other sick natives. After three months and loaded with presents, they sailed for Syracuse in Sicily, then Rhegium. then Puteoli, where they stayed for seven days, and finally they arrived at Rome. Christian brothers came from as far as Appius' Forum and Three Taverns to meet them, and Paul gave them thanks and encouragement. In Rome Paul was given permission to live by himself. Three days later he invited the leading Jews of the city to visit him. He told them of his innocence, how he had "committed nothing against the people, or customs of our fathers," how the Jews spoke against his release from the Romans, and how he was "constrained to appeal unto Cesar; not that I had aught to accuse my nation of." The leading Jews of Rome say they had not received any letters from Judea about Paul, nor any news of him whatsoever, but they did express a curiosity to hear his views on the sect which is denounced everywhere. Many Jews then came on an appointed day and were persuaded that Jesus comes out of the law of Moses and the sayings of the prophets. His talk lasted from morning till evening, and some believed—some did not. Paul's last words before they left is a quote from Isaiah: "Go unto this people, and say, Hearing ye shall hear, and shall not understand." The Jews are blind and dull and deaf, and therefore salvation is only possible for the Gentiles, who will heed the message of Christ. Paul stayed two years in rented lodgings, welcoming everybody and preaching openly and un-hindered the Good News.

COMMENT: Very likely the other prisoners on the boat were being sent to Rome as lion fodder. Luke shows poor knowledge of the seas of the Levant, says the scholar Ramsay (William Ramsay: *St. Paul the Traveller and Roman Citizen*, 1894). The fast Paul tells them to break aboard is the Fast of the Atonement, a Jewish holy day occurring late in September or early October. In 59 A.D. it fell on October 5. In the crisis they were forced to drop four anchors from the stern after losing their paddles (steering paddles), which had been hung over the side to prevent damage to them from the anchor chains. The last "we" passage occurs in the notice of the arrival of Paul and his companions in Rome. Note the generous conditions of his imprisonment in Rome, but still under the guard of a soldier (verse 16 of Chapter 27). The final two interviews with Jews seem more propaganda than reality, but it is a ringing conclusion to the book of Acts, a conclusion that the only true Judaism is Christianity; and since the Jews reject it, the only true followers of Christ in Judaism are the Gentiles. Since the only true Judaists are the Christians, the author Luke is saying, then the Romans should give them the same rights and liberties they allow the Jewish cult. Obviously, Luke knew what happened to Paul in Rome, but he does not care to relate his last days and end. The same is true for his omission of the account of the last days of Peter. Nevertheless, the fate of the two greatest apostles still remains a mystery, although Roman Catholics still affirm their belief that Peter was the first Bishop of Rome and was there martyred.

THE EPISTLES: A PREFACE

DATE: See the commentary in the individual sections.

AUTHORS: The problem of authorship of the epistles is one of the thorniest in Biblical scholarship. The orthodox position usually maintains that most of the epistles are genuine; the liberal position admits to some "interpolations" in several of the epistles; the historical critics find some to be outright forgeries parading under some famous apostle's name, such as Paul or Peter. A few epistles are deemed forgeries, even by orthodox scholars. The controversies surrounding some of the epistles is given in the individual sections. Generally speaking however, Paul is certainly the author of most of the epistles credited to him.

THEMES: Again the individual sections should be referred to. Paul had been preaching the gospel for 25 years throughout the eastern provinces of the Empire. Then he fixed his eyes on the western provinces, like Spain, for his missionary efforts, and it is while he is on his way to Spain that he visits the small congregation of Christians in Rome. Paul, the great missionary-statesman whose "interests embrace East and West, Jerusalem, Rome, Spain" (Goodspeed, p. 349), makes a final effort at attempting to unite both Jew and Greek under the banner of Christianity in his epistle (letter) to the Romans. His other letters also often attain the sublime, but he is usually busy patching the rents in the fabric of his churches, hauling in the wayward Faithful, exposing and denouncing incipient heresies—in all, he produces in his letters a significant body of doctrine which has been as influential in the shaping of the course of church history as the gospels themselves.

DETAILED REVIEW AND COMMENTARY ON THE EPISTLES

ROMANS

(Chs. 1-8) After a salutation (1:1-7) and an introductory section (1:8-15) Paul talks of the "saving power" of the gospel. God gave man a way of righteousness, which means a right relationship with God, from whom we receive righteousness in ourselves and in our life with other people. Now all men need this basic rightness with God, although some men do not recognize this need. We think we are good, but before God we are all sinners when we fail to live up to God's requirements. The Jews were given a great advantage by being provided with the Law of Moses, which is the revelation of God's will through the mouths of the prophets—but the Jews have been wilfully disobedient and contrary to the Law. All men then need God's help; they need justification and "acquittal" before God's judgment seat. Justification cannot be had by observing a complex Law, which only serves to distinguish what we really are from what God really wants us to become. Good deeds alone will not justify us but only faith in Jesus Christ, who carries to us God's grace and mercy. Through Christ God comes to our aid, out of his complete and freely given love for man ("grace"). The gift of God's grace through Jesus, man did not merit, but he can rightly and gratefully accept that gift. The Jews rejected his gift, but both Jew and Gentile can now freely receive God's grace because God so wills it. Salvation is not earned by keeping God's commandments; salvation can not be *earned*; all we can do is *accept* and be strengthened by its power. God forgave man by offering Christ to atone for his sins, and through his sacrifice only are we "justified."

When we respond to God's love as revealed in Jesus, we are displaying faith, as did both Abraham and David in the Old Testament. Ignorance of God's laws is no excuse for sinning, however, nor is knowledge of God's love an excuse for continuing to sin. Baptism washes our sins away and from it we rise with Christ to a new life. Henceforth, God's free gift of forgiveness and washing us clean of sin imposes upon us a task to behave like called "saints." Our daily lives must reflect God's great gift to us—the sacrifice of his only Son.

The life of a Christian is an inner struggle between the "flesh" and the faith in Christ. Following the law cannot break the grip of evil within all of us; it will merely enhance the bitterness of the struggle. Law tells us what to do without giving us the power to do it. Neither do our good judgment and intentions help us, for they lack performing and continuing power. Our will-power is both weak and wrong in its direction—only Jesus Christ can set our wills right and give them performing and continuing power. This is what the Christian life does in fact: utter faith and loyalty to God, the adopted children of God (not his spoiled brats). We have no prior claim or rights on God, but his grace is all-encompassing. Since God has broken the grip of sin upon our lives and hearts, it is left to us to break the grip of sin in actual fact, to live in truth as the children of God. Nothing can tear us from God's love, which was made plain in Jesus Christ our Lord (8:38-39).

(Chs. 9-11) What is the meaning of human history? Why did the Jews reject Christ when they should have been the first to recognize him? The answer: God has his own purpose in history; he can do as he wishes with man, events, and time. It was God who made the Jews his chosen people, but it was also God who willed that the chosen people would reject his son. Throughout history he selects some and rejects others— as he willeth! Yet the Jews had heard the good news of Christ, which was freely offered to them; still they reject on their own responsibility the true Messiah. Note however the great good done by the Jewish rejection: Christianity has become universal, all part of God's plan of turning evil into good. And when the Gentiles have taken in Christ, the Jews will be taken in too by the will of God! He will show mercy for all. Paul says he does not understand the nature of God, but he trusts in it completely.

(12:1 to 15:13) All Christians live together as members of the organism that works for Christ in the world. Every deed and thought in the Christian should be molded in love for his fellow, in common sympathy and trust and obedience. Good Christians live peaceful, orderly lives, respect and obey the political and legal authorities. Our duty to man is to love him. Those members who follow

Jewish food laws should be respected, but they must not accuse the non-followers of laxity. All must respect one another and live together in harmony. Paul then gives his brothers in Rome his benediction.

(15:14 to 16:27) Paul sends personal greetings to many friends of his, whose names he gives in a long list, and he concludes with a statement of glory in Jesus Christ: a doxology.

COMMENT: This letter, ostensibly addressed to the Christians at Rome, has as its aim a statement of his teaching principles and a preparation for an oncoming visit to Rome, a city which he has not as yet seen. It is more a pamphlet than a letter, and except for the beginning and ending, it is all pamphlet. The opening sentence of 93 words in Greek (about 130 in the RSV) stresses Paul's doctrines and his own unique importance; in addition, verse 3 preaches a historical Jesus ("born of the seed of David according to the flesh": 1:3), one of the very few times that Paul mentions a historically living Jesus. Some critics hold the first sentence to be non-Pauline and verse 3 an attempt to fasten a historical Jesus upon an essentially gnostic (God = logos = idea = spirit; see above, commentary on gospel of John) Paul. Chapters 6 and 8 speak of the mystical identity between Christ and the Christian community; 12 refers to an extension of the idea: the Church is the body of Christ, which is the doctrine found in I Corinthians 12

(q.v.). Christ is depicted with two characters in this letter: 1. A divine power manifest in the Christian community, a concept essentially gnostic. 2. A historical figure in man's flesh as seen in the gospels, especially the synoptic ones. Chapter 13 enjoins the brethren to submit to the Roman Empire as a state ordained by God, etc., which indicates the letter to have been written before the Neronian persecutions of 64 A.D. Chapters 3 and 4 use texts from the O.T. to prove justification by faith; the same is also true of 9, 10, and 11, which in addition speaks of the downfall of Jerusalem, indicating to some critics interpolated material—i.e., non-Pauline. These critics feel that such matter was added because by the end of the first century Christianity had broken with Judaism, and church leaders were anxious, indeed over-anxious (as some of their weak, argumentative "proofs" show), to demonstrate that the O.T. was on the Christian side of the quarrel. In 6, 8, 12, 13, and 14 Christ is a divine being with whom one unites in a mystical manner, but in 3, 4, and 5 we see the man Jesus Christ who was sacrificed on the cross for our sins. Paul's mystery divinity contrasts with the Jesus who atoned for man's sins. Note the epistle seems to finish five different times; perhaps one postscript is Paul's—but that all five are seems unlikely. Note that Paul could not have known all the Romans he greets at the end of the letter since he had never been there. The best theory is that they are Christians who *came* from various parts of the Empire, people Paul had known personally.

I CORINTHIANS

(Chs. 1-11) To the Christians in Corinth Paul writes that he is opposed to schisms (SIZZ ums) in the Church, no matter whether they followed Paul, Apollos, or Cephas (Peter). The Holy Spirit reveals the mysteries of the earth to all Christians, no matter what their weakness and foolishness.

Paul calls the Corinthians still carnally inclined, still unable to partake of the solid food of the spirit. God alone will judge us, says Paul, and he lists the pain, travail, and suffering of the Christians even now. In Chapter 5 he asks that a wicked fornicator be put away (a case of incest), and he scolds the Corinthians for not having "rebuked" this man. In Chapter 6 he tells them to avoid law courts, to seek redress in their own courts; better yet, not to seek redress at all in the true way of love. The first of all sins is fornication, and he tells them to glorify God by remaining clean of lust. Celibacy is best, but instinct being what it is, it is proper for men to get married, a state which is not an evil one. Paul allows separation in marriage but not remarriage to others. Circumcision makes no difference in belief; and the unmarried condition is better than the married one since time devoted to God is much longer in the former. Chapter 8 asks the Corinthians to abstain from eating meat which has been offered to idols, even though Christians do not take such idols seriously. The gods these idols represent are of the inferior variety anyway. Chapter 9 is concerned with Paul's affirmation that he is a true apostle, that he is celibate, that he remains without salary, and that he labors hard for the Cause. Hence, his converts ought to support him. Men should pray bareheaded, women covered. At the Lord's Supper (a meal eaten in common by Christians with a sense of strong bondage, called the Agape or Love Feast, which later became the mass sacrament) Paul objects to their lack of dignity, the greediness and drunkenness of some (11).

(Chs. 12-16) The Church is the body of Christ, and all should love one another even though God's spiritual gifts differ in each of us: some can cure, some prophesy, some can go into ecstatic trance-like ravings ("speak with tongues"), but all such gifts issue from the Holy Spirit (12). Love covers and encompasses all things, and gifts are rendered valueless without it (13). Speaking with tongues helps only the speaker—no one else. Prophecy (moral instruction) teaches both the utterer and the listener. Speaking with tongues edifies no one, but prophecy does. Moreover, speaking with tongues gives outsiders the impression we are mad, but prophecy leaves strangers instructed. Women are to be quiet in church; let them learn the answers to their questions from their husbands when they reach home. Decency and order is the keyword (14). Christ was resurrected as he demonstrably proved, and all Christians will be raised who believe. The body rises to God uncorrupt, glorified, spiritual; a body of finer substance than our bodies in life, and full of the Spirit. When the trumpet of God sounds the judgment, the dead shall rise in uncorrupt bodies and be changed to spiritual life (15). Paul tells of his wish to visit the Corinthians and ends with salutations and a benediction.

COMMENT: Comment will follow II Corinthians.

II CORINTHIANS

(Chs. 1-7) Paul greets his brothers in Corinth and asks them to forgive a man who has already been punished enough. The old Jewish ministry with its law is a veil which has been removed by Christ, who is Spirit and gives us liberty. Paul does not mind how he suffered for Christ, for in this way he is brought nearer to him who has suffered most of all! He goes on to warn them not to deal with the heathens. Paul tells how he has wronged no one, corrupted no one, and taken advantage of no man. He refers to an almost savage letter he had previously sent them (unpreserved as a document), which had brought about the repentance of the Corinthian Christians.

(Chs. 8-13) Paul congratulates them for their large contributions to the Jerusalem church, and asks them to receive Titus kindly, since he is sending Titus to them (8-9). Paul tells of his own humbleness, his spiritual strength against the enemy, a power received on the road to Damascus. His enemies say he writes strong, bold letters but acts weakly when in their presence, which Paul denies. He tells that he does not steal glory from others (evidently others had tried to steal the glory of the conversion of the Corinthians from Paul). Paul urges them to avoid and disregard certain doctrines preached to them by others (rival Christian preachers), since Paul's right to being a true apostle is equal to that of the twelve. Paul admits to his rudeness in speech (ineffective orator) and his sufficiency in learning. He charges his enemies with being false apostles, deceitful workers, whereas Paul is a Hebrew like them, an Israelite, a seed of Abraham, a minister of Christ, more abundant in his labors, more whipped than they (five times whipped, thrice beaten, once stoned, thrice shipwrecked, much traveled, much imperiled by rivers, robbers, countrymen, and the Gentiles). Paul tells of his spiritual visions, his thorn in the flesh (a physical deformity?) which makes him more perfect in his weakness. He announces his third visit to them and expects to find them in a proper state.

COMMENT: These two letters are all that remain between Paul and one of his most important churches. We obtain a deeper knowledge of the meaning of Christ for the early Church and Paul. But besides that we get a glimpse of concrete problems arising in the early Church: party strife, litigation, marriage, social relation with pagans, food customs such as the one of eating animals sacrificed to pagan deities, the tendency of the more emotional members to take over in worship ("speaking with tongues"), the agape; altogether we see how violent and stormy the relations of Paul with one of his churches really were! Paul runs the gamut of emotion in these two letters, but the break in mood between II Cor. 1-9 and 10-13 is so sharp that some critics believe that some editor has combined two different letters. Some say that 10-13 is a fragment of the letter mentioned in II Cor. 2:3-4, the one written with many tears and in great distress. Note that collection of money for Jerusalem implies a wish to heal a breach between Jew and Greek, for which there is much evidence. One problem was to teach asceticism to former Corinthian pagans who were, shall we say, accustomed to excess. But total abstinence from sex, wine, etc., would be impossible; hence, we have Paul's compromises on celibacy and sex. Lastly, note the advice to keep the same occupation, to keep in the same state without change, circumcision, etc. Why? The Judgment Day; the Son of Man would be coming soon in *their lifetime!* Stay put — and stay the same! Resurrection implies not merely a spiritual ghost but also a new, uncorrupted body.

GALATIANS

(Chs. 1-6) Paul greets the Galatians (a Roman province in central Asia Minor to which Paul had been several times). He tells how although he had made converts everywhere, he had also made numerous enemies, especially among the Jewish-Christians ("Judaizers"), who tried to stir up trouble for Paul as soon as he would leave. Their special approach was to denounce violations of the Law (with its minute rules concerning dietary habits, etc.) and thus to bring schism and trouble into the movement. Paul tells how he was converted from Judaism to Christ, how he had been liberated from the Old Law and gained New Freedom in Christ; his enemies claim authority from the scriptures but Paul obtains his from God himself! His gospel too comes from the same source. The Jewish law is impossible to live up to with its manifold requirements, but God does not require it. Faith in Jesus is required; repentance, trust in God, and a life in freedom. Customs of religion and heritage of race have nothing to do with opening the way to the new life. No class distinctions, no sets of rules are necessary—through Christ, a belief in his atonement (sacrifice for our sins), we shall obtain hope and freedom. All people are included and can seek the Way. "To all who live by this principle, to the true Israel of God, may there be peace and mercy! . . . I carry on my scarred body the marks of Jesus."

COMMENT: As to who the Galatians were, one theory holds they were the people of Lystra, Antioch, Derbe, and Iconium (mentioned in Acts as places Paul had visited). This letter reflects trouble: the Judaizers were people like Peter and the other apostles, Jews who believed in the law and circumcision, in works, in the scriptures, etc. It was inconceivable to them that anyone believing in the Jewish Messiah could violate God's laws given to Moses, the rites of circumcision, etc. Jerusalem was the focus of this group. Naturally non-Jews favored Paul's much easier entrance requirements!

EPHESIANS

(Chs. 1-6) Paul addresses the faithful in Ephesus and in other places and praises God for what he has done for the Christians. We are one in the Church because Christ is one; he is the fountain of our faith, its source. Through Christ, God wills that the church repair all rifts and act as one. Human history reveals one divine purpose: Christ, its center, sums all before and after. His Holy Spirit guides us always. Everything everywhere is bound up in one—made one by Christ. Before Christ, God had hidden from us this uniting purpose of His, but now we know! Christ unites all the Christians into one in his church. The walls of suspicion and hostility are broken down by Christ, and we are made one, says Paul.
The thing to do is maintain this unity of spirit, to keep together in ties of single peace. There is only one Lord, one faith, one baptism, but unity is not simply conformity; it comes by working together in each other's interest, under the guidance of Christ, our silent partner as it were. The love of man for wife is like that of the Church for Christ. A Christian's

life is not easy, not a bed of roses: there is hard work before victory!

COMMENT: Paul wrote this letter from prison, just as he had written letters from prison to the Colossians and Philemon. The deliverer was named Tychicus and it dates around 62 A.D. The best manuscripts delete *at Ephesus;* indications are that these people are not well known to Paul and are not Ephesians. This letter closely resembles the one to the Colossians; yet it is one of the noblest in the New Testament. The theme of unity has special relevance today, and it is often read. The un-Pauline and unhistorical emphasis of the Church is more appropriate to a period much later than Paul, but most orthodox scholars treat the letter as genuine, since characteristics such as style and emphasis are subjective elements. Nevertheless, the emphasis on the Church as the bride of Christ and the fervid mysticism in this union are matters unusual for Paul. Was the letter forged then? It would be too crude to state this flatly, but the best answer would be a "perhaps" and left at that. Note that the letter is addressed to the whole Church, and is concerned with the total meaning of the Church's life itself. The style is less rugged and colloquial, more smooth, sophisticated, and flowing, than Paul's. The stress on unity is no longer between Jewish-Christians and Gentile-Christians but on unity in the face of new schisms threatening the entire Church. Of this, more later.

PHILIPPIANS

(Chs. 1-4) Paul tells how anxious he is to see his beloved brothers once more. He tells how imprisonment has aided his work, not hindered it. In fact Paul feels that he shall soon be out of prison, but no matter how it all ends, Christ will be necessarily glorified! He encourages them to live like good Christians, hold well to the faith, and even to suffer for the Lord's sake.

We must pay attention to our salvation with fear and apprehension ("fear and trembling"), for is it not God who is working away within us? What they have begun let them complete in "the day of Christ." He mentions that this letter will arrive by Epaphroditus, the messenger. Paul mentions the Judaizers who are his enemies at Philippi, and he too could brag about his Jewish ancestry; but he has put that all by now that he is an apostle. But he does know that he is going in the right direction, and is willing that they (the Philippians) use him as a kind of model. We must not become anxious and embroiled in the sight of earthly enemies. Our Christian life will be in heaven when our mortal bodies will be transformed into spiritual and heavenly beings like Christ.

COMMENT: Philippi is mentioned in Acts 16, which tells how an earthquake released Paul and Silas from prison and converted the jailer. The Philippian Christians had always loved Paul and had sent a gift to him via Epaphroditus, and it is to him Paul entrusts the letter. Paul is in prison in Rome and writes this letter of reassurance and affection to his beloved brethren. There are some noble thoughts in this warm and lovely letter, and we see intimately into Paul's character. This letter may be divided: 1. A warning against the Judaizers, and an acknowledgment of the gift, and 2. An urgent plea that they remain harmonious and unselfish, with an explanation why Epaphraditus is being sent back.

COLOSSIANS

(Chs. 1-4) Paul and Timothy salute the church at Colossae, a city to which Paul has never been. Paul says the universe was created in and for Christ; no greater claim could be made for him, and it follows then that Christ only is necessary for salvation of all men. The false teachers (pagan religious) do not have Paul's focussing view: Christ is the Father's image; the Father was at the beginning, and Christ carries forward the will of God throughout history. Even the angels (those universal powers of the Colossians) are subject to the Lord! Then Christians should be still more loyal to Christ, for he is God's own gift to man, the sign of God's forgiveness. We cannot rise to God by rules and practices; we are to be humbly dependent upon the risen Lord — not a matter of do's and dont's; it is all a matter of being in Christ. We must leave our old habits and wrong ways of life; we must "put on love" and let Christ's peace rule in our hearts. Common love and alert help is most precious in family living.

The letter closes with Paul commending to them Mark and Justus, and sending greetings from their former neighbor Epaphras (EPP uh FRASS) and Aristarchus (AIR ih STAR kuss). Tychicus (TIE kih kuss) will carry the letter to them. He asks that his letter be read at a church nearby, and the one to that church be read to the Colossians.

COMMENT: The practice of reading a letter in round-robin style came to be known as *encyclicals,* and a direct result of such practice is the New Testament. This letter is primarily directed at the false teachings of those who would deny the all-sufficiency of Christ. The date of this letter is about 60-62 A.D., while Paul was a prisoner at Rome. Note the freedom given Paul to consult with friends like Epaphras, the minister from the church at Colossae in the Roman province of Asia. Certain pagans who in Platonic fashion worshipped angelic beings in various hierarchies (Christ being one of them) until God was reached are the objects of Paul's wrath, even though they professed Christianity.

I THESSALONIANS

(Chs. 1-5) Paul salutes the Thessalonians (Thessalonica, a seaport in northern Greece) in the name of himself, Silvanus, and Timothy. He reminds them of his work with them; never flattering or greedy; never a glory-seeker; never were Paul and his companions a burden to them. The Thessalonians have suffered many persecutions for their belief and have remained brave and steadfast. Paul is glad that Timothy, his messenger, has returned to him with good news that all was well with

them. Paul warns them against fornication (a sure sign of a Gentile community!), tells them to love each other, and mind their own business. Paul tells them that those Christians who had died prior to the second coming will be raised again when Christ returns on judgment day. The blessed dead will rise along with those blessed alive ones into heaven to meet Christ, who will greet them at the half-way mark. Then all will ascend into heaven! No one knows the time of the Coming, but we must watch, wait, and comfort each other, aid the weak, and pray.

COMMENT: In 50 A.D. Paul wrote this letter and with it he began the writing of the New Testament. It is in Corinth that Timothy brings him the good news of their welfare. Paul corrects their view that the Day of the Lord had come. He showed this was impossible, for the Antichrist had not yet made his appearance (Jewish lore said that before the Messiah there would come a false one—the Antichrist). Note the difficulties of the very early church and the keen interest Paul had in it.

II THESSALONIANS

(Chs. 1-3) Paul repeats the same salutation as in I Thes., and speaks again of their suffering in persecution. He speaks of the Antichrist (see commentary to I Thes.). Again he warns them to avoid false doctrines and to work diligently: those who don't work, don't eat, says Paul flatly! Paul ends the letter with "the salutation of Paul with mine own hand, which is the token in every epistle: so I write. The grace of our Lord Jesus Christ be with you all. Amen."

COMMENT: This letter is written from Athens and repeats somewhat the contents of I Thes. Note that Paul replies as to his integrity and lack of greed; evidently someone had slandered his motives. The injunction *no work — no food —* sounds drastic and implies that the little socialist communities were having troubles either with idlers or with those who kept staring into the sky waiting for the coming of the Messiah! Hence the eager questions to Paul on various signs of the second coming. What Paul wanted them to do was to go about their work, for the coming would be unexpected, even though it would be preceded by the Antichrist, who will eventually be defeated by Christ.

I TIMOTHY

(Chs. 1-6) Paul warns the leaders of the church against two evil kinds of teaching, the purely speculative and the bare legalistic. What is necessary is a sound and solid doctrine to maintain the church. Worship within the church must include prayers for the leaders of the state in order to obtain a peaceful and harmonious community life. Women must be unobtrusive and quiet. As for Paul, he again makes a defense of his call from God as an apostle. The officeholders of the church such as the bishops must be personally impeccable from sin; they must be good administrators and good fathers; they must be strong in faith and widely respected by the community. Deacons too should be proven in faith, serious of mien, and in good standing with the community. The same should be true of the women.

Christianity does not follow a series of "don'ts!" God is not better served by following rigid dietary laws or remaining unmarried; all God had created is good and is to be taken in thanks with gratitude. A true Christian follows a kind of discipline in order to set his hope on the living God. Although Timothy is young, he has a great gift, which needs cultivation and practice.

Attention must be paid to the support of poor widows since there has been laxity in this department. Moreover, children or grandchildren who are solvent enough should take care of their widowed mothers or grandmothers and not leave such burdens to the church. The elders must not be gossiped about or slandered, but all such charges must be publicly disclosed. This will make for simple justice in the church. Christians who are slaves must hold their master's good name in honor. Wealthy men must not think that right living is the only way to riches, for greed may lead them to ruin: the love of money is the root of all evils.

II TIMOTHY

(Chs. 1-4) Paul addresses his second letter to the evangelist Timothy by telling him to guard the truth, to be bolder in his teaching, not to be timid nor ashamed before the members. Like Paul, he must not fear to defend Jesus before all his attackers. Above all a strong, durable discipleship to Christ is vital—not a love for quarreling or controversy, nor an overcritical attitude to others.

Things are going to become more difficult and Timothy must be able to stand the stronger stresses which are to come very soon! The forces of evil are bracing themselves for the final conflict before the second coming of Christ. Paul has suffered much from the enemies of Christ, for some have deserted the gospel and others have opposed it, but Paul's conscience is still true and good. Paul concludes by saying he has fought the good fight, he has finished the race, and he has kept the faith; he sends his benediction.

COMMENT: The thought of a speedy second coming so overshadowed the minds of some Christians that care for organization and order fell before high zeal and enthusiasm. But as time went on and no Messiah, more attention was paid to prosaic details like church organization and church officials. Efficiency can only come through organization. To bring this about, a Greek follower of Paul at some time about the middle of the second century wrote these letters to Timothy (and to Titus). They take the form of a "Paul" writing to his young lieutenants, Timothy and Titus, telling them about matters of policy and organization. Incidentally, they attempt to refute a heresy (Marcionite) which denied the inspiration of the Jewish scriptures. Note the condemnation of asceticism and Gnosticism and Marcionism. These are practical letters — not prophecy or poetry.

TITUS

(Chs. 1-3) Paul salutes Titus (a Greek follower of Paul), who is in charge of the church at Crete. Bishops should be men who are blameless in character and strong in morality. The natives of Crete, who have a bad reputation, are rebuked; hence sound teaching of the gospel and sensible behavior are urgently necessary for those who follow Christ. It should be much easier for Christians than for non-Christians to work honestly, to abstain from quarrels, and to display courtesy to others. And those followers of the Way who are impervious to right conduct should simply be left strictly alone—for their behavior condemns them! Be especially wary of the Jews who, in their greed for money, will subvert Christian doctrines for personal gain. Servants must obey their masters in all things; obedience to one's superior is essential. Another essential is to avoid quarrels about the Law. Paul closes his letter with the usual greetings to his friends, commending certain of the members for their good work within the church. A benediction closes the letter.

COMMENT: See the comment on the Timothy letters. The Titus and Timothy letters are often known as the Pastoral letters because they contain largely a set of directions, advice, and personal comment on the conduct and administration of the church. Pastoral = shepherd = leaders or elders (known as bishops later) who are directed to heed and make effective the advice and directions in the letters. Most scholars find these three letters non-Pauline but evidently written by one quite familiar with Paul's opinions. A few scholars call the letters outright forgeries of the second century, at least a hundred years after Paul's genuine letters had been written. Prosaic matters are discussed and there seems to be a feeling of urgency to defend the church from attackers of its doctrines, especially from various heresies then flourishing.

PHILEMON

(One Chapter) Paul salutes Philemon (a Pauline convert) and tells him that he is sending back Onesimus, who had fled his master with stolen goods; Paul earnestly asks that Onesimus (own ESS ee muss) be forgiven his sins and be returned to Paul, since he had been of some service to Paul in addition to his having been converted by Paul. He even promises to make good any losses Philemon (FILL uh munn) might have suffered. Paul ends his letter with the usual benediction and wellwishes.

COMMENT: Philemon's slave Onesimus had been a slave in Laodicea (lay oh DISS ee uh) and had robbed and run away from his master only to be found by Paul and be converted. The penalty for a runaway slave could have been death by Roman law, and that is why Paul recommends Onesimus to the neighboring church at Colossae (Koh LOSS ee) as well as to Philemon *and* his household. Hence, Philemon is surrounded by advocates of mercy, Paul very cleverly forcing his hand. The question often arises as to why Paul endorsed the vicious institution of slavery, since slaves formed a good number of the members of the Church. But Paul was no revolutionary, as we have seen before many times; perhaps he wished to undermine that institution from within, as some critics suggest. A more realistic outlook suggests that he was content with that institution, feeling that eventual salvation in Christ was reward enough. A militant campaign by the Church to free slaves would most assuredly have brought the wrath of the Roman state on its head. This is a personal letter of Paul's, which makes it unique, but the lessons of practical righteousness, Christian brotherhood and courtesy, and Christian love are what make it priceless.

HEBREWS

(Chs. 1-6) This epistle begins without a salutation. "Christ the son of God is better than the prophets: God, who at sundry times and in divers manners spake in the past unto the fathers by the prophets, hath in these last days spoken unto us by his Son, whom he hath appointed heir of all things, by whom also he made the worlds." The Son is better than the angels also, for the angels are merely his messengers and servants. The writer warns: we must observe more acutely what God has done in Christ, who assumed human nature and form, who took on human trial and temptation. This assumption of humanity makes Christ superior to the angels. In order to deliver man from sin, he must first be made man in form and flesh and be sacrificed on the cross to redeem man from sin. Christ is superior to Moses, who gave the Jews their laws; Moses is God's servant, but Christ was his son. *Exhortation*: Do not fall away from the living God, nor like the Israelites be refused the promised land because of our disobedience and stubbornness. Today, of all times, is the time to keep faith in God.

Jesus is a high priest in his utter sympathy for man and his divine authority from God. He knows and understand's man, is gentle with him, identifies with him. Hence, he can plead our cause before the living God perfectly. Unlike the Jewish high priests, Christ does not place himself superior to man, but identifies himself with man, intercedes for him with God — their passionate pleader and defense counsel! God appointed Jesus to sit on his right hand in heaven because Jesus suffered humiliation, torture, and death for man. Who but God himself would deign to stoop so low for the love of mankind?

The writer says Jesus is like the king of ancient Salem and high priest of God and the Jews (Genesis 14:18-20 and Psalm 110:4), Melchizedek (mel KIZZ uh deck), who, having met Abraham (the father-patriarch of all Jews), both fed and blessed him. As in Psalm 110, where Melchizedek is the Eternal Priest-King in whose manner the Christ is to be divinely ordained, Christ too is an eternal priest whose office cannot be usurped by another. Just as Melchizedek had blessed Abraham in ancient times, Christ too is eternally seeking for his followers at all times blessing from God.

(Chs. 7-13) In addition to being man's high-priest intercessor with God, Christ is perfect in the offering of his sacrifice—thus setting aside the commandments of Moses and the Jewish priesthood. Therefore, our hope is more complete in that we can draw nearer to God. Christ is not the holy of holies of the Jewish Temple, but rather he sits on God's right hand in heaven; he is superior to all earthly, Jewish priests, who are but copies of the heavenly God. Jeremiah 31:31-34 shows that the Lord told the Jews of a new covenant unlike the one he had made with the patriarchs: this covenant has become effective in Christ, who by perfect sacrifice for our sins greatly overshadows Jewish sacrifice, which sprinkled animal blood to wash away sin. Christ shed his own blood and purified man. Thus the New Covenant (contract, bargain, agreement) supersedes the old. Christ alone is our hope, the only high priest, the only purifier of sins, the only intercessor. Angels, Moses, Joshua, Temple sacrifice of animals can offer no hope at all. It is vital then to hold fast to the Way now, just as Christians held fast before under persecution.

Faith is like a great pilgrimage of the soul. Abel, Enoch, Noah, Abraham, Isaac and Jacob, Joseph, Moses, Joshua, Rahab, and many others were heroes in faith, which is "the substance of things hoped for, the evidence of things not seen." These ancient heroes were like pilgrims with desires for better shores who tramped the highways to God's promise, who trudged, toiled, and persevered to the very end. Long before Christ arrived they lived in faith and by faith. To this glorious company of pilgrims all Christians belong! Christians too have been fed to the lions, won strength out of weakness, suffered mocking, scourging, and torture—even chains and prison. We have but to imitate these heroes, to enter into similar pilgrimages, to persevere in the race, looking for Jesus—the pioneer and perfecter of our faith. He took the cross, the shame he despised, and now sits with God.

Faith and the habits of daily life are related. The Christian pilgrim takes a step at a time, clings to every advantage, moves with hope and confidence into the future of achievement. Hospitality, brotherly love, concern for the unfortunate, sexual purity, scorn for money, loyalty to the others, and constant prayer must be the daily concern of the Christian pilgrims. "Now the God of peace . . . make you perfect in every good work to do his will, working in you that which is well pleasing in his sight, through Jesus Christ; to whom be glory for ever and ever. Amen."

COMMENT: Sometime after the persecutions of Nero, in the later years of the first century, the churches were largely made up of second generation Christians who had not won their faith in struggle but had inherited it from their parents and neighbors; consequently, apathy and indifference "were their worst failings, and when the collision with the Empire over emperor worship threatened them with persecution, they were in no condition to meet it (Goodspeed tr., p. 502)." So the Letter to the Hebrews was written to counteract indifference and to convince the brothers in faith of the eternal values of the Christian faith. Most important—the writer prepares and strengthens his brethren for the new and difficult tribulations of that very hour. Point by point Judaism suffers in comparison with Christianity. The writer (an imitator of Paul) uses the letter form and the allegorical method so popular with Greek and Jewish thinkers of the late first century; but the document more resembles a great oration whose breadth and poetry makes it the greatest of the letters. The divisions are the following: The great salvation; the rest of God; our Great High Priest; the New Covenant; the superiority of the faith-way; the worship and walk of the believer-priest. Some major points: Christ is better than angels, Moses, Aaron, and the Levite priests; his sacrifice is greater than those of the Jewish Temple; faith is defined; the O.T. were heroes on a pilgrimage; and the new pilgrimage. Note the stress on faith in Jewish history and the dependence of the Christians on faith too. The author is unknown; there is no salutation but there is a letter close: this is very likely an addition. The people addressed are Jewish-Christians who have been losing their faith in Jesus as the Jewish Messiah; hence the use of Jewish sources for proof. The author is unfamiliar with genuine Judaism but he did know his Old Testament through reading; for example, the Temple had been destroyed long ago, and blood sacrifice had stopped long ago. Note too that Jesus here seems gnostic-like, as in John's logos and similar concepts in Ephesians and Colossians.

JAMES

(Chs. 1-5) After a short salutation to the twelve tribes of the "Dispersion" (Jews outside of Palestine), James gives advice on facing the troubles of daily life. We should not blame God for sending us troubles and tribulations but accept them as part of God's plan. If we do so, we shall transform them into blessing! Temptation causes sin and sin causes death; but in reverse: faith brings loyalty and firmness, which in 'turn bring personal fulfillment. God helps his humble petitioners and his will should be the blueprint of our lives. Profession of faith is not enough: neither God nor our neighbors are fooled; the heard word is forgotten but the word achieved in *deed* does God's work and remains fresh and alive. Patience is vital to the Christian. We should be "quick to hear, slow to speak, slow to anger"; calmness is basic to all Christian virtues. All men, whether rich or poor, are equal in the sight of God; the poor are chosen by God to inherit God's kingdom. People must not be treated according to their wealth in property but according to their true natures in the sight of God. Indeed, the church must not be segregated—rich from poor—but united as equals. To segregate denies Christianity! "Even so faith, if it hath no works. is dead, being alone . . . shew me thy faith without thy works, and I will shew thee my faith by my works." Watch the tongue: it is capable of blessing and cursing. We must speak with reverence, with frankness, and with honesty. This is especially true of teachers, in whom speech is influential upon others. James opposes the taking of oaths, since a Christian always speaks the truth anyway. Faith is revealed in works for the teacher too. Real wisdom is not clever display and clever debate but "is pure, then peaceable, gentle, and easy to be entreated, full of mercy and good fruits, without partiality, and without hypocrisy." Wisdom is more revealed in action than in words. Desire and greed bring on wars: "Ye lust (desire), and have not: ye kill, and desire to have, and cannot obtain: ye fight and war, yet ye have not, because ye ask not." Draw near to God, and he will draw near to you: "Cleanse your hands, ye sinners; and purify your hearts, ye doubleminded (doubters)." Speak no evil of your brothers and judge not your neighbors. The man who knows what is right and fails to do it, he is guilty of sin.

"Go to now, ye rich men, weep and howl for your miseries that shall come upon you. Your riches are corrupted and your garments are motheaten. Your gold and silver is cankered (rusted) . . . Behold, the hire of the labourers who have reaped down your fields, which is of you kept back by fraud, crieth: and the cries of them which have reaped are entered into the ears of the Lord." James tells them to be patient and await the coming; to confess their faults to one another, to pray, for "the effectual fervent prayer of a righteous man availeth much." He who converts the sinner from error saves a soul from death, "and shall hide a multitude of sins."

COMMENT: This is not an epistle but a sermon—the only one of its kind in the New Testament. As such it is often inconsistent and irrelevant, miscellaneous and passionate. The aim was moral stimulus and regeneration to its hearers. It is filled with apostrophe, anecdote, dialogue, and invective. But it is also "searching, intensely practical, mingling scorn and humor with tenderness and moral passion . . . keen interest in democracy, philanthropy, and social justice strikes a responsive note in our times" (Goodspeed tr., p. 526). Simple, honest, direct, hating sham, strong in satrical exposure of hypocrisy, and great in espousing the rights of labor and the poor.

I PETER

(Chs. 1-5) Peter salutes the churches in Pontus, Galatia, Cappadocia, Asia, and Bithynia. His readers must regard their troubles and persecutions as tests of faith; hence faith must be maintained and strengthened. Christians are the elect of God; they are to be respectful of the laws of society, and servants must obey their masters even if the masters are unjust! A far greater virtue is it to bear *undeserved* punishment without complaint as Christ did, even though he was without sin.

Wives should obey their husbands, even if their spouses are pagans; this should convert their husbands. Wives, "the weaker vessel," are to be treated with kindness and consideration. Most important is it to live in goodness and virtue. Christ preached the good news to the dead in hell also "that they might be judged according to men in the flesh, but live according to God in the spirit." The end of the world is at hand, so virtue and the good life is essential. All Christians should lead sinless lives so that if they suffer persecution, it will be as Christians and not as criminals.

The elders are told to be good models for the faithful, and the younger members are exhorted to obey their elders. God especially dislikes the proud and will strike them down in the middle of their pride. Peter closes with a benediction and a salute from "Marcus my son."

COMMENT: A Roman Christian (not the apostle) about 94 A.D. used the apostle's name to address the churches of Asia Minor. The great problem then was the persecution under Trajan—how to meet persecution: by battle or submission? The latter was the answer. If the former had been adopted, the Christians would have been revolutionists (like the Zealots of the gospels) and lost the cause. This pacifist way, which the Christians adopted, eventually won the day for them. The Book of Revelation counseled resistance, a vindictive hate of Babylon (Rome), and gloated over the fall of Babylon. The Roman church is represented here in the name of the apostle Peter; it shared the glory of having been the place where two of the greatest apostles, Peter and Paul, had labored. Since Rome tended their graves and memories, it was entitled to be the spokesman of the two greatest apostles. Peter tells them to be obedient to the state, the same counsel as that given by Christ; moreover, love should be displayed even towards one's enemies, as Christ had taught. The references to persecution could not have applied to the days of Nero as the letter implies, since the persecution had not yet spread that far. It is far more likely that the letter refers to the times of Emperor Trajan, when Christians were persecuted merely for the sake of having been Christians; this would be about the beginning of the second century. Orthodox scholars prefer the time of Nero, however. Note that the martyr "complex" is developed here: suffering for the faith, for being a Christian, identifies one with Christ, the suffering servant of God. This explains the cheerfulness with which many Christian martyrs met their deaths.

II PETER

(Chs. 1-3) Second Peter (like Jude; see below) denounces gay living and physical indulgence and stresses the strength and purity of the Christian life. Peter denies that the physical body is entirely inferior and separate from the spiritual one. God made all things and called all things good, including the physical body. It interacts with and is inseparable from our spiritual bodies. Hence, the true Christian is just as responsible for his body as his soul. The gay and immoral life is not to be tolerated!

JUDE

(1 Ch.) Jude salutes all Christians, calling himself the brother of James (the brother of Jesus), and tells them of the new heresy arising which denies Christ. He accuses them of immorality, and just as God destroyed immoral practicers in the O.T. so will he now. Jude exhorts his readers to increase in faith and defy the heretics who desire to corrupt their beliefs.

COMMENT: Like the Adventists today, the early Christians eagerly expected Christ to return and rejudge the world. Christians were uncertain whether Paul was right in declaring there would be an actual Second Coming or whether the Johannine gospel was right in saying the coming would be one of the Spirit. Both Peter and Jude set forth the second coming in similar fashion. Jude passionately denounces those who would deny it, calling them heretics. The "heretics" are probably the Marcosians, a sect supposedly reeking of sins, greed, sexual license, and black magic. Second Peter knows his four gospels and Paul's letters, which are being misused by the Marcionites to deny Judaism in Christianity. Date then: middle of second century.

I JOHN

(Chs. 1-5) John attacks the Docetists (heresy: Jesus only *seemed* to have a human body, only *seemed* to be flesh and blood on earth, but he was simply spirit divine, logos etc.). Did not the disciples see, touch, hear, and feel the living son of God? Unlike the gods of the Greeks, Christ is not a myth but a real human being who, although sinless, came to redeem man of sin. This is the *full* teaching of Christ. Certain "knowers" (Gnostics) think they are better than baser Christians, that they are an elite, an aristocracy in religion who had peculiar insight and virtue not gained by others. They even deign not to associate with their lower brothers:

"If a man say, I love God, and hateth his brother, he is a liar: for he that loveth not his brother whom he hath seen, how can he love God whom he hath not seen?" Some Christians are unwilling to see sinfulness in themselves, and declare themselves virtuous; but among the truly faithful and just one freely confesses his sins, and God will forgive him and free him from all unrighteousness. We are truly Christians in faith when we are fellowed with God in our hearts and behave with brotherly love toward our brothers in the faith. God's nature is love: hence, one shows love within as well as without.

COMMENT: The author is perhaps the John of the fourth gospel, for the ideas are very similar. The style is also similar, and may have been written in Ephesus, as was the gospel of John in about 110 A.D. John's aim is to strengthen his Christians in spirit and to expose Docetism, which denied some basic Christian doctrines, one of which was that such a belief left Christ's crucifixion empty of significance. This is the longest of the three epistles of John. Note the odd mixture of rationalism and mysticism.

II JOHN

(Ch. 1) The author salutes a "lady and her children" and tells them of the importance of love, defined as following the commandment of God: "let us love one another . . . be guided by love." Impostors deny Christ as having been human: they are impostors and Antichrist. Hold the teaching of the church and you will not lose God. "If anyone comes to you without bringing this teaching, do not let him come into the house or bid him good morning. For anyone who bids him good morning shares in his wicked work."

III JOHN

(Ch. 1) The author, an elder, salutes his dear friend Gaius and is glad to hear that they retain the teachings of the Church. He especially commends Gaius for his hospitality to wandering Christians. The author objects to a certain Diotrephes (die OTT truh feez) who will not listen to John, and even accuses John; moreover, he refuses to welcome Christian brothers and "casteth them out of the church." Those who do good are of God, but those doing evil have not seen God. He bids Gaius an affectionate goodbye.

COMMENT: John urges fellowship in love as against the Docetists who claimed special enlightenment, more nearness to God, more knowledge of the Truth, and complete freedom from sin. This great declaration of love in John's three letters, this bond of Christian brotherhood in love, this God who is love and love who is God are the supreme expressions of religious love, the epitome of the Johannine writings. The writer calls himself the "Elder," sending letter one to the churches of Asia, letter two a covering letter, and three a personal note to Gaius.

REVELATION: A PREFACE

WRITER: John, a prophet of Ephesus, said by many *not* to be the same John as the one of the gospel and epistles.

DATE: About 90 A.D.

THEMES: See the prologue and the last verse of this mighty book for a statement of the theme by John himself; and see the individual commentaries. The Book of Revelation is one of the most stirring of all books, and next to the gospel of Matthew has had the most influence upon the language and literature, indeed upon the very speech patterns, of the western world. It is a beautiful call to love God, but it is also an appeal to destruction and woe for the ungodly. The target is Rome, concealed beneath the symbol of the beast and the Whore of Babylon. The symbols alone in this poem—for it is more poem than prose—have become an integral part of the symbology of the Church as well as our own great literary heritage. No man can call himself well-read without knowing this book and assimilating its abundance of striking imagery. As for the message—one is not very likely to miss it in spite of the cryptic apparatus of symbols and numbers: it is woe to Babylon and glory to the Faithful, who will see the Millennium and sit with God and the Son at the love feast in heaven!

DETAILED REVIEW AND COMMENTARY ON REVELATION

CHAPTERS 1-2

CONCERNING THIS BOOK (1:1-20): This book was communicated by God to his slave John, who is the witness of all that he saw—to the message of God, and the testimony of Jesus Christ. "Blessed is he that readeth, and they that hear the words of this prophecy, and keep those things which are written therein: for the time is at hand."

JOHN'S GREETING AND ASCRIPTION: John addresses the seven Christian churches of Asia. He bids them grace. and peace "from him which is, and which was, and which is to come; and from the seven Spirits which are before his throne" (perhaps a reference to the Holy Spirit and his seven gifts). Behold, John says, Christ is coming on the clouds; all shall see him, and they also which pierced him (the Romans?): ". . . and all kindreds (tribes) of the earth shall wail because of him. Even so, Amen. I am Alpha and Omega (the first and last letters of the Greek alphabet = God's infinite nature), the beginning and the ending, saith the Lord, which is, and which was, and which is to come, the Almighty!" I, John of Patmos, heard on the) Lord's day (Sunday) a great voice "as of a trumpet" telling me to write in a book and send it to the seven Asian churches: Ephesus, Smyrna, Pergamum, Thyatira, Sardis, Philadelphia, and Laodicea. John turned and saw seven golden candlesticks, in the midst of which "one like unto the Son of Man, clothed with a garment down to the foot, and girt (belted) about the paps (breast) with a golden girdle (sash); his head and hair were white as wool, as snow, and his eyes blazed like fire; his feet like fine brass (bronze) as if they burned in a furnace (i.e., refined); and his voice as the sound of many waters. In his right hand seven stars; in his mouth a two-edged sword." When John saw him he fell at his feet as if dead, but the being reassured him and told him to write the things he had seen, "and the things which are, and the things which shall be hereafter." John is told that the stars and candlesticks are the angels of the seven churches.

SEVEN LETTERS TO CHURCHES IN ASIA: *The first letter* to the angel (bishop) of the Ephesus church: the Lord knows their work and labor and how they found the false apostles to be liars. But the Lord is somewhat displeased because "thou hast left thy first love," and he tells them to repent, "and do the first works"; or else the Lord will remove the church. The deeds of the Nicolaitans are hated both by the Lord and by the Ephesians (perhaps a sect of pagan moral laxity). If the church overcomes its failings the Lord "will give to eat of the tree of life." *Second letter to Smyrna:* the Lord detests the blasphemy of those false Jews, the synagogue of Satan (the Gnostics?). Some of them will be cast into prison; the faithful will be rewarded and shall not be harmed by the second death (after the Milennium, the death before Judgment). *Third letter to Pergamum:* The bearer of the two-edged sword knows where the throne of Satan is (i.e., in Rome), but there are some in Pergamum who are troublemakers and fornicators as well as some Nicolaitans. They must repent! Those who do will be given "hidden manna," and will be given a "white stone, and in the stone a new name written" (*manna:* eucharist; *white stone:* admission ticket to God's kingdom). *Fourth letter to Thyatira:* this church "sufferest that woman Jezebel which calleth herself a prophetess" (inspired), who teaches the eating of idol-sacrificed meat and immorality. Unless she and her followers repent, she will be made sick ("cast her into a bed") and the others troubled. God will strike her children dead. Those who overcome evil and keep God's works "will I give power over the nations (heathen), and he shall rule them with a rod of iron; as the vessels of a potter (earthen jars) shall they be broken to pieces!"

CHAPTERS 3-4

Fifth letter to Sardis: God knows what they are doing; you are supposed to be alive, but you are dead! I have found nothing good in you: hear, obey, and repent. If you do not wake up, "I will come on thee as a thief." Only a few are good in Sardis, and they shall walk with me in white, "for they are worthy." *Sixth letter to Philadelphia:* I will bless this church because it has kept my word. I will also keep you from "the hour of temptation" which will come in judgment time. Upon the good I will write the name of the city of my God, "which is new Jerusalem" (the New Kingdom). *Seventh letter to Laodicea:* You are neither cold nor hot, "I will spew thee out of my mouth." Repent! "I stand at the door, and knock: if any man hear my voice, and open the door, I will come in to him, and will sup with him, and he with me."

156   THE NEW TESTAMENT

COMMENT: The first three chapters are concerned with seven of the Christian churches in Asia Minor. To each John applies the necessary pats on the back, scoldings, threatenings, and dire vengances. The various symbols are explained within parentheses in the text. The early Christians were viciously persecuted by Nero in A.D. 64, but with Domitian persecution commenced anew; the Christians were arrested, tortured, and killed merely for refusing to take the religious oath of loyalty to the Emperor. To prevent Christians compromising their faith by compliance, John writes his book. John, a prophet of Ephesus, calls upon the seven churches not to give in to Satan (Rome). The letters reflect Paul's letters, but where Paul would compromise and conform, John would sound the blast of resistance and destruction! Now will follow three great visions in the standard metaphors of the old Jewish apocalypses (dire predictions of an end of the world and the coming of the new Messiah to destroy all evil and raise the good; a new paradise on earth, and a new kingdom in heaven of peace, joy, and plenty with God enthroned). The message is cast like a super-opera, with arias, antiphonies, and choruses; the orchestra are the harps, trumpets, thunders, earthquakes, and great waters. "Rome itself, the mightiest empire the world had seen, would fall, for above the emperor, the Autokrator, stood the Pantokrator, the Omnipotent" (Goodspeed tr., p. 565). The bewildering array of complex images and symbols, the intricate allegory, successfully concealed from the Romans the hatred felt for Rome, the Babylon, the seat of Satan, the evil dragon, the whore!

Too successfully concealed is that same meaning today; but the early Christians were tremendously consoled by its message of hope and fierce resistance!

HEAVENLY WORSHIP (4:1-11): Then a door opened in heaven, and the same trumpet voice invited him up to see what must take place in the future. John saw a throne in heaven with one on it who looked like "jasper and a sardine stone" (*jasper and sardius*: precious stones) and who was surrounded by an emerald-colored halo. Round about the throne were 24 elders in white with golden crowns. From the throne came lightning, thunder, voices: seven lamps of fire burned before the throne. Before the throne the floor seemed like a sea of glass, and near it were four beasts covered with eyes "before and behind"; the first was a lion, the second a calf, the third a beast with a man's face, and the fourth a flying eagle. All four had six wings each and kept saying "Holy, holy, holy, Lord God Almighty, which was, and is, and is to come!" All 24 elders fall down to worship the Lord.

COMMENT: The elders represent mankind in the heavenly palace of God, giving him homage. 12 O.T. patriarchs + 12 apostles = 24. Lion = all that is noble (symbol of Mark); calf = all that is strong (symbol of Luke); man = all that is wisest (symbol of Matthew); eagle = all that is swiftest (symbol of John). All creation is seen paying homage to God. The eyes = ceaseless vigilance of nature and God's power operating in it (Westminster Bible).

CHAPTERS 5-6

(5:1-4) On the right of God near his throne was a book "written within and on the back side (a parchment roll with writing on both sides), sealed with seven seals. John weeps that he is not able or fit to unseal the roll, but one of the elders says, one of the line of David "has been victorious so that he can open the roll and break its seals." Then John saw a seemingly slaughtered lamb with seven horns and seven eyes (they are the seven spirits of God), that took the roll and while doing so, the elders and four animals sang a hymn of how with the lamb's blood had been bought for "God, men from every tribe, tongue, people, and nation" (meaning: slaughtered lamb = Christ crucified, who, by his sacrifice, saved man for God—all men of the world). Then all creatures everywhere sang a hymn to God and the Lamb.

THE OPENING OF THE FIRST SIX SEALS (6:1-17): The Lamb broke *the first seal* and a white horse with a rider carrying a bow and wearing a crown rode forth like a conqueror (either the Parthians who had defeated the Romans or Christ and Christianity victorious); *second seal broken*: red horse, "and power was given to him that sat thereon to take peace from the earth, and that they should kill one another"; *third seal broken*: black horse, rider with scales in his hand (War rides the red horse; Famine rides the black); *fourth seal*: horse is ashen-colored; its rider Death "and Hades followed him." They were given power over one quarter of the earth "to kill with sword, and with hunger, and with death, and with the beasts of the earth"; *fifth seal*: those killed as Christians appear under the altar and cry for vengeance and judgment of the earth. Each was given a white robe and told to be quiet a little longer, until there were a certain number of their brethren killed; *sixth seal*: a great earthquake, the sun turning black as sackcloth, the moon like blood, the stars fell from the sky "even as a fig tree casteth her untimely figs, when she is shaken of a mighty wind." The sky was torn apart, the world shook, and the kings, great and rich men, slave and free men of the world, hid themselves and said, "Hide us from the face of him that sitteth on the throne, and from the wrath of the Lamb: For the great day of his wrath is come."

COMMENT: The Four Horsemen of the Apocalypse represent Conquest (the white horse), War (red horse), Famine (black horse), Death (pale horse). The Christians who had died for the faith (martyrs) have but to wait a little while = until the second coming of Christ! The sixth seal brings on an earthquake, an eclipse, etc. The end of the world is at hand!

CHAPTERS 7-8

AN INTERMEDIARY VISION, AND THE OPENING OF THE SEVENTH SEAL (7:1-17): Four angels standing on the "four corners of the earth" are prepared to destroy all when a fifth angel from the east carrying God's seal stops them from destroying the earth until the servants of God were marked on their foreheads with the seal. All the twelve tribes of Israel were sealed, 144,000 in all, twelve thousand from each tribe. Then numberless people from all nations clothed in white appear. John explains that they came out of great persecution, who "have washed their robes, and made them white in the blood of the Lamb" (i.e., become Christians via baptism and eucharist). These people shall hunger no more; the Lamb will feed them; they shall be led "unto living fountains of waters: and God shall wipe away all tears from their eyes" (i.e., Christians).

THE SEVEN TRUMPETS (8:1-13): A half-hour silence follows, the *opening of the seventh seal* (silence = expectancy of all on earth). An angel ministers at the altar; then the seven angels blew their trumpets in turn: *first trumpet*: a storm of hail and fire mixed with blood; much of the world is burned up; *second trumpet*: volcano erupts and turns one-third of the sea to blood; one-third of all live creatures perish and one-third of all ships destroyed; *third trumpet*: a star called Wormwood (Aosinthus) falls and turns one-third of sea into wormwood (bitter herb), killing numbers of people; *fourth trumpet*: one-third of sun, moon, stars blotted out; an eagle in midair weeps for the destruction to be summoned by the three remaining trumpet blasts!

CHAPTERS 9-10

(9:1-21) The *fifth angel sounded his trumpet*: a star fell from heaven, and to him (Satan, who had been the angel Lucifer in heaven, and had rebelled) "was given the key of the bottomless pit." Locusts, smoke descend upon the earth issuing from Hell, and torment for five months those men without the seal of God on their foreheads (pagans, heretics, etc.). "And in those days shall men seek death, and shall not find it." The locusts resembled war-horses armed, crowns on their heads, faces like humans, women's hair, tails and stings like scorpions, and the king of the locusts was the fallen angel of the bottomless pit: Abaddon in Hebrew, Apollyon in Greek ("the destroyer"). The *sixth angel blew his trumpet*: the four angels that were bound "in the great river Euphrates" were let loose to kill one-third of minkind. Twice 10,000 times 10,000 horsemen are let loose to kill by fire, smoke, and sulphur that poured from the mouths of their horses! Yet the remainder of mankind did not repent, nor did they give up idolatry, murders, magic arts, or their immorality.

(Locusts = evil spirits; the plagues are taken from the plagues of Egypt in Exodous; the Euphrates = eastern frontier of the world beyond which lay the terrible Parthians = the horsemen?)

AN INTERMEDIARY VISION AND THE SEVENTH TRUMPET (10:1-11): An angel with feet "like pillars of fire" came with a little book in his hand (contains God's revelation of the future), placed his right foot on the sea and the left on the earth, and seven thunders accompanied his cries; but John, who was about to write these things down, is told to seal up his book and "write them not!" The angel swore that there will be no more delay, but that at the sound of the seventh trumpet "the mystery of God shall be finished." John asks for the little book (scroll) and eats it, "and it was in my mouth sweet as honey: and as soon as I had eaten it, my belly was bitter" (see Ezekiel 3:3 for the scroll-eating image: *sweet* = divine communication and *bitter* = the events foretold). The angel tells John that he must prophesy "before many peoples, and nations, and tongues, and kings."

CHAPTERS 11-12

(11:1-19) Then John is given a measuring rod and is told to measure the temple of God; the holy city (Jerusalem) "shall they tread underfoot" for forty-two months. God's two witnesses will prophesy for 1,260 days clothed in sackcloth (42 = symbolic of the time of Christian persecution—(see Daniel 7:25). The two witnesses: (O.T. prophets Elias and Enoch?); when they shall have finished their testimony, "the beast that ascendeth out of the bottomless pit shall make war against them, and kill them" (*beast* = Satan = Rome killing Peter and Paul?), but they after three and a half days went up to heaven in a cloud. *The seventh trumpet*: great voices in heaven cry, "The kingdoms of this world are become the kingdoms of our Lord, and of his Christ; and he shall reign for ever and ever and ever!" The 24 elders worship and announce the Judgment, the time of reward and destruction. The temple of God is thrown open, the chest containing his covenant is seen, and there are great disturbances of lightning, thunder, storms, and earthquake. (3½ days = fraction of 3½ years of persecution; the covenant must have been the commandments given to Moses; at last we have the announcement of the Final Judgment of God on all mankind with the peal of the seventh trumpet!)

THE SEVEN SIGNS: THE WOMAN AND THE DRAGON (12:1-17): A woman "clothed with the sun, and the moon under her feet, and upon her head a crown of twelve stars (i.e., the Church of Christ and also the mother of Christ, Mary; here John could be reading the contents of his "little book"). The woman was pregnant and in birthpains; and there appeared a "great red dragon, having seven heads and ten horns, and seven crowns" on his seven heads. He stood ready to devour her child, but she gave birth to a "man child, who was to rule all nations with a rod of iron: and her child was caught up unto God, and to his throne." The woman fled into the desert to a place prepared by God and stayed there 1,260 days: (the dragon = Satan). John then describes the war in heaven between the dragon and the angels, the dragon being cast out, "that old serpent called the Devil, and Satan," along with his evil anged-accomplices. The dragon persecutes the mother of the child (Christ), but she is given two wings to flee the dragon-serpent. Furious, the dragon "went to make war with the remnant of her seed (Christians)."

CHAPTERS 13-14

THE BEAST RISING OUT OF THE SEA (13:1-18): An animal came out of the sea with ten horns and seven heads, and with ten diadems ("crowns") on its horns, and blasphemous titles on its heads. It resembled a leopard with the feet of a bear and a lion's mouth; and the dragon gave it great authority (*the beast* = the Roman empire, *the titles* being the Emperor's demand to be worshipped as a deity; see

Daniel 7:4f. for more on this beast). It laid waste to the world for forty-two months, constantly blaspheming God. It persecuted the saints of the church and ruled the world, forcing all to worship its gods. "If any man have an ear, let him hear. He that leadeth into captivity shall go into captivity (whoever is meant for captivity will go into captivity); he that killeth with the sword must be killed with the sword. Here is the patience and faith of the saints." Another beast arrived with two horns like a lamb and the voice of a dragon; and it brought the earth to worship the first beast, which had been wounded (probably the Roman priesthood who organized emperor worship); the animal's number or name corresponding to its number is 666 (probably "Nero Caesar," which in Hebrew letters equals 666 if taken numerically—a kind of "numbers game" popular at that time. Note that 666 = the height of evil since it stops just short of the most perfect of all numbers 7, which denotes the Apocalypse: 7 is perfect because God made the world in six days and rested on the seventh; the seven planets; the seven-day phase of the moon; the seven patriarchs, etc.)

THE LAMB AND THE VIRGINS (14:1-20): John sees a Lamb standing on Mount Zion (*Jerusalem* = Jewish Nation = Church of God = Heavenly Jerusalem; Lamb = Christ) and with him 144,000 people with Christ's and God's names on their foreheads. They are the saved of the earth, the sexual virgins, celibates, Christ-followers, irreproachable in their truth and purity! Another angel announces the eternal good news: "Fear God, and give glory to him; for the hour of his judgment is come!" Another angel cries that Babylon (i.e., Rome) is fallen, "is fallen that great city, because she made all nations drink of the wine of the wrath of her fornication!" A third angel announces that anyone worshipping the beast and his image (gods) will be "tormented with fire and brimstone in the presence of the holy angels, and in the presence of the Lamb." Then John saw a white cloud and on it one like a man wearing a gold crown and carrying a sharp sickle. He is told to reap the harvest of the earth (good Christians), and the "man" did so. Likewise he gathered the grape harvest and flung the grapes into the "great winepress of the wrath of God (*grapes* = the wicked), "And the winepress was trodden . . . and blood came out of the winepress, even unto the horse bridles, by the space of 1,600 furlongs" (the blood from the winepress flowed bridle-high for 200 miles!).

CHAPTERS 15-16

THE SEVEN ANGELS AND THE SEVEN VIALS (15:1-8): Last to express God's wrath with sinners are the seven angels with seven plagues: "And I saw as it were a sea of glass mingled with fire," and on it the good Christians with harps singing hymns to God. The seven angels are given seven golden vials (bowls) full of God's anger, containing in them the plagues (this could refer to the end of the Roman Empire or the Judgment).

THE PLAGUES (16:1-20): *First angel pours out bowl upon the earth*: painful sores afflict sinners of earth; *second*: turns sea to blood and kills all animals in it; *third*: rivers and springs turn to blood: "For they have shed the blood of saints and prophets, and you have given them blood to drink as they deserve!" *Fourth*: these contents of the bowl dreadfully scorch all sinners, who are still unrepentant! *Fifth*: the animals' throne (Nero's?) and the kingdom are plunged in darkness, "and they gnawed their tongues for pain"—but still unrepentant! *Sixth*: the Euphrates river dries up, to prepare the way for the eastern kings; three frog-like spirits issue from the dragon's mouth and muster all the earthly kings for the battle "of that great day of God Almighty." (This is the great battle called in Hebrew Armageddon (ARM uh GHED un): the final battle on earth between the forces of good and evil); *seventh*: a voice of God: "It is done!"

Then thundering and lightning and earthquake, the greatest ever seen: the great city (Rome) is broken into three pieces, the heathen cities fall; huge hailstones, each the weight of a talent (about a hundred pounds) fall on mankind, which cause men to revile God for their misery.

COMMENT: The plagues resemble those of the Egyptian exodus of the Jews. The dried Euphrates makes way for the Parthians, the great enemy of Rome. Armageddon = Mount of Megiddo, a great battlefield in Palestine, a symbol of disaster. The enemies of the Lamb will be disastrously destroyed!

CHAPTERS 17-18

THE GREAT BABYLON (17:1-18): John sees a woman sitting upon a scarlet-colored beast, "full of names of blasphemy, having seven heads and ten horns." She was dressed in purple and scarlet, decked in precious jewels, carrying a golden cup "full of abominations and filthiness of her fornication" ("full of accursed things, and the impurities of her)immorality," Goodspeed tr., p. 589). On her forehead was written: "MYSTERY (mighty) BABYLON (Rome) THE GREAT, THE MOTHER OF HARLOTS AND ABOMINATIONS OF THE EARTH." The scarlet whore "drunken (drunk) with the blood of saints, and with the blood of the martyrs of Jesus" strikes John with amazement. The angel explains that the seven-headed beast is really seven mountains (i.e., the seven hills upon which Rome was built); they also represent seven kings (the crowns), "five are fallen, and one is, and the other is not yet come" (Roman Emperors, Domitian, the reincarnation of Nero = "was, and is not and is to come": he was assassinated in 96 A.D. = the end of the beast). The

ten horns, explains the angel, are ten kings (nations under Roman rule who for a short time ("an hour") are allied with Rome to persecute Christians, but they shall be defeated by the Lamb! The ten horns (allies of Rome) shall hate the whore, "and shall make her desolate and naked, and shall eat her flesh and burn her with fire!"

THE FALL OF BABYLON (18:1-24): Another angel from heaven cries out in a mighty voice, "Babylon the great is fallen, is fallen, and is become the habitation of devils, and the hold of every foul spirit, and a cage of every unclean and hateful bird!" Another voice warns the people of the city to leave, vengeance is near: "So much torment and sorrow give her: for she saith in her heart, I sit a queen, and am no widow, and shall see no sorrow." No longer shall the kings commit fornication with her and live "deliciously" with the whore, but there shall be burning and torment only. No more trade in gold, silver, precious stones, pearls, fine linen, silk, scarlet, all kinds of citron wood ("thyine" wood), and cinnamon, perfume, frankincense, wine, olive oil, flour, wheat, cattle, bronze, iron, marble, "and sheep, and horses, and chariots, and slaves, and souls of men!" A mighty angel took up a great stone and cast it into the sea, saying, "Thus with violence shall that great city Babylon by thrown down, and shall be found no more at all!"

CHAPTERS 19-20

VICTORY: DEFEAT OF THE BEAST (19:1-21): The multitudes in heaven sing a hymn of praise and joy at God's judgment, as do the 24 elders and the four animals. They sing that the "marriage of the Lamb is come, and his wife (the Church?) hath made herself ready," and John is told to write, "Blessed are they which are called unto the marriage supper of the Lamb." Then John saw heaven open and a white horse ridden by one called "Faithful and True"; his eyes were flaming, and on his head many crowns with a name written therein that only he knew; he is clothed in a cloak dipped in blood and his name is "The Word of God." An army clothed in white linen bestriding white horses follows their leader, who has written on his clothes and thigh a name: "KING OF KINGS AND LORD OF LORDS." An angel calls on all the birds to "come and gather yourselves together unto the supper of the great God" (to dine on kings, captains, soldiers, horses of the enemy). The beast is captured, as is the "false prophet that wrought miracles before him (did miracles in behalf of the beast), with which he deceived them that had received the mark of the beast, and them that worshipped his image. These both were cast alive into a lake of fire burning with brimstone"; the enemy is defeated and the birds gorged themselves upon their bodies (the false prophet was mentioned in 13:11, the Roman imperial priesthood, the subsidiary beast).

THE VICTORY OVER SATAN (20: 1-15): An angel came from heaven with the key to the bottomless pit (hell) and a great chain in his hand. The dragon-Devil-Satan is bound in chains and cast into the pit for a thousand years! "And after that he must be loosed (freed) a little season." The heavenly Judges resurrect the dead Christian martyrs to live and reign with Christ a thousand years, but all other dead remain dead until the Millennium, (a thousand years) is over: this first resurrection of the martyrs will last a millennium; after the Millennium, Satan shall be freed; he will lead astray the heathen of the world, Gog and Magog, "to gather them together to battle: the number of whom is as the sand of the sea." They surround the heavenly city, but they are destroyed by God's fire from heaven, and their Satan again cast into the lake of fire where the beast and the false prophet already are lying; and they "shall be tormented day and night for ever and ever!"

COMMENT:. The thousand years symbolize the period from Christ's coming to his Second Coming; here it represents unalloyed joy and divine love for a thousand years in heaven—but only for the martyred saints: the *"first resurrection,"* the period of grace. The *second resurrection* is the physical rising of the dead at the end of all time (cf. John 11: 25-26). The non-saints are those who die in a state of sin and will not enjoy any sort of resurrection until after the Millennium. Gog and Magog = earthly enemies of God.

The books of Judgment are opened and the dead from the earth and the underworld ("hell") ascend; each is judged "according to his works" (deeds in life). Anyone whose name is not found in the "book of life" is flung into the fiery lake, Hell!

CHAPTERS 21-22

THE NEW JERUSALEM (21:1-27): John sees the holy city, the New Jerusalem "coming down from God out of heaven, prepared as a bride adorned for her husband." God will now dwell with men, a voice cries, and he shall wipe away all tears from their eyes; "and there shall be no more death, neither sorrow, nor crying, neither shall there be any more pain." The good will inherit all things, but the evil will suffer a second death in the burning lake.

John is carried away in a trance to a high mountain and is shown the New Jerusalem:

1. A high wall with twelve gates, upon which were carved the names of the twelve tribes of Israel.
2. On the foundation stones of the walls were carved the names of the twelve apostles.
3. The city was square, each side measuring 12,000 furlongs (about 96,000 miles); the walls were 144 cubits (about 216 feet high and made of jasper (precious stone).
4. The city itself was pure gold, as transparent as glass, and the foundations stones ornamented with precious stones like jasper, sapphire, chalcedony, emerald, etc. The twelve gates were twelve pearls.
5. No temple was needed since God and the Lamb are its temple.
6. No sun or moon needed: the glory of God lighted it, and the Lamb is its lamp. There will never be any night.
7. The splendor and wealth of the heathen will be brought to the city, but nothing unclean will ever enter it.

THE PARADISE OF GOD (22:1-21): From the throne of God and the Lamb flows a river clear as crystal, a water of life, and it ran down the middle of the main street of the city; on both sides of the river grows the tree of life; it bears twelve different kinds of fruit, one for each month, and its leaves are a cure for the nations (heathen). The inhabitants shall see the face of God and the Lamb, "and his name shall be in their foreheads."

EPILOGUE: The angel told John that all he had said was faithful and true, and that God had sent this message to be relayed to mankind. The angel tells John not to seal his book but to broadcast it, for the time of the fulfillment is very near: "I, Jesus, have sent my angel to give you this testimony for the churches . . . I am the bright morning star . . . Let everyone who is thirsty come . . . if anyone adds anything to it (John's book), God will inflict upon him plagues that are described in this book." Jesus adds: "Behold, I come quickly: blessed is he that keepeth the sayings of the prophecy of this book." Final benediction: "The grace of our Lord Jesus Christ be with you all. Amen."

End of New Testament

COMMENT: For a long time this book was deemed difficult, farfetched, fantastic, and utterly bizarre! Especially mystifying was the unending procession of weird beasts, men, and women. Even the Heavenly Jerusalem seems more a nightmarish dream than a reality; and as for the blood and thunder, death and devastation, warnings and imprecations, the exalted prophecies and promises—what is one to make of all that! *Now we know*, for today we live in a world threatened with a similar destruction. Flaming gasoline rains fire from the skies, atomic-hydrogen bombs rain thunder, lightning, disease, and pestilence from heaven! Surely the beast has taken over the world, the scarlet Whore of Babylon is riding us to destruction. Certainly, there is need today for direction, for peace, for certainty. And some will find just that by reading John's supposedly fantastic book of the revelation of God. For the more rational of us I offer in startling contrast to the more orthodox theories contained herein, an interpretation for rationalists, one which can be taken or left as the reader pleases:

Very little or no reference, is made to the career of Jesus on earth, the historical Jesus. Instead, he is here the Lamb dealing reward and death, an enthroned Christ with angels and the books of judgment. In the Pauline epistles Jesus is also very seldom referred to as a historical figure; rather he is more gnostic than anything else, a figure in a divine mystery of faith. But in John the attitude is nationalistic, and fiercely anti-Roman—in strong contrast to the Pauline attitude of cooperation and approval of Rome. This is the most Jewish of the books in the New Testament, probably written by a Jewish-Christian about 94 A.D. in Asia Minor; perhaps a Jew who had escaped the destruction of Jerusalem some twenty years before. He writes Greek as a foreign tongue, unlike the author of the gospel of John. He is steeped in the imagery and language of the old Hebrew prophets. Such books called *apocalypses* were popular in the late first century, but John's book is white-hot with passion, very

likely the work of a Jewish revolutionary who fiercely desired the destruction of Rome and the creation of a New Jerusalem. But more, he hates all those who preach submission to the Roman harlot—and one of the giants who preaches such submission was Paul himself! Paul and his followers are of the "synagogue of Satan," the false apostles, the false prophets, and the false Jews! John writes in ungrammatical Greek, but there is no mistaking his congratulations to the churches of Smyrna, Ephesus, and Philadelphia for not having been seduced by the false apostles and Jews. He, John, commends the majority of the faithful for rejecting the "deep things of Satan" (a parody of Paul's "deep things of God"). Especially detestable are the churches of Sardis and Laodicea.

John's kingdom of God is materialistic, almost exotic—certainly sensuous and splendid in things! He recognizes no priestly hierarchy within the Church, unlike the apostle Paul. John's anger and ferocity is blazing with hate for the evil and the Roman! John's Messiah is a general in bloodstained garments; Paul's is almost a gnostic logos of faith. The end of Revelation seems to have been much handled: the New City comes down to earth twice; the writer falls down to worship twice and is rebuked twice: in short two alternative versions have been lumped together by some editor.

The book was extremely popular in its day and was early taken in as canonical by the Church; but its anti-Romanism embarrassed many church fathers. Nevertheless, the masses loved its promise of a material millennium and paradise, its denunciation of the powerful and great, its sympathy for the good and poor—and so it is part of the inestimable treasure of the New Testament.

QUESTIONS AND ANSWERS ON THE NEW TESTAMENT

1. What are the basic four classes of literature in the N.T.?

The basic four classes of literature in the N.T. are the following:
1. Gospel (the four gospels: Matthew, Mark, Luke, and John).
2. History (the book of Acts).
3. Correspondence (the letters or epistles of Paul and others).
4. Apocalyptic (the book of Revelation).

2. Are the books of the N.T. placed in their chronological order?

The books of the N.T. are *not* arranged in their chronological order of writing but in order of *importance*. The persons who gathered these books together into a collection were not, as we are today, interested in a scientifically historical and chronological scheme. *Content* was their sole criterion for placement.

3. What are the earliest writings of the N.T.? Discuss.

The earliest writings of the N.T. are letters or epistles written to the various Christian churches; they are mostly occasional in nature, answering questions on various matters of practice and belief that then beset the early Christian communities: questions like "When will Jesus come again?" "Whom do we follow, Paul or Peter?" "How do we observe the Lord's Supper?" etc. Paul was the writer of most of the epistles, sometime between 52 and 64 A.D. Of course, there is much in the letters that is not specifically occasional.

4. Discuss the importance of the letters of Paul.

Paul's letters are extremely important in the following four ways:
1. Their *antiquity*: Even well before the composition of the earliest gospel (Mark), these letters were written, read, perused, studied, and passed about as a single collection.

2. Their *autobiography:* Paul is second only to Jesus as the greatest figure in the history of Christianity! Consequently, his words have carried tremendous significance for Christians. Their doctrinal influence alone has been stupendous, not to mention their great literary and ethical import.

3. Their *historicity*: Paul's letters reveal how the early Christians thought, behaved, felt; their customs and problems are revealed with great candor and insight.

4. Their *personality*: The letters reveal the inner life "in Christ" of one of history's supreme religious personalities. This alone makes the letters of inestimable value.

5. What about their dating and authenticity? Discuss.

This is one of the thorniest problems in biblical scholarship; however, the scholarly consensus of liberal theologians is the following:

I, II Thessalonians 50-52 A.D.		Authentic
Galatians 53 A.D.		Authentic
I, II Corinthians 54-57 A.D.		Authentic

Romans	
56-58 A.D.	Authentic
Philippians	
60-64 A.D.	Authentic
Colossians	
60-64 A.D.	Authentic
Philemon	
60-64 A.D.	Authentic
Ephesians (?)	
60-64 A.D.	Questionable
Pastoral Epistles	
(I, II Timothy; Titus)	Questionable
Hebrews	
80-90 A.D.	Questionable

6. What are the so-called Catholic Epistles? Dsicuss.

The Catholic Epistles are made up of seven letters: James, I and II Peter, I, II, and III John, and Jude. These letters are *catholic* in the sense that they are more general in character than Paul's. Except for I Peter and I John, the rest have not attained the authenticity (canonicity) of the others, even in the eyes of the early Church fathers like Eusebius.

7. What is meant by the so-called synoptic problem?

"Synoptic" in Greek means "to see together" and applies to the "synoptic" gospels of Matthew, Mark, and Luke because they tell almost the same story about the life of Christ. They agree often to the smallest detail very frequently, often for many passages. Indeed, the three books are so alike that a "harmony" alignment can be made of them by arranging the three books in three parallel columns. The reader should consult the Harmony Chart at the end of this book for an insight into the correspondences of the three gospels. On the other hand, there are striking variations amongst the three gospels as well: hence the "synoptic problem." The problem is how to account for both the similarities and differences among the three books. This is one of the most complicated and disturbing cruxes in biblical criticism; and the results of such investigations can be of tremendous import. Example of synoptic parallelism: Mark 12:36-37; Matthew 22:43-45; and Luke 20:42-44.

8. What is the best scholarly solution to the "synoptic problem" proposed thus far?

The *documentary theory* is the best proposed so far:
1. There must have been a common earlier written source, a finished gospel, which Mark used as his source; Matthew and Luke then reproduced the bulk of Mark later in their texts. For Mark as earliest, see Eusebius' *Ecclesiastical History,* iii. 39, 15.
2. Matthew and Luke can be reconstructed on the basis of Mark, but the reverse is not true. Mark then served as the written source for Matthew and Luke.
3. What about the "double tradition"; that is, some 200 verses of teachings which are identical in Matthew and Luke and not to be found in Mark at all? This points to a second documentary source for Matthew and Luke. Papias, a bishop of Hierapolis in Phrygia (first half of second century), wrote that Matthew composed the *Logia* in Hebrew and all understood them as they were capable (see Eusebius, as cited above). Conclusion: Matthew and Luke depended upon a second written source (now lost, as was the first document) called the *Logia* or "Q" (German *Quelle* = source). Matthew collected the *Logia;* and that is why in all likelihood the gospel is named after him.
4. The documentary theory is known as the Two-Source theory.

9. What is the Four-Source theory? Explain.

The Four-Source theory adds two other sources to the Mark and Q sources. There is a small amount of narrative and teaching material in both Matthew and Luke which is unique to each. The unique material for Matthew is called the *M* source and for Luke the L source. Both sources are hypothesized from internal evidence. Proto-Luke refers to an earlier form of Luke's own gospel. See B. H. Streeter, *The Four Gospels: A Study in Origins* (London, 1930).

10. What are some stylistic characteristics of Mark's gospel?

Mark's gospel carries the stamp of historical authenticity; it is terse, economical in words, avoids abstractions; Mark reflects strength, vigor, realism, honesty, and directness.

11. What was Matthew's chief purpose in writing his gospel?

His chief interest was to show to his readers that Jesus was the actual Messiah so often alluded to in the Old Testament. Jesus, said Matthew, was the fulfillment of O.T. messianic prophecy. Matthew especially liked often to use the *proof-text* method: the O.T. is quoted over and over again (usually out of context!) to show that Jesus was the fulfillment of the messianic quotation. For example, in 2:14-15 he quotes Hosea 11:1: "When Israel was a child, then I loved him and called my son out of Egypt," to prove that the flight to Egypt of Jesus, Mary, and Joseph was the fulfillment of the eighth century Hosean quotation (which reminds the Hebrews how God cares for them)!

12. Just how was the Sermon on the Mount delivered?

It was supposedly delivered all at one time — the entire substance of his teaching! Actually, it is an editorial collation of diverse sayings of Jesus into one solid sermon, so to speak.

13. What is the substance of the Sermon on the Mount?

They are the ethical discourses and teachings of Jesus Christ, and the basis of all Christian ethics and teachings:
1. The Beatitudes: requirements for enrollment in the Kingdom of God (5:1-12).
2. Social responsibility in Jesus' followers (12-16).
3. Spirit of religion as against the letter of the law (17-48).
4. Worship is internal rather than outward show (6:1-18).
5. Things are not so important as values—the purpose of life rather than the means by which we exist (19-34).
6. Golden Rule (7:1-12).
7. Conduct over mere creed: "By their fruits ye shall know them." (13-23).

14. What are the important periods of decision of Jesus' life?

The Baptism, the Temptation, the Transfiguration, the Triumphal Entry, Gethsemane; the whole climaxed by his Crucifixion.

15. What is Luke's literary style like?

Luke is a non-Jew, a gentile writer who writes in polished classical Greek (only the epistle to the Hebrews is as classical in style), a style far more elegant than the rest of the N.T., which is more colloquial. Luke is a writer with fine instincts, taste, sensitivity, and a commanding sense of form and structure: "the most beautiful book ever written" said Renan.

16. Why is Luke's book often termed the Social Gospel?

Luke seems to emphasize social reform and humanitarianism. The very greatest of Jesus' parable of humanitarianism occur here: those of the

Good Samaritan and the Prodigal Son, for example.

17. What makes the fourth gospel unique?

The gospel of John is a world unto itself. The language, viewpoint, concepts, theology, and style are all radically different from the synoptic gospels. We go from a gentle humane and lovable Christ to an aloof, distant, impassioned, and thoroughly self-conscious Messianic Christ. We go from interest in the life of Jesus in the synoptics to emphasis on doctrine. Jesus in John's book is the Eternal Word, the Son of God. He is abstract, abstruse, almost metaphysical. In short, Jesus in the fourth gospel is part of the divine Godhead himself! Remember that John's gospel was written at a much later date than the synoptics, about 110 A.D., and in a much different milieu.

18. Give three reasons for Luke's authorship of Acts.

1. The Prologue tells Theophilus how the author had formerly dealt with the life of Jesus (i.e., the gospel of Luke).
2. The so-called "we-sections" in Acts. The author on four occasions refers to himself and his companions inadvertently as "we," abruptly switching from the third person plural to the first person plural. From internal evidence it can be shown that Luke is one of the "we" referred to.
3. The style and vocabulary is strongly reminiscent of Luke's gospel.

19. What was Luke's intent in writing the book of Acts?

Acts describes the birth and growth of the early Church, its rise and consequent spread—tremendously important to the history of Christianity. Luke wants to show how and why and where the early Church grew from a devoted group of apostles to a widespread band of churches circling the Mediterranean. He is especially intent on showing how the Romans did not hinder the Church in its growth, Here is a rough chronology of Acts:

Crucifixion of Jesus	29-30 A.D.
Conversion of Paul	35 A.D.
First Visit to Jerusalem	38 A.D.
Second Visit to Jerusalem	44 A.D.
First Missionary Campaign	45-47 A.D
Council at Jerusalem	48 A.D.
Second Campaign	49-52 A.D.
Third Campaign	52-56 A.D.
Imprisonment in Caesarea	56-58 A.D.
Arrival in Rome	59 A.D.
Death of Paul	64 A.D.

20. Why was John's book of Revelation written?

Much nonsense has been circulated about this book, such as its use to predict wars and to date the end of the world, and there have been many vain attempts to interpret its vast symbolism. Actually, the book was written to give the Christians courage and firmness against emperor-worship and Roman persecution.

BIBLIOGRAPHY

The author expresses his deep indebtedness to the following commentaries: *The Cambridge Bible Commentary; The Interpreter's Bible* (Abingdon); *The Pelican Gospel Commentaries; Peake's Commentary.*

Especially useful was the Goodspeed *Parallel New Testament* in which the King James' version and Goodspeed's translation are arranged in parallel columns. The Phillips' translation, *The New Testament in Modern English* (Macmillan), was extremely useful for its title headings and its unparalleled clarity. H. B. Sharman's *Records in the Life of Jesus* (Harper) provides a parallel harmony that proved enlightening.

For the definition of biblical terms I am indebted to H. C. Jenkins' *A Modern Dictionary of the Holy Bible* (Locllyn, 1958). Of invaluable aid and insight into the historical position were Alfred Loisy's *The Origins of the New Testament* (tr. L. P. Jacks; Collier Books) and Charles Guignebert's *Jesus* (tr. S. H. Hooke; Knopf). Finally, a delightful and handy review of essentials is R. Haz-elton's *New Testament Heritage,* 1962.

BACKGROUND BIBLIOGRAPHY

General Introduction:

Scott, Ernest Findlay: *The Literature of the New Testament.* (Columbia University Press, 1932).

Moffatt, James: *An Introduction to the Literature of the New Testament.* (Scribner's, 1918).

Peake, Arthur Samuel: *A Critical Introduction to the New Testament.* (Scribner's, 1910).

Studies of Special Subjects:

Hastings, James (ed.), *A Dictionary of the Bible.* (Scribner's, 1905).

Mackinnon, James: *The Historic Jesus.* (Longmans, 1931).

Dodd, C. Harold: *The Apostolic Preaching and Its Developments.* (Willett, 1937).

Charles, R. H. *Eschatology, etc.* (Macmillan, 1913).

Especially good: the life and times of Jesus in volumes by M. Goguel, H. E. Fosdick, E. J. Goodspeed, and A. C. Headlam.

A Harmony Table of Synoptic Parallel Passages

A TABLE OF THE SECTIONS IN MARK
WITH THEIR PARALLELS IN MATTHEW AND LUKE
(Raised numbers signify Chapters)

Mark.	Matthew.	Luke.
^{1}1-8.	^{3}1-6,11f.	^{3}1-18.
^{1}9-11.	^{3}13-17.	^{3}21f.
^{1}12f.	^{4}1-11.	^{4}1-13.
^{1}14f.	^{4}12-17.	^{4}14f.
^{1}16-20.	^{4}18-22.	^{5}1-11.
^{1}21-28.	^{4}13b,^{7}28f,^{4}24f.	^{4}31-37.
^{1}29-34.	^{8}14-17.	^{4}38-41.
^{1}35-39.	^{4}23-25.	^{4}42-44.
^{1}40-45.	^{8}1-4.	^{5}12-16.
^{2}1-12.	^{9}1-8.	^{5}17-26.
^{2}13-17.	^{9}9-13.	^{5}27-32.
^{2}18-22.	^{9}14-17.	^{5}33-39.
^{2}23-28.	^{12}1-8.	^{6}1-5.
^{3}1-6.	^{12}9-14.	^{6}6-11.
^{3}7-12.	^{12}15-21.	^{6}17-19.
^{3}13-19.	^{10}2-4.	^{6}12-16.
^{3}20-30.	^{9}32-34, ^{12}22-32, 36f.	^{11}14-23,^{12}10.
^{3}31-35.	^{12}46-50.	^{8}19-21.
^{4}1-20.	^{13}1-23.	^{8}4-15.
^{4}21-25.	^{5}15, ^{10}26, ^{7}2, ^{13}12, ^{25}29.	^{8}16-18,^{6}38,^{11}33,^{12}2,^{19}26.
^{4}26-29.	Nil.	Nil.
^{4}30-34.	^{13}31f., 34f.	^{13}18f.
^{4}35-41.	^{8}18, 23-27.	^{8}22-25.
^{5}1-20.	^{8}28-34.	^{8}26-39.
^{5}21-43.	^{9}18-26.	^{8}40-56.
^{6}1-6.	^{13}53-58.	^{4}16-30.
^{6}7-13.	^{9}35-38, ^{10}1,5-16, ^{11}1.	^{9}1-6,^{10}1-12,^{18}22.
^{6}14-29.	^{14}1-12.	^{9}7-9,^{3}19f.
^{6}30-44.	^{14}13-21.	^{9}10-17.
^{6}45-56.	^{14}22-36.	Nil.
^{7}1-23.	^{15}1-20.	Nil.
^{7}24-30.	^{15}21-28.	Nil.
^{7}31-37.	(^{15}29-31.)	Nil.
^{8}1-10.	^{15}32-39.	Nil.
^{8}11f.	^{12}38-42, ^{16}1-4.	^{11}29-32.
^{8}13-21.	^{16}5-12.	^{12}1.
^{8}22-26.	Nil.	Nil.
^{8}27-^{9}1.	^{16}13-28.	^{9}18-27.
^{9}2-13.	^{17}1-13.	^{9}28-36.
^{9}14-29.	^{17}14-20.	^{9}37-42,^{17}5f.

9 30-32.
9 33-50.
10 1-12.
10 13-16.
10 17-31.
10 32-34.
10 35-45.
10 46-52.
11 1-11.
11 12-14.
11 15-19.
11 20-25.
11 27-33.
12 1-12.
12 13-17.
12 18-27.
12 28-34.
12 35-37.
12 38-40.
12 41-44.
13 1-37.
14 1f.
14 3-9.
14 10f.
14 12-16.
14 17-21.
14 22-25.
14 26-31.
14 32-42.
14 43-52.
14 53-65.
14 66-72.
15 1-5.
15 6-15.
15 16-20.
15 21-32.
15 33-39.
15 40f.
15 42-47.
16 1-8.

17 22f.
18 1-9, 5 13.
19 1-12, 5 31f.
18 3, 19 13-15.
19 16-30.
20 17-19.
20 20-28.
(9 27-31), 20 29-34.
21 1-11.
21 18f.
21 12f.
21 20-22, 17 20, 6 14, 18 35. Nil.
21 23-27.
21 33-46.
22 15-22.
22 23-33.
22 34-40.
22 41-46.
23 1,6f.
Nil.
24 1-36.
26 1-5.
26 6-13
26 14-16.
26 17-20.
26 21-25.
26 26-29.
26 30-35.
26 36-46.
26 47-56.
26 57-67.
26 69-75.
27 1f.,11-14.
27 15-26.
27 27-31.
27 32-44.
27 45-54.
27 55f.
27 57-61.
28 1-10.

9 43-45.
9 46-50, 17 1f., 14 34f.
16 18.
18 15-17.
18 18-30.
18 31-34.
22 24-27.
18 35-43.
19 28-38.
(13 6-9.)
19 45-48.
Nil.
20 1-8.
20 9-19.
20 20-26.
20 27-38.
20 39f., 10 25-28.
20 41-44.
11 43, 20 46f.
21 1-4.
21 5-33.
22 1f.
(7 36-50.)
22 3-6.
22 7-14.
22 21-23.
22 15-20.
22 31-34.
22 39-46.
22 47-53.
22 54f.,63-71.
22 56-62.
23 1-5.
23 18-25.
Nil.
23 26-43.
23 44-47.
23 48f.
23 50-56.
24 1-11.

NOTES

NOTES

NOTES

MONARCH® *NOTES* AND STUDY GUIDES

ARE AVAILABLE AT RETAIL STORES EVERYWHERE

In the event your local bookseller
cannot provide you with other
Monarch titles you want —

ORDER ON THE FORM BELOW:

Simply send retail price, local sales tax, if any, plus 35¢ per book to cover mailing and handling.

TITLE #	AUTHOR & TITLE	PRICE
	PLUS ADDITIONAL $1.00 PER BOOK FOR POSTAGE	
	GRAND TOTAL	$

Mail to: **PRENTICE HALL PRESS,** c/o Simon & Schuster Mail Order Billing, Route 59 at Brook Hill Drive, West Nyack, NY 10994

I enclose $ .... to cover retail price, local sales tax, plus mailing and handling. (Make checks payable to Simon & Schuster, Inc.)

Name _____
(Please print)

Address _____

City _____ State _____ Zip _____

Please send check or money order. We cannot be responsible for cash.